TWIRLYMEN

TWIRLYMEN

The Unlikely History of
Cricket's Greatest Spin Bowlers

AMOL RAJAN

Yellow Jersey Press
LONDON

For Pattabiraman Varadarajan, Sunanda Joshi,
Keertichandra Rajan, Farrah Hossain, and Charlotte Rosemary Faircloth

Published by Yellow Jersey Press 2011

2 4 6 8 10 9 7 5 3 1

Jiggery Pokery
Neil Hannon and Thomas Walsh © Sony/ATV Music Publishing
All rights reserved. Used by permission.

First published in Great Britain in 2011 by
Yellow Jersey Press
Random House, 20 Vauxhall Bridge Road,
London SW1V 2SA

www.randomhouse.co.uk

Addresses for companies within The Random House Group Limited can be found at:
www.randomhouse.co.uk/offices.htm

The Random House Group Limited Reg. No. 954009

A CIP catalogue record for this book
is available from the British Library

ISBN 9780224083232 (hardback)
ISBN 9780224083249 (trade paperback)

The Random House Group Limited makes every effort to ensure that the papers
used in its books are made from trees that have been legally sourced from well-managed and
credibly certified forests. Our paper procurement policy can be found at:
www.rbooks.co.uk/environment

Mixed Sources
Product group from well-managed
forests and other controlled sources
www.fsc.org Cert no. TF-COC-2139
© 1996 Forest Stewardship Council
FSC

Printed and bound in Great Britain by CPI Mackays, Chatham, Kent ME5 8TD

CONTENTS

WHY I SPIN

I wish I could say, as George Orwell did, that from a very early age I knew that when I grew up I should be a writer. Given how things have turned out, were it true that might be a source of solace to me now. But the fact is I didn't. From a rather early age, in fact the age of nine years and eleven months, I knew that when I grew up I should bowl leg-spin.

At least that was my intention. I can trace its origins very precisely. It was 3 June 1993, and I had several hours earlier returned from primary school. It was a ritual of my father's to watch *The Nine O'Clock News*, as it then was, and I was in the habit of ignoring all of it until the sport came on. But in the headlines at the top of the programme – I can't remember the newsreader – I saw approximately one and a half seconds of sport that would change my life.

Shane Warne, an enigmatic young Australian whose peroxide blond hair gave every indication of his being cricket's answer to Debbie Harry, bowled over the wicket to Mike Gatting in the Old Trafford Test. It was his first ball in an Ashes match. Upon release, the ball swerved viciously in the air from left to right, dipped sharply and then turned dramatically in the opposite direction to hit the off-stump. Gatting was dumbfounded. Dickie Bird, umpiring, was similarly perplexed, and Richie Benaud, commentating, gave it the heavily accented understatement: 'He's done it, he's started off with the most *beautiful* delivery.'

Nothing would ever be the same again.

I had played Kwik cricket at school, and in long afternoons on Tooting Bec Common, but until that moment I had never understood the potential innate in a cricket ball, or realised the beauty there was in a leg-break. Batting had a rawness to it, as fast bowling did, and other sports had something similar; but spin bowling – beating the bat in the air and off the pitch – that was something new, something calculated, something that could be learned, even if you were obese, as I was (and Warne threatened to be).

The significance of this last point is tremendous. The generosity of my boyhood girth equipped me only for a form of bowling wherein my approach to the crease would be an amble rather than a sprint, and if I was to dream of sporting glory, as I did for the next decade of my life, leg-spin specifically it would have to be.

Having failed through a combination of injury and indolence to become a leg-spinner of renown myself, my motivation here is essentially that of the admiring critic. But it should be mentioned that this book is, in a very fundamental sense, the product of my own failure to warrant a place within the pages to come, alongside these heroes. I devoted my childhood to spin, and leg-spin in particular. I cycled to the nets at my local club, Sinjuns CC in Wandsworth, south London, before school, and ripped the lower part of my uniform climbing over the main gate so as to snatch a couple of overs in which to practise. My portly frame was incongruous with the athleticism of my ambition. Until the age of fourteen, when I remained resolutely more spherical than the newest cricket ball, less supportive parents than mine could have been forgiven for making me choose between leg-spin and the penny sweet cola bottles I gulped by the hundred on a daily basis, ensuring I would remain rotund.

It was this very frame that had led my first coach and mentor, Kevin Molloy, later Director of Sports at Alleyn's Junior School in south London, to christen me Mushtaq – or Mushy for short – after the great Pakistani Mushtaq Ahmed, when I first turned up at Sinjuns aged ten and a half. This new name caused me to have a very clearly split childhood personality: I was Amol at school, but the real person I wanted to be, the personification of my dreams and ambitions, the person in whom was invested genuine emotion, was 'Mushy'. So wholly did I embrace this nickname – this persona – that after seven years at Sinjuns, many of my very closest friends and associates, people with whom I had grown up, frequently had reason to ask, when invited by a third party, what my real name was. On a thousand scoresheets of the Fuller's League in Surrey, I am known to the world as M. Rajan; though if I took a particularly decent haul I made sure the home scorer knew my initial was an 'A'.

This double life intensified my devotion to spin. Awarded some book vouchers for a modest academic achievement, I escorted my father to Foyle's in central London, whereupon he had hoped to initiate in his second son a lifelong devotion to literature. I can remember very precisely the look on his face as I steered him away from the section containing Dostoevsky and Conrad, and towards two books that changed the course of my life forever. He didn't think Peter Philpott's *The Art of Wrist-Spin Bowling* and Brian Wilkins's *Cricket: The Bowler's Art* would stimulate the intellectual activity he so longed to see, but his decision to sanction their purchase laid the foundation for a personal agenda of industry and diligence from which I am still recovering.

Wilkins's book told me about the tradition of spin; Philpott's told me how to become part of it. So I set to work, paying especially close attention to Philpott's recommendation for 'close focus' exercises. They enabled the bowler capable of really spinning it but lacking in accuracy – that is, the personified globule of mediocrity that was my adolescent self – to land the ball on the right spot more regularly. I even moved to a better club, just down Burntwood Lane.

Eventually I had trials, in an indoor school in Guildford, for Surrey Under-17s. Every kid was late because it was snowing. With my parents watching from the gallery above, I managed by divine providence not only to land a series of deliveries on the mat used for spinner's nets in indoor schools, but actually to hit a decent length and make the ball perform right angles. This hitherto unknown personal feat led to my selection for the Surrey youth side, so that I would follow in the footsteps of that great medium-paced spinner George Lohmann in graduating from the fields of Wandsworth Common to the Oval.

But no sooner had I attended my fourth net session at the Ken Barrington Centre than the anointed coach ended it by calling me and two other boys over for a debrief. I had been struggling with painful tendons in my finger and, more acutely, in my elbow, for several weeks. I was already hugely intimidated by the presence of all these public schoolboys, with their easy confidence, classical techniques and air of intense competence, so that when this summons came I instinctively suspected ill was afoot. I will never forget being warmly told that it fell to this head coach to reduce the size of the squad, with far too many players having being selected after the trials, and would I and the other two lads, one of whom was at least nearly as fat as me, mind awfully staying at home for next week's nets. I went upstairs and changed, and haven't cried like that since.

Weeks later I resolved to prove a point by getting reselected for the Surrey side. But the physiotherapy I was getting for the tendon trouble led to one particularly honest session which concluded with an X-ray – possibly taken just to scare me – and a stern warning from the consultant. If I wanted not only to avoid five decades with an arthritic elbow, but also to own a functioning right arm at all by the time I was thirty, I should give up spin bowling – not cricket, not bowling; spin bowling – immediately, which of course, devastated, I duly did.

The following pages are, then, an extended apology, mainly to the cricketer I might have been. Beyond that pathetic self-pity, two distinct but related propositions form their basis, though there is a broader argument too, which I shall outline in a moment. The first asserts that spin bowling is the most exceptionally beautiful art form within a sport already characterised by elegance. The second asserts that we are living through spin bowling's greatest age. During this time, not only have Warne and Muttiah Muralitharan, who spin the ball in opposite directions, become the leading wicket-takers in history, but the most exciting bowler in the world, Ajantha Mendis, is bowling unlike almost anybody seen since the 1950s. Meanwhile Twenty20, which many predicted would be the death of spin, is in fact handmaiden to its latest flourishing. And in the 2011 limited overs World Cup, a plethora of spinners opened the bowling (albeit in helpful conditions) to prove their importance in that form of the game.

Both propositions are essentially optimistic, so that while almost all of the literature on spin bowling written in the past thirty years has taken the form of a lamentation, and the tone of elegy, the pages that follow are unapologetically celebratory.

In speaking on and off the record to hundreds of spinners, journalists and fans of the game before settling down to write this book, people whose knowledge of not just spin bowling but cricket in general varied hugely, I soon realised that these pages could be radically enhanced by explaining some of the basics graphically. As a journalist, and here as a lover of the game, my chief occupation is descriptive rather than prescriptive; but expanding on the *when, what, why* and *who* of spin bowling to incorporate the *how* seems a pleasant necessity. This is not a coaching manual (some good ones are recommended in the bibliography); nor is it a detailed investigation into the science of spin (again, see the bibliography); but given that spin bowling is as much an art form as it is a practice, I hope that the Interludes will be of use to those minded to join the spin doctor's club. Almost certainly it is worthwhile reading the pages to come with a cricket ball perched close to you, and within reach of your spinning hand.

Fittingly, I hope, for a historical book, the Interludes reach their apogee with two deliveries – the doosra and the carrom ball – which are innovations by their most illustrious modern practitioners, Saqlain Mushtaq and Ajantha Mendis, respectively a great bowler and one destined for greatness, and then a delivery that I believe a new generation of Twirlymen will find irresistible once they have mastered it. I call this Rajan's Mystery Ball.

As an activity, spin bowling speaks to a frame of mind, a spirit and attitude, that is eccentric, manipulative, relaxed about deceitfulness, brave in the face of adversity, curiously obsessed with the twisting motion of spherical objects, and bent on ingenuity (never were disabilities put to better use in able-bodied sport than Muttiah Muralitharan's crooked arm, or Bhagwat Chandrasekhar's polio-withered elbow, as will become clear). My concern therefore is not just to explore the art, but the characters conducting it, the cultures from which they spring, and the idiosyncrasies common to all. This I begin to do in my exploration of the Spinner's Spirit.

My aim is not to produce an encyclopaedic overview of spin bowling; rather, by focusing on the most successful purveyors of a precious art, I hope to chart the vicissitudes of its evolution. All histories must contain some element of chronology, and all chronologies must be susceptible to division into composite parts – that is, eras. I have split spin bowling into eras that bleed into one another, much as the indelible qualities of their characters do. Sydney Barnes, for example, who came closer than any other man before or since to being the complete bowler, could be categorised alongside what I have called the Swift Pioneers – the bowlers of the late nineteenth century who spun the ball at medium pace – but for chronological reasons I have made him the starting point of what I call spin bowling's First Flourish.

There are three different theoretical approaches which illuminate what I am setting out to do. They come from the spheres of biology, history and literature.

The unwritten sub-headline of this book is 'A Darwinian Approach to Spin Bowling' or, if you like, 'An Evolutionary Approach to Spin Bowling'. Lewis Wolpert, the brilliant scientist, has written: 'The key evolutionary idea related to our minds is adaptiveness'; and so it is with spinners, too. The Twirlymen of cricket constitute a sub-species, whose survival has been threatened by the remorseless destruction of their habitat by man, and who have been pushed to the very brink of extinction. And yet they have survived, by adapting: whether through the invention of magical new deliveries, the adoption of new approaches more amenable to the latest laws or the rediscovery of old rituals and practices that helped their forebears. What is more, it has often been their very chosen method of adaptiveness that has been a later source of success.

Historians, meanwhile, examine the past with wildly different preju-dices about what can and cannot be deduced from their observations.

'Long ago,' Simon Schama has written, 'we were told by the French historians of the Annales School that spectacular events – the storming of the Bastille, the assassination at Sarajevo, and the decisions of individuals, be they Roosevelt or Hitler – were but spume on the crest of history's waves: that what really shaped the shoreline was the invisible pull of deep tides and currents far beneath the surface. Long-term influences are what change the world.' But other historians take the opposite line: for them, the acts and decisions of individuals really are the drivers of history, the change-makers that push old forms into modernity, and create the possibility of anachronism. These historians hold that history is best understood through the prism of Great Men, and I suppose the title of this book is a confession of my subscription to that model of historical thinking.

Above all, I believe the art with which we are concerned generously repays consideration, and my starting point is akin to that of T. S. Eliot, in his epochal *Tradition and the Individual Talent*: 'No poet, no artist of any art, has his complete meaning alone. His significance, his appreciation, is the appreciation of his relation to the dead poets and artists. You cannot value him alone; you must set him, for contrast and comparison, among the dead. I mean this as a principle of æsthetic, not merely historical, criticism' – and so do I. The ghosts of Bosanquet, Barnes, O'Reilly and Iverson look on with pride each time Warne, Muralitharan, Mendis and Vettori approach the crease. It is only by placing modern Twirlymen in the context of the tradition they have inherited, inhabited and updated, that their ostensibly individual achievements can be fully admired, and understood.

Just as great writers borrow devices from ancient texts, occasionally pastiche them, and create a conversation between themselves and the tradition they inhabit, so too are modern bowlers conversant with their forebears. This can take extreme and controversial forms, as when Trevor Chappell in 1981 bowled a pea-roller to Brian McKechnie, doubtless annoyed that spectators and pundits alike failed to recognise his doing so had nothing to do with denying New Zealand a victory in the final of the Benson and Hedges World Series Cup at the Melbourne Cricket Ground, and everything to do with reawakening the spirit of the very first bowlers, who used to 'bowl' in the literal sense of sending the ball along the floor. Similarly, when Dilip Vengsarkar bowled an over of lobs in 1984–5, as reported by Graeme Fowler in his book *Fox on the Run*, he was doing no more than expressing solidarity with the great lob bowlers of the early Victorian era, and possibly even George Simpson-Hayward, the last of the lobsters, who plied his trade in an England shirt at the start of the twentieth century.

There is a canon of great bowlers, I contend, and my irksome task has been not so much to select those who deserve a place in it, as to judge why so many great bowlers don't. Why don't Tim May and Bob Appleyard, or Intikhab Alam and Mushtaq Mohammad, get chunkier treatments? I don't have an answer that will satisfy all. The bowlers I have profiled were exceptional either in their preservation of an inherited tradition, or in their capacity to update it: they helped spin bowling survive through what economists too fondly call cyclical downturns. Many fine bowlers have not made the cut, as it were, and in some cases, when the lesson learned from a bowler's career is so obvious as to be superfluous to the argument, they have been elided.

As to the basis of that argument, it contains several strands, to which I hope the details to come are convincing appendages. First, it seems to me a far too little observed fact that spin bowling, which hovered on the very brink of extinction so recently, is now in the ascendant, so that we have lived through an age in which not one but two of the very finest spinners ever have been a constant sight, and a dozen or so outstanding Twirlymen have clamoured for our attention, too.

Not many books are written about spin bowling these days. If you look at ones written not all that long ago, their titles and chapter headings tell you how morbid were the prospects for spin even in very recent memory. That classic work, John Emburey's *Spinning in a Fast World* (1989), is just one example. Patrick Murphy's *The Spinner's Turn* (1982) asks: 'What hope for spin?'. And the opening chapter of Trevor Bailey and Fred Trueman's *The Spinner's Web* (1988), 'Where and Why have all the spinners gone?', says it all. We have gone from there to living in possibly spin bowling's greatest age in a mere two decades. This re-emergence seems to have merited little comment; and it is only by returning to the era immediately previous to the present one that we can see how close spin was to virtual extinction, and so appreciate the extraordinary bowlers we have before us today.

Second, this wonderful renaissance has happened *despite*, rather than because of, the rule changes successive generations of selfish, myopic and lucre-loving administrations have pushed through. Looking over cricket history it seems highly plausible that there was a conspiracy against spinners, because at every stage overlords of the game seem hell bent on making their lives miserable. Shorter boundaries, the advent of pinch-hitting with the one-day game, covered, lifeless wickets, and now, for goodness sake, two-faced bats (which effectively double the batsman's hitting range), all have worked in the batsman's favour and against the spinner. In the early years of video technology, spinners were also undone by the fact that opposition batsmen could study their every trick in minute detail. This remains a huge problem, of course, but it has been mitigated by the fact that Hawk-Eye technology, and the consequent willingness of umpires to give more leg-before decisions, has been of some use to spinners, especially English ones such as Graeme Swann and Monty Panesar. Still, the vast slew of legislation enacted over cricket history has been detrimental to the art of spin. That it should still have survived leads me to conclude, in the chapter on the Spinner's Spirit, that the defining quality of all great spinners, after physical skill, is stamina – a fact borne out by many of their inspirational biographies.

Third, bowling, as it emerged from its very immature beginnings, was in fact dominated by spin. To the modern eye, so accustomed to raw pace and seam and swing bowling, it seems almost unfathomable that bowling attacks should be dominated by spin. The modern Indian spin quartet of the 1970s, like the South African googly quartet of the early twentieth century, show this need never be the case; but it is still refreshing to discover that for the first century or so in which cricket was played, spin was the first weapon of choice, and pace was a mere secondary consideration. This was largely because round-arm bowling – that is, bowling with the arm at 90 degrees to the body – wasn't legalised until well into Queen Victoria's reign, of course. But considering the history of the game as a whole, we should welcome the fact that, compared with pace bowling, spin has the longer, deeper heritage. The dominance of medium or raw pace at the top of bowling rankings for roughly the period the historian Eric Hobsbawm calls the short twentieth century – 1914–89 – should, with the aid of this historical knowledge, be rightly understood as a kind of decades-long aberration.

Fourth, in spin bowling as in all spheres of sport, all patents are fraudulent. I document the willingness of spinners to propagandise on their own behalf, and so widespread is the ignorance of spin bowling that whenever a bowler claims to have invented a new delivery, or set of new deliveries, their opponents naively believe them. Ahead of one Ashes series, Warne put it about that he had sixteen deliveries. This could just mean his stock ball bowled from sixteen marginally different positions on the bowling crease. English batsmen, far from taking a moment to think clearly about what was being put to them, were hypnotised with fear.

Throughout the history of mystery, spinners are claiming to invent their own 'magic ball' or 'other one'. In almost each and every instance, the vacuity of their braggadocio can be exposed. This will be a recurring theme: whereas human history is rectilinear, the history of ideas is not. There is no such thing as an original idea. One very useful instance is in the falsity of claims made on behalf of the flipper, where endless devotees of the game who should know better claim it was invented by Clarrie Grimmett. In fact it was being bowled nearly a century before Grimmett used it in a match. The Australian should be credited with reawakening a dormant delivery, not with creating it from scratch.

Neither was the googly invented by the suave Englishman Bernard Bosanquet. And what about the doosra, the ball 'invented' by Saqlain Mushtaq? That, I suppose, could be called an original idea – if you erase from history Jack Potter, the off-spinner who went on Australia's 1964 Ashes tour and had a delivery which went the other way.

Fifth, off-spin, for so long thought of as an ugly duckling in cricket despite the extraordinary achievements of bowlers such as Jim Laker, Hugh Tayfield and Lance Gibbs, remains even today the victim of outrageous slurs. I propose some theories as to why this may be the case in my chapter on the Two Dichotomies that have governed spin bowling. For now, suffice it to say that, at the time of writing, the best spinner in the world is an orthodox English off-spinner, very much in the mould of Laker, whose exceptional success should alone debunk the idea, sympathetic though I was with it in my childhood, that off-spin is at the very best no more than Robin to leg-spin's Batman.

Sixth, while mystery is temporary, mastery is permanent. Of course the exoticism of the mystery spinners, those unknown and seemingly unknowable bowlers who are the subject of gossip and scurrilous rumour, and who occasionally burst on to the scene from nowhere, is a huge attraction to us. But the intriguing thing about mystery is that it often runs in inverse proportion to success. Paul Adams, the frog-in-a-blender South African, was a mystery spinner who briefly lit up Test cricket in the 1990s. Yet his chief service to the game was to prove indubitably that a bowler will not succeed at the highest level if, at the point of delivery, his head is speared into the ground and he is looking at his front knee. Masterful bowlers, on the other hand, such as Warne and classic slow left-armers like Wilfred Rhodes and Bishen Bedi, owe their longevity at the summit of the game to their complete mastery of the basics. They are supremely orthodox rather than mysteriously unorthodox.

Next to all this, the linear simplicity of medium and fast pace has, I contend, all the romance of genital warts. Spin bowling is just as attacking, just as aggressive, but more intellectually so. Far from being content with such uncomplicated weapons as speed or swing or seam, beautiful as those things may be, the spinner sends down his missives spiced with sinister infelicity. There were, of course, those spinners who, bowling marginally more quickly, sent arrows rather than grenades in the batsman's direction, and elicited a kink rather than a kick from the pitch. These recur through the eras, but were most prevalent in the age of the great spinning medium-pacers, which I have called the age of the Swift Pioneers. More broadly, the eras bled into each other, so that the archives hum with periods in which bowlers adopted different styles, and the history of mystery is really one long, rowdy conversation between cerebral revellers: a merry band of men, delighting in each other's company.

We should be thankful, above all, that the conversation is still not over – despite having threatened abrupt closure only recently. In fact, there is a sudden plethora of voices, and they're talking more raucously than ever. How did we get here?

Chapter One

BRAVE ORIGINALS

The development of bowling from its base form, when it took the meaning of the word in its most literal sense of rolling the ball along the ground, owes as much to revolution as evolution. It should be granted at the outset that the chief agitators in the former category, who by sheer willpower forced cricket into modernity, were bowlers who determined to bamboozle batsmen rather than brutalise them. Between the middle of the eighteenth and nineteenth centuries, a series of spinners would regularly risk the wrath of players and umpires alike, defying convention, custom and courtesy to overcome the resistance of an older, inferior game. That opened the path to today's sport. Only once this premise has been accepted can the actions of the first spinners – they were spinners, incidentally, genuine tweak merchants rather than merely slow bowlers – be fully understood. They were progenitors not just to modern bowling greats but to all those who had ambitions to put more variation into bowling than was permitted by molehills, hollows, lumps and fox holes.

It was those natural occurrences that in the early days of cricket were a bowler's best hope. Until around the middle of the eighteenth century, bowling was conducted along the lines of ten-pin bowling: delivered by an under-the-shoulder action, with the ball on the surface almost immediately upon leaving the hand, and the arm swinging through from a crouched position, with the opposite foot outstretched. Both knees were bent, that of the bowling side on or just above the ground. Slow deliveries were called 'trundles'; quick deliveries were called 'skims'.

Crucially, the bowling side themselves could choose where to lay the pitch. This was one of few compensations for the bowler, who had to accept what, to modern eyes, is the indignity of his undeserved absence from the scorecards. For many years only wicketkeepers and fielders were credited with dismissals; a bowler's name would appear on the scorecard only in the event of the batsman having been bowled. But the privilege of choosing where to lay the strip for a game was exploited mischievously by many early bowlers, and purveyors of spin in particular.

It was probably around 1770 that bowlers first started to give the ball air, and there is no record of who was the first to do so consistently. One bowler who did, and who best utilised the freedom to place the strip, was Edward Stevens – known only as 'Lumpy' in scorecards from his playing days. A gardener by trade, his bowling was so effective it earned him work on the Walton-on-Thames estate of the Earl of Tankerville, an early patron of Surrey cricket and formulator of cricketing laws. Of Lumpy, who once won £100 for his lordship by hitting a feather with a ball four times in a row, was the verse written:

Honest Lumpy, who did 'low
He ne'er could bowl, save o'er a brow.

And it was his effort, in a single wicket match on 22–23 May 1775, where he beat the Hambledon batsman John Small three times in quick succession, but with the ball going each time between the two stumps that then constituted the wicket, that prompted his patrons to introduce a third (middle) stump, if only to quell Lumpy's vociferous disgust.

His efforts were best reported by that first and literally foremost of cricket hacks, John Nyren. Our debt to him, as with so many chronicles of cricket, is beyond measure. The son of Hambledon Club captain Richard Nyren, raised in the legendary Bat & Ball Inn, wrote a kind of *Plutarch's Lives* for the second millennium when recording his reminiscences of the great players at the turn of the nineteenth century. He wrote of bowlers and batsman alike, though, pleasantly enough for our purposes here, he seemed especially to admire the former. Given that a majority of bowlers in his time were spinners, this preference is to our lasting benefit. His reports go a long way towards compensating for the otherwise scattergun accounts of the period. Prone occasionally (and forgivably) to hyperbole, it is his descriptions that give us our most vivid portraits of the early spinners.

Nyren's dysphemism for spin was 'twist', which moves the focus of attention to the wrist action instead of the revolutions on the ball in the air and off the ground. He was wont to contradict himself in his attitude to the early Twirlymen. Indeed, other than an obvious zeal for the game and a crime reporter's attention to detail, we cannot discern a coherent ideology of bowling from his writings. At times he seemed fantastically in awe of the possibilities offered by 'twist'; at others he would warn against its employment at all costs: 'I cannot approve of his recommending a young player to give a twist to his balls,' he wrote of William Lambert, 'for in the first place, there are a hundred chances against his accomplishing the art and ten hundred in favour of the practice spoiling his bowling altogether.'

This caution, as we shall see, stands in direct opposition to the risk-taking innovation promoted by modern greats, from Benaud to Warne, who recommend young spinners try to really give the ball a rip before acquiring accuracy. Lambert, incidentally, was the five-foot-ten Surrey man with giant hands who fell from grace when accused of throwing a match at Lord's, but not before becoming a spinner of renown.

At other times, a kind of childish exuberance seems to overwhelm Nyren, and he indulges all the devious possibilities of spin with relish, as we see in his account of Lamborn, 'the Little Farmer', who played for Hambledon between 1777 and 1781:

Right-handed, and he had the most extraordinary delivery I ever saw. The ball was delivered quite low, and with a twist; not like that of the generality of right-handed bowlers, but just the reverse way, that is, if bowling to a right-handed hitter his ball would twist from the off-stump into the leg. *He was the first I remember who introduced this deceitful and teasing style of delivering the ball* [my italics]. When All England played the Hambledon Club, the Little Farmer was appointed one of our bowlers; and, egad! this new trick of his so bothered the Kent and Surrey men, that they tumbled out one after another, as if they had been picked off by a rifle corps. For a long time they could not tell what to make of that cursed twist of his

The language here is wonderfully evocative, from the military metaphor ('rifle corps') to the almost serpentine sibilance of 'cursed twist' and the constant sense of magic, with reference to teases and tricks and deception. Lamborn, we surmise, probably bowled the first under-arm off-spinners, but didn't know quite where to pitch them, constantly landing them on leg-stump rather than outside off. 'Ah, it was tedious near you, sir!' he would shout at the Duke of Dorset every time the ball went down the leg side, and eventually it got boring, so he learned to bowl a better line, something a few English off-spinners in recent times have been reluctant to do, even at Test level. Deprived by time of his forename, despite living to be eighty-five, he was described by Nyren as 'a plain-spoken little bumpkin' and 'very civil and inoffensive' (read: simple), and learned to spin the ball by hours of practice against a hurdle while tending his father's sheep. Such ingenuity united Lamborn not only with the likes of Clarrie Grimmett, who trained his fox terrier to fetch balls after he'd bowled an over in his back garden, but with contemporaries such as Tom Boxall, David Harris and Tom Walker, too.

Boxall, who in 1801 published the earliest known cricket manual, *Rules and Instructions for Playing the Game of Cricket*, was no more than five foot five, and according to Arthur Haygarth, the author of *Scores and Biographies* (published in fifteen volumes between 1862 and 1879), probably bowled the first under-arm leg-breaks. He had practised them indoors in winter in a specially converted barn built for him by the celebrated Kent patron Stephen Amherst. This indoor training was also the method favoured by David Harris – prompting Simon Hughes to suggest he invented indoor schools – and also Tom Walker, so that we can probably update Hughes and say all three were pioneers of indoor practice. It seems curious to us that indoor practice should have flourished in this humble manner over two centuries ago, but accounts of the time are clear that they did.

David Harris, a potter by trade, became the greatest bowler of his day, but was eventually overwhelmed with gout. He was so dominant that he was permitted to walk to the middle on crutches, complete his over and then rest in an armchair rather than field. Lord Frederick Beauclerk, the irascible gambler who was a leading figure in the game around this period, called his bowling 'one of the grandest sights in the universe'. Not the least of Harris's charming attributes is that he is the father of the hat-trick – now hijacked by other sports – having been presented with a gold-laced hat after a game in the mid-1780s, in recognition of his taking three wickets in three balls.

He was, further, a man who owed a significant portion of his reputation to his capacity (literally) to make mountains out of molehills. Like 'Lumpy' Stevens, he had a propensity for choosing strips that favoured his unorthodox under-arm delivery, and a penchant for the rough unpredictability of molehills. The other striking feature about his method was the bounce he could generate. Again Nyren is invaluable and, as ever, the clues can be uncovered by looking to the language:

His attitude when preparing for his run previously to delivering the ball would have made a beautiful study for the sculptor. First of all, he stood erect like a soldier at drill; then, with a graceful curve of the arm, he raised the ball to his forehead, and drawing back his right foot, started off with his left. His mode of delivering the ball was very singular. He would bring it from under his arm with a twist and nearly as high as his armpit, and with this action push it, as it were, from him. How it was that the balls acquired the velocity they did by this method I never could comprehend. In bowling, he never stooped in the least in his delivery, but kept himself upright all the time. His balls were very little beholden to the ground when pitched; it was but a touch, and up again; and woe to the man who did not get into [sic] block them, for they had such a peculiar curl, that they would grind his fingers against the bat: many a time have I seen blood drawn in this way from a batter who was not up to the trick.

'Very singular' could apply as much to Harris's unique action as to Nyren's prose. Spin is conjured up here by the ever-ready 'twist', the evocative 'peculiar curl', and the slightly revolting but irresistible image of the revolutions on the ball inducing a grinding of batsman's fingers against bat, and drawing blood. There is more of the magician's vocabulary ('trick') and another military metaphor ('soldier at drill'). Harris's 'upright' action is an example through the ages, and compares favourably with many later spinners who didn't make full use of their height (a repeated criticism of Tiger O'Reilly, in fact). Above all, we have received from Nyren an early description of spin causing pace off the wicket, fizzing on to the bat in a manner that O'Reilly himself, and other bowlers in his mould, such as Anil Kumble, emulated.

The other spinner to bamboozle batsman with his pace off the wicket, having practised indoors, was Tom Walker, known as 'Old Everlasting'. He was described as the first 'lobbing slow-bowler' by 'Silver' Billy Beldham – an all-rounder so named because of his prematurely greying hair and ranked, in 1997, as one of *The Times*'s one hundred greatest players ever. It is Walker who is thought to have first stretched out his arm to the horizontal, and consciously bowled round-arm in defiance of the spirit of the game. He did this in the 1780s, and was immediately called for 'throwing' – though by use of that term his contemporaries were chastising him not for straightening his arm but for raising it too high. In other words, they thought he was a cheat rather than a chucker – not that such a distinction would be much comfort to the legion of spinners (most notably Muralitharan) to whom both those insults have been attached in more recent times.

In Walker as much as any other bowler we see the revolutionary impulse of the early Twirlymen rear its head. He was an agitator, and proudly, too. Walker was one of a celebrated brotherhood from Thursley, near Hindhead in Surrey. Harry and Tom were described by Nyren as a pair of 'anointed clod-stompers', but their brother John played more sporadically. Tom Walker induced mixed feelings in Nyren, who said both that he 'never thought much of Tom's bowling', and later added he was 'one of the most fox-headed fellows I ever saw', a nod to his cunning with the ball. Later still Walker would prompt an admiring outburst from Nyren, who was in awe of his 'hard, ungain, scrag-of-mutton frame' with 'skin like the rind of an old oak', and knuckles that were 'handsomely knocked about' but never bled (unlike those of Lance Gibbs, Benaud, and, for that matter almost every other bowler mentioned in these pages). Beldham refuted this last point, saying, 'I have seen Tom Walker rub his bleeding fingers in the dust!', but we get a picture of Nyren's adulation.

It was as an opening batsman of astonishing patience that Tom Walker acquired fame, as well as his nickname, once facing 170 balls from David Harris to score just one run. But his contribution to the development of the game is most profound in relation to that notorious, arm-outstretched delivery in the 1780s. He was far from being simply reprimanded for 'throwing'; a special council of the Hambledon Club was convened to discuss the matter, and they lamented the foul play. In doing so, however, they gave the incident publicity, so that when later rebels also ate from the tree of cricket knowledge, of whose fruit round-arm and over-arm bowling were especially ripe picks, they cited 'Old Everlasting' as an early and shining example.

Towards the end of the eighteenth century, another major catalyst for the development of bowling was, perhaps unsurprisingly, the development of batting. Indeed, new batting techniques were central in forcing the pace of change. That late, brilliant historian and cricket nut Derek Birley attests batsmen were generally from a superior social standing, and thereby at greater liberty to innovate. Around 1765, John Small, from Empshott, just north of Petersfield in Hampshire, had become one of the first to make a habit of playing with a straight bat, and in two senses: first, he used a bat shaped like modern bats – that is, rectangular – rather than the inglorious hockey stick used previously; and second, he actually played 'straight', with a vertical rather than horizontal stroke. This gave a new role to the top hand. The Hambledon man Tom Seuter is the first batsman recorded as leaving his crease, and so popular did that technique become that it was quickly adopted as the orthodox method. Harry Hall, the gingerbread baker from Farnham, Surrey, proselytised about the 'high left-elbow' method, and Billy Beldham employed it to great effect.

A few decades later, a stylish young man named William Fennex, from Buckinghamshire, bucked the new trend for batsmen to jump out of the crease towards the pitch of the ball, instead playing it by lunging with his front foot while still stationed in the crease. This made him a progenitor of the cover drives that bring such happiness to spectators today. It also caused his watching father to shout in anguish, 'Hey! Hey, boy! What is this? Do you call that play?'

All these developments had vast ramifications. Eventually the laws of the game had to keep up, and it is here that the myth of Christina Willes springs up. In 1806 John Willes, a Kent player, became the first man to bowl round-arm at Lord's. Contemporary accounts suggest that he had been inspired by his sister who, bowling in their garden at home, was so inconvenienced by her lead-weighted dress that she raised her arm to waist height, soon to discover that by doing so she obtained the secondary benefit of making it easier to control the ball. Sir John Major, in that invaluable work, *More Than a Game*, has debunked this account. Hooped skirts, of the kind suggested by the purveyors of this myth, were simply not in fashion at the time of the Napoleonic Wars. Christina's crinolines couldn't have come into it.

John Willes attracted opprobrium for this shocking new method, and would on occasion defy certain rebuke to bowl it in matches. He was another proud agitator. In 1816 the game's first Laws of Cricket, written in 1744, were updated to the following effect:

> The ball must be bowled (not thrown or jerked), and be delivered underhand, with the hand below the elbow. But if the ball be jerked, or the arm extended from the body horizontally, and any part of the hand be uppermost, or the hand horizontally extended when the ball is delivered, the Umpires shall call 'No Ball'.

This they duly did when, with blatant disregard for the new laws, Willes, who had by now been pushing the boundary of the law for close to fifteen years, delivered a round-arm delivery while bowling for Kent against MCC at Lord's on 15 July 1822. Outraged by the continuing rigidity of the laws, Willes threw the ball down in disgust, called for his horse and promptly rode off into the sunset (literally and metaphorically: he all but retired after that match, ostracised by the cricket fraternity for his outlandish behaviour). For the next thirteen years, round-arm was tolerated unofficially and, in 1828, the MCC moderated Rule 10 to allow the hand as high as the elbow. In 1835 the laws were moderated again: by now the relevant passage was 'if the hand be above the shoulder in delivery, the umpire must call "No Ball"'. In 1845 this rule was reinforced with the removal of the benefit of the doubt going to the bowler, but so impossible was this to adjudicate that by 1864 the authorities finally succumbed and legalised over-arm bowling.

If, to modern or myopic minds, this eventual permitting of over-arm bowling seems inevitable, it is worth reminding ourselves how far from certain such progress was. It took a full four decades between Willes's tantrum at Lord's in 1822 and eventual legalisation of over-arm; and it took just under six if we go back to his first round-arm delivery at the home of cricket in 1806. The intervening period is an extraordinary segment in the history of spin. The taboos surrounding the legality of round-arm encouraged risk-taking and, with it, innovations for which future Twirlymen would owe a debt of gratitude. Yet it was also a period in which the looseness of the laws and their enforcement meant bowlers of several different types flourished at the same time. Cricket matches regularly witnessed the early round-armers bowling their leg-breaks at one end, while from the other, old-school under-armers plied their trade in a more traditional fashion, sometimes reprising the off-breaks pioneered by Lamborn. It made the modern spectacle of almost complete over-arm delivery dominance seem positively monotonous by comparison, and one of the charming aspects to those middling decades of the nineteenth century is that spin bowlers were clearly beginning to develop a sense of self-awareness, of themselves as merchants of mystery, and employers of variation. Of the growing numbers doing this, four stand out. Each was called William.

The first, the aforementioned William Lambert, of whose technique Nyren was sceptical, employed infamously enormous hands to turn the ball sharply from leg. In *Scores and Biographies*, Arthur Haygarth wrote, that Lambert was 'one of the most successful cricketers that has ever yet appeared'. Lambert also happened to be the finest batsman of his day, though he never recovered from the accusation that he threw a match at Lord's.

The second, William Ward, was a Wykehamist who saved Lord's by injecting it with cash just as it was about to be sold off, an act which led Nyren to dedicate one of his books to him. A director of the Bank of England, Member of Parliament and owner of the record score at Lord's (278) between 1820 and 1925, he wielded a 4lb bat and once bowled seventeen maiden overs on the trot. Ward opposed round-arm bowling, saying it was too hard for the batsman, though ironically his own success with the bat undermined his argument. He insisted on bowling under-arm, which he did to great effect, spinning the ball sharply from leg to off.

William Clarke thought he could achieve a more substantial break from leg bowling under-arm, and so returned to that method, achieving huge success along the way. He was the Kerry Packer of the 1800s. A one-eyed wanderer referred to as 'Old Clarke' ('old' was clearly a popular motif in cricket circles of the time), he used to walk around the nets on the morning of a match, watching opposition batsmen and psyching them out, hands always tucked under his coat flaps, counting aloud his wickets in advance, deciphering the 'exact pitch' – that is, length – at which a batsman would be most discomfited, and referring to this as their 'blind spot'. He would have a glass of soda water and a cigar every lunchtime, a combination he described as 'most satisfying – with no after-effects of indigestion', which presumably isn't altogether different from the justification Warne proffered when defending his definition of a balanced diet 150 years later ('a cheeseburger in each hand'). And he was cantankerous, too: about as cantankerous as the great Sydney Barnes. Once, when a station master asked for a porter's assistance in forcing the stubborn Clarke to put out his cigar, he responded by stubbing it out on the porter's hand. Another time, when a grocer asked how he should become a great spinner Clarke responded: 'Get your fingernails cut.' Of modern spinners, perhaps only the perennially argumentative Harbhajan Singh could compete in this regard. At night Clarke dined alone, with a penchant for demolishing an entire Michaelmas goose single-handedly.

Clarke learned most of his craft from William Lambert, always wore a tall hat and had sight in only one eye because of an accident when playing fives in his twenties, where the ball hit his right eye on the court behind the Bell Inn in Nottingham. It was in Bunker's Hill, Nottingham, that he had been born on Christmas Eve, 1798. Intriguingly, Haygarth described his having a 'cruelly deceptive' slower ball, launched from armpit height, as his main variation from the under-arm skimmers he usually sent through. Clarke must thereby have been one of the very few under-arm bowlers to slow his pace down when graduating to round-arm. The author James Pycroft wrote that he delivered the ball from around the hip, 'with a little chuck or fling from the hand' to impart spin, but he appears to have reverted to under-arm leg-spin when he realised this gave him both more 'twist' and better control. It gave him so much of those, indeed, that he is the only player ever to take a first-class hat-trick that included the same player twice – John Fagge, the Kent batsman, being snared over two innings. He had a well-disguised and speedy faster ball, too, and received the rare treat, in mid-nineteenth-century terms at least, of having a book written about him: *How to Play Clarke*, by Nicholas 'Felix' Wanostrocht, a renowned Kent batsman. A totem of the pivotal role he played in popularising not just the round-arm style but genuine spin was his celebrated denunciation of the master at a public school who was trying to coach his pupils to bowl fast. Outraged at the sight of this 'wild style of bowling', he described it as 'cruelty to animals'.

Shrewd in his field placings and use of conditions, he demanded the Pavilion End at Lord's, so that the slope would counter his sharp leg-spin and help generate bounce. He was said to conquer batsmen by making them overplay their favourite strokes, and left a remark as supporting evidence which has been heard, and acted upon faithfully, by modern bowling greats. Asked how he overcame good batsmen, he said, 'Nothing easier, sir: I bowl him three balls to make him proud of his forward play, and then with the fourth I pitch shorter, twist, and catch him at the slip.' It is wonderful to think how, more than a century and a half ago, this giant of the game probably left the cover area vacant, tempted batsmen by goading them into successive drives through that region, luring them into overconfidence, and then bowled a delivery slightly shorter, with more side-spin, and watched enemy after enemy nick it to slip. The best methods are the oldest, and with good reason.

His tactical awareness informed a successful bout of captaincy as well as his later business career, which flourished after he gave up bricklaying for the life of a publican. Clarke married a widow named Chapman and took over the running of her pub, which happened to be the Trent Bridge Inn. He laid out a pitch on the meadow behind his establishment and, caring for its turf obsessively, became the father of Nottingham's modern Test match venue. After moving up to London, where he was a practice bowler in the nets at Lord's (an activity that would unite him with our fourth William), he spotted an opportunity to promote an All England XI match. This involved embarking on nationwide, money-spinning tours, taking famous names to small villages in widely publicised fixtures. Though his failure to pay the players sufficiently led to many joining John Wisden's breakaway group in 1852, Clarke's vision helped the game expand internationally. It was his successor as manager of the All England XI, George Parr, who embarked on that team's first tour, to North America in 1859. John Arlott described Clarke as 'the greatest missionary [cricket] ever knew, or ever can know'. His playing career at competitive level lasted forty-one years, and he took a wicket with the last ball he ever bowled. Clarke's contribution to the game is remembered by the stand named after him at Trent Bridge, but no tombstone or epitaph marks his final resting place in a Norwood cemetery.

The fourth William is the grandfather to an early cricketing dynasty. F. W. (William) Lillywhite gave his name to the store opened in London's Haymarket in 1863, and that now occupies a corner of Piccadilly Circus.

His sons profited more from it than he did. One of William Clarke's original All England XI, Lillywhite was like Clarke in being both a practice bowler at Lord's and a former bricklayer, having originally worked for his father on the Duke of Richmond's Goodwood estate. (He was unlike Clarke, however, in having an obelisk paid for by public subscription on his grave in Highgate cemetery, just yards from Karl Marx.) He was one of the most rambunctious, truculent, and fat players of all time – and a brilliant spinner. Matched in obesity among the great spinners, never mind players, probably only by Warwick Armstrong, his roundness was accentuated by a diminutive, five-foot-four-inch frame. Nicknamed 'the Nonpareil', he rarely batted if he could get away with it, insisting bowlers, the workhorses of the game, exerted themselves sufficiently with the ball in hand. 'Look here, sir,' he once said to a recalcitrant captain, 'when I've bowled the ball, I've done with hur [sic], and I leaves hur to my field.' Another time, displaying an arrogance to match his laziness, he exclaimed, 'I bowls the best balls in England, and I suppose if I was to think every ball, they'd never get a run!' The trouble for his interlocutors was that such a claim was probably justified.

It has been suggested by Hughes with some plausibility that Lillywhite took a long time to make an impact on the game 'because he couldn't get his under-arm past his belly'. Nevertheless, once he did, his record was excellent, even with the caveat that it was only in this period (the mid-nineteenth century) that reliably comprehensive records were being maintained. Over one three-year period, he took 685 wickets, and over twenty-seven seasons obtained at least 1,576 wickets in 237 matches, at an official average of 10.36. His probing round-arm deliveries were referred to as 'peculiars', and he had a mesmeric looping ball, probably not far off what we would call a moon ball today, referred to as a 'tice', a now anachronistic word for a ball on a tricky length, which doubled up charmingly as a shortened version of 'entice', which is exactly what it did.

He and his Sussex colleague Jem Broadbridge were self-styled round-armers who, knowing the greater difficulty of bowling an accurate line with a round-arm action – release it too early and it goes leg-side; too late and it veers to the off – became among the first to popularise going around the wicket. A secondary advantage of this was that they avoided hitting the umpire, something regular and bitter experience of bowling over the wicket had led to. But, having gone round the wicket, Lillywhite's accuracy was exceptional. It is said he bowled fewer than a dozen wides in his entire career and, responding to a bowler who claimed he could land it on a piece of paper, he said, 'Yes, but I could shift the paper and still hit it.' So conscious was he of the need for a good line that he explained, 'Three balls out of four straight is what we calls mediogrity [sic].'

Lillywhite also left one of the first non-Nyren descriptions of how to impart spin. Coming from a bowler renowned for his mastery of flight and variation, it has especial value. In a handbook published in 1844 he wrote: 'By holding the ball slightly askew, with the thumb well across the seam, you will find by working the wrist as the ball leaves the hand, it will assist to cut and rick at the wicket, such balls are very troublesome to stop, to get rid of.' We have no pictorial evidence of this grip, alas, but it is one of the earliest coaching efforts in relation to spin. 'Working the wrist' stops tantalisingly short of pronouncing on direction – clockwise for off-spin or (more likely) anti-clockwise for leg-spin? – and it's noticeable that there is no mention of fingers getting involved. It's unlikely that the wrist did all the work for Lillywhite, but his emphasis on it gives us licence to call him a wrist-spinner rather than a finger-spinner. The idea of a fiercely spun delivery being difficult to 'get rid of', as if it were a lingering odour or an annoying child, puts us in his frame of mind: Lillywhite sought to cause a nuisance as often as possible.

Through such exertions did he take up the baton handed to him by previous Williams, renegades all, and accelerate the development of bowling. Ironically, it was his son, John Lillywhite, who, when umpiring in a game between Surrey and All England at the Oval on 26 August 1862, called the left-arm Edgar Willsher, who always had an unsmooth action, for a no-ball six times in succession when he bowled over-arm. In the same vein as Willes decades earlier, Willsher threw the ball down and stormed off. Unfortunately, he had no waiting horse, but this was compensated for by the action of his teammates who, in a coordinated protest, walked out. Lillywhite Junior was replaced as umpire, Surrey released a statement saying he had 'fulfilled his duties as umpire according to his honest convictions' and the correspondent from *The Times* acquired the view that his actions had been 'perfectly justified'.

To quell the ensuing palaver, the MCC changed Law 10 ahead of the 1864 season. Now the bowler could bring his arm over at any height, provided it was straight. Dark mutterings were heard suggesting Lillywhite Junior had been bribed, and even (less plausibly) that he had contrived the controversy to speed up the change in the law, and so complete the unfinished business of his father. The later business association between him and Willsher seemed to back this conspiracy theory, but its basic improbability has led several authors (notably Birley) to dismiss it.

One way or another, the work of Lillywhite and his spinning comrades had caused irreversible changes to the game. Other spinners became notorious for their deceptive methods and innovations. Robert Clifford of Kent bowled effective under-arm leg spin in the 1780s, despite a childhood accident causing the two shorter fingers of his right (and bowling) hand to be pressed into his palm. He was regularly lauded for his all-round performances, and Haygarth makes a point of recognising his attention to detail. John Sparks, a small man from Cambridge who bowled under-arm leg-spin, was referred to as the 'best slow bowler in England'.

The essential point here is that the greatest bowlers during cricket's infancy had two predominant features; first, a preparedness to be radical; second, a propensity for imparting Nyren's infamous 'twist'. Let's examine them in reverse order.

Throughout this hugely formative period in the game's history, when it emerged from humble Hampshire origins into modernity, and acquired the laws that make it recognisable today, spin – under-arm, round-arm and over-arm – was dominant. In the grand narrative of bowling history, pace is an afterthought. Spin, not speed, was the favoured weapon of the original bowlers. Of course, this is largely a product of circumstance. It is difficult to generate discomfiting pace bowling under-arm, so other weapons had to be employed. There are only so many molehills in England, which led quickly to the 'working the wrist' that later gave the elder Lillywhite cause for glee. These wrists would generally have been worked in an anti-clockwise fashion because, such is the physiology of the arm, it is as natural to bowl leg-spin under-arm as it is to bowl off-spin over-arm. (That is why Lamborn's first off-break sent shock waves through England: it went against the prevailing orthodoxy.) In part because bowling under-arm places much less strain on the body – in particular the shoulder, which doesn't have to undergo a huge rotating circle – a striking feature of many of these early spinners is their longevity.

It is a myth that, in the modern game, spinners generally last longer because they somehow exert themselves less over the course of a career than quicker bowlers (ask Shane Warne). But it is true that, in the age of under-arm and then round-arm bowling, many successful bowlers played for decades and conducted their greatest endeavours when middle-aged. David Frith has charmingly suggested that this is because they acquired 'cunning ... pure cunning' as they got older, in a way that fast bowlers don't. That is probably true. But it's also simply the case that, unlike in the modern game where over-arm is so dominant, bowlers' bodies could cope with the strain of under-arm for many years longer. Even when, as was so often the case during this period, and with Lillywhite in particular, the spinner in question was monstrously fat.

That last point shouldn't distract us from the overtly cerebral dimension to their play. Few of those discussed above excelled academically, but it is fascinating when reading Nyren and other accounts of the period to note that, as a language of self-consciousness emerges among the bowlers of the game, it is through the vocabulary of cunning, deceit and trickery – that is, a spinner's jargon – that this development is expressed. Not for nothing did Derek Birley refer to bowlers of this period – spinners, predominantly – as the 'march of intellect' bowlers. We should recall that with no professionalised coaches, most of these bowlers learned largely on their own, practising against hurdles, in makeshift barns, anywhere they could find spherical objects and a patch of earth they thought could take spin.

Under-arm leg-spin was to them an emancipation from the tedium of reliance on uneven, molehill-infested strips. And possibly because the laws of the game were not as punitive, and were in any case not enforced as frequently, there was more leeway for a game still finding its way out of infancy. Early bowlers exploited this by trying several different methods to remove batsmen. Lamborn's off-break might have been a shock, but he kept bowling it, experimenting with different lines, and eventually it had such efficacy as to become part of other bowlers' armoury, too. As we have seen, other bowlers who imparted spin on the ball were pilloried by fellow players, and forced in some cases (as with John Willes) to abandon the game altogether. But their stamp on history is deep and ineradicable: it was the preparedness of early bowlers – and Twirlymen, at that – to bend the spirit of the laws, which eventually benefited all those who now take an active interest in the game. From Tom Walker's outstretched arm and Willes's repeated round-arm deliveries, to Clarke's persistence in bowling under-arm and Willsher's consecutive no-balls, it was a spirit of defiance, invariably from purveyors of spin, that led to modern bowling forms and forced the laws of the game to adapt.

This will be a recurring theme of ours. Revolutionaries shimmer through the history of spin: when we come to the First Flourish, we'll see that the first mainstream googly merchants were lambasted for their officious forwardness, and told to drop their act; and yet they gave cricket a new dimension. At the same time, a curious lob bowler emerged in England, bowling slow moon balls as if teleported from the era we have just considered to one that thought it had said goodbye to old orthodoxies.

All these bowlers were also, simply by virtue of the stage they occupy in the game's evolution, overtly conscious of themselves as part of a tradition: specifically one in which bowlers of around what we would call medium pace sought to add variation to their bowling by imparting spin on the ball. They were categorically different from those we have just considered, not just in occupying a different era, but in being faster too. But they developed spin bowling, and laid the foundation for bowlers of a similar ilk to flourish later– most strikingly, Sydney Barnes. All this made them what I call cricket's Swift Pioneers. But before we get to them, and to the two basic methods they sought to deploy and the limits thereof, it's worth reflecting on what it is that these great men had in common with their modern successors – what it was that animated the spinner's spirit.

Interlude One

LEG-BREAK

Grip   *Batsman's Point of View*

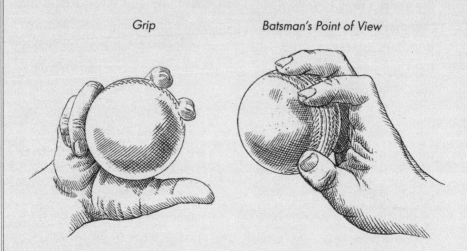

The basic grip for the leg-break is, as Warne calls it, 'Two up, two down'. The tops of the first two fingers are across the seam. The spin is imparted by the third finger, which straightens from a bent position. On entering the delivery stride, the back of the hand starts off facing the sky. As the arm comes round, the wrist unfurls in an anti-clockwise direction, or from right to left, so that at the moment of release the back of the hand points towards the bowler's face. The seam should be spinning along its own axis, which by now points to the third-man region. The thumb can be on or off the seam until release.

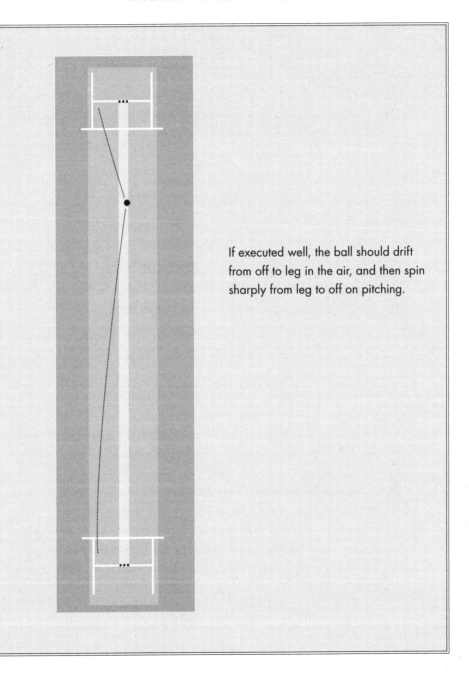

If executed well, the ball should drift from off to leg in the air, and then spin sharply from leg to off on pitching.

Chapter Two

THE SPINNER'S SPIRIT

The word 'spin' has been hijacked by political operatives of late, but from its very origins it connoted non-linearity and entanglement. Its usage dates back to at least the fifteenth century, where it was a term meaning 'draw out and twist fibres into a thread'. The modern incarnation retains the original notion of weaving, but fibrous materials have been replaced by (usually political) narratives. In those narratives, spin doctors, as we now call them, are concerned to manipulate public knowledge by controlling what enters the public sphere, and so distort history. They do this by keeping a certain amount of information secret, thereby creating false impressions – that is, being deceiver to the receiver.

Deception is similarly the forte of the spin bowler to a degree unique, not just in cricket, but across all great sport. It is the single most leaned-upon word by spinners trying to account for their motivation as bowlers, and it entered every interview I conducted for this book. Those looped offerings to the batsmen contain none of the conviviality their lack of pace initially seems to intimate. In time, the batsman will come to prefer extreme pace, due to its relative simplicity. It is much harder to argue with brain than brawn.

If there is one thing a spinner must do more than his faster and seaming counterpart, then, it is cause the batsmen not just to think intensely, but to think wrongly – that is, to become confused. 'To stay ahead of the batsman,' Johnny Gleeson, a mystery spinner of the 1970s says, 'you have to make him think, convince him that you are doing something.' By this demand spin bowling becomes cricket's most overtly intellectual habit. Once thrown the ball by his captain, the spinner is as one of two interlocutors engaged in ferocious debate. Unlike standard dialogue, which is oiled by a modicum of honesty, and whose meaningful conduct depends on trust, this conversation contains lies, verbal shortcuts and false segues. The spin bowler cannot extricate his opponent by employing sheer power; his weapons are more cerebral than that, based on subtleties and strategies whose execution can only be effective with extensive practice. He makes batsmen fearful, not of pain, but of ignominy.

And, like a chess grandmaster who offers a gambit down one flank only suddenly to open up the opposite one, the spinner must impart every one of his deliveries – every blast into enemy territory – with the power to confuse by deception. He must make his every action – before, during and after the delivery – incorrigibly polysemous. He must pay heed to the old saying, if the batsman thinks it's spinning, it's spinning. A slower delivery here, a wider angle on the crease there, an extra man in the slips; the spin bowler is an actor, performing his role in the unfolding drama with more versatility than any other character on stage.

His disposition therefore is, of necessity, attacking, risk-taking, unconservative, selfish. Where the pace man seeks to make a batsman cringe, the spinner seeks to make him cry. The great E. H. D. Sewell was getting at just this when he wrote, in *Well Hit, Sir!*: 'There is real art in bowling opponents out or in getting them caught or stumped out by the clever pitching of a well-spun ball. There is none whatever in trying to frighten them out.' Well said, sir.

It is no coincidence that the greatest spy in history used the language of Twirlymen to advance his espionage ambitions. It is a little-known fact that Kim Philby, the high-ranking member of British Intelligence who worked as a spy for the Soviet Union, used nothing less than the googly to examine the merit and integrity of his contacts. In Chris Petit's essay 'The Stiletto of Fiction: Or, the Chinaman', from *London: City of Disappearances* (edited by Iain Sinclair), we learn of a meeting between James Jesus Angleton, later head of the CIA, and Philby in London.

Petit reports a conversation in which the novelist Graham Greene – recruited to MI6 by his sister Elisabeth, and counting Philby as his mentor – is implicated:

Philby asked if Angleton knew what a Chinaman was.

'A left-handed googly.'

Greene looked irritated. 'I thought Yanks weren't supposed to know about cricket.'

Philby said: 'All right, Mr Know-it-all. What's a googly?'

Angleton told them it was an off-break delivery, disguised by sleight of hand to resemble a leg-break action, deceiving the batsman into thinking the ball would break the opposite way from the other one it would really turn.

Philby said: 'You offer the other fellow three googlies. He gets one chance to read it, one to play it and the third you give him the real leg-break, which he misreads and doesn't know where he is, if you get my drift.'

This passage indicates more than simply that Philby was a cricket nut. It tells us that what espionage relies on is what spin bowling relies on – deception; that the language of spin bowling itself has an evocative power, suggestive of deviant methods; and that the greatest spies civilisation has known thought it fit to code their intentions in the vocabulary of Twirlymen. Spinners should be understood in this context, as purveyors of trickery from beyond enemy lines.

It may seem a stretch, given the degree of variety among the characters that fall under the label, to think it possible that Twirlymen could share common ground at all; that it's possible to decipher a philosophy of spin or a spirit of spinners from so broad a canvas. But several traits do recur among them. First, as we have seen, a propensity for deception. Second, immodesty, and a consequent willingness to propagandise about one's own talents (that is, brag). Third, intelligence and a tendency to the eccentric. Fourth, alertness to the comic aspect of human relations. Fifth, sensitivity to the prevailing cultural mood in one's own nation. And sixth, and perhaps most important, extreme stamina – fortitude in the face of adversity, and the ability to do what Churchill demanded of Roosevelt: 'Keep buggering on!'.

From its very conception cricket is illuminated by the lights flickering in the minds of spin bowlers intent on deception and duplicity, on calculating possibilities and recalibrating strategy. 'There is so much variety in spin bowling,' says Anil Kumble, the modern Indian great, 'so much deception, so much analysis. And at the end of it you can't terrorise a batsman. You have to get a wicket by deceiving him and trying to apply pressure with whatever variations you have. I am sure all of us spinners, when we are not really at our best, would like to just hit the batsman with a bouncer.'

The great Bernard Bosanquet, known wrongly to history as the pioneer of the googly, would have concurred with Kumble's sentiment.

'The whole art of bowling,' he said, 'is to make the batsman think that the ball is going to be of one kind when it is really of quite a different nature.' That sentiment reflects the keenly felt spirit of the spinner long before that of a speedster, and has been a kind of guiding principle of many of the great Twirlymen. The Australian Clarrie Grimmett, sometimes known as 'the Fox', so cunning was his method, often clicked his fingers with his left hand as he came in to bowl with his right, trying to confuse batsmen along the way by overloading their radars with stimuli.

Closely tied to the art of deception is the instrument of propaganda. More than any other type of cricketer, spin bowlers seek not to speak truth to power, but to lie on its behalf. They do this because they know that by spreading disinformation they can buy themselves cheap wickets. So spinners, always and everywhere, make claims on their own behalf which lack the ring of truth. They know they can trade on the relative mystery in which their methods are generally thought concealed: the ignorance of batsmen and pundits the world over gives them space to exploit. It's no wonder, given this love of story-telling, that so many spinners have a background in journalism (like Benaud) or become great journalists themselves (Benaud, Laker and now Warne must be three of the finest pundits or commentators across all sporting history).

'What matters is not always how many deliveries you possess, but how many the batsman thinks you have,' Warne says. 'Half of the battle is sowing doubt in his mind.' We know of his boast of possessing sixteen deliveries ahead of an Ashes series. And as he showed during the summer of 2005 in England, when he claimed to dismiss Ian Bell with a perfect slider – in fact, it was simply a leg-break that failed to grip – he's not afraid of boasting about his own armoury, even if it involves lying publicly.

Most of the time it's pure nonsense that the spinners propagate: they lay claim, as Mike Atherton once put it, to more deliveries than an NHS midwife. Saqlain Mushtaq, when marching into cricket history with his brilliant doosra – meaning 'the other one', and being a ball that looks like an off-break but spins away to leg – put it around that he had a 'teesra', yet another delivery that looked like the doosra but was in fact the off-break. It was garbage, of course, but caused batsmen, particularly those on the county circuits, sleepless nights. Similarly, Grimmett did briefly try to develop a 'wrong' wrong'un – wrong'un being the Australian term for a googly – which looked like the googly but in fact spun like a leg-break. Again, he never really got it going, but the non-entity achieved the desired aim of its progenitor by spreading terror. Ajantha Mendis, knowing the excitement his arrival on the Test scene had generated, said he only had five balls but was working on a sixth. 'This is different from the carrom ball,' he said. 'I was testing this ball in the nets during net sessions earlier, but I might use it during match time.' That quote got around. It contained a threat, not despite but *because* it was so utterly devoid of specifics.

Many a commentator and ignoramus amateur has not only complied in the spread of this propaganda, but been the main source of it. The ignorance surrounding the various deliveries available to a spinner is extraordinarily wide, and it is a modest ambition of these pages to help remedy it. One common confusion, for example, is between the googly and the flipper, two deliveries whose only common qualities are that they are generally delivered by a wrist-spinner and come in from the off. Their trajectories are completely different. Other times, it is simply ignorant batsmen who spread the fear. Benaud's New South Wales teammate Barry Rothwell hardly did his colleague a favour by whispering to him, when he was preparing to play Johnny Gleeson, having heard much about his threat, 'this bloke's bowling Iversons', so invoking the spirit of a bowler whose name was synonymous with indecipherability.

In fact, a surprising number of commentators are equally stumped. In a recent Test match, Rangana Herath, the scintillating Sri Lankan left-arm spinner, bowled a delivery from round the wicket that, on pitching, spun into the right-hander, causing (in this instance) the Indians no end of trouble. In the commentary box, Sunil Gavaskar, the second most distinguished cricketer his country has produced and a legend of the game, was almost lost for words. 'There it is that … [pause] *finger-tweaker*,' he said, choosing those words only in the forlorn hope they would erect a sense of puzzlement on behalf of the batsman, while in fact merely revealing his own. He has no vocabulary for what his eyes present him with – though the vocabulary exists with which to describe Herath's carrom ball.

Such mischief is a consequence of the fact that, perhaps more than any other category of cricketer, spinners have tended to be intellectuals. Any docile thinker can make a reasonable go of the game; but the great spinners have never failed to be alert to the most minor detail, the deeply obscured plan and the most complex possibility. The Australian Tiger O'Reilly, who was the best bowler of the 1930s, said of Grimmett that he was 'perhaps the best and most consistently active cricket thinker I ever met'; the great Ralph Barker wrote that Grimmett 'delighted in deceiving the batsman for the sake of deception, whether he got him out or not'.

Extra-curricular habits, or academic records, are often a sound indication, too. Among the Indians who toiled successfully at the top level, Anil Kumble, Erapalli Prasanna and Srinivasan Venkataraghavan were qualified engineers. So, too, was the Australian Gleeson, a culture vulture who was known as 'Cho' because he was around during 'cricket hours only' on tour, so fascinated was he by the discovery of local customs and traditions. Sonny Ramadhin, the brilliant West Indian off-spinner, was obsessed with motor mechanics. Australia's Stuart MacGill is a wine connoisseur, also known for his tendency to pack for each tour with an extra suitcase stuffed with a dozen books, which he would invariably devour before the series was up. Phil Edmonds took a First from Cambridge.

Equipped with a reputation for being cerebral, spinners have been the great innovators of the game. Their thirst for experimentation, and the knowledge yielded by it, makes Copernicus look like the class dunce. Arthur Mailey, the humble Australian leg-spinner of the early twentieth century, developed strong fingers by working as a glass-blower. Ramadhin's obsession with motor mechanics was key to his developing stronger digits. Gleeson reckoned he owed the dexterity of his hands to working on his parents' farm; while for Bishen Bedi, the lithe Indian left-armer, it was a combination of yoga and the fact that he washed his own clothes. Teddy Peate, one of the first of the great Yorkshire left-armers, trained as a clown and then bowled at bales of 'mungo'.

Spheres of all different sizes have succumbed to this innate curiosity: Iverson had a nervous tic with the table-tennis ball; Saqlain used the same to master the doosra before graduating to a tennis ball on the rooftops of Lahore. Ramadhin bowled with tropical fruit to make his fingers supple; Warne and Abdul Qadir spun oranges at each other one evening at the latter's house.

According to the accounts of that occasion it was full of laughter and back-slapping camaraderie. This is in keeping with the spinner's feel for comedy. Twirlymen have a peerless proclivity for practical jokes. Wicketkeepers are also among the great eccentrics of the game, wearing silly hats, observing curious rituals, imitating nature with indecipherable noises and adorning themselves with regrettable facial hair; but it is spinners who know a knave when they see one, who cohere a team with their outrageous pranks, and who could find a point of humour on the edge of a knife.

That may be why, on the classic album *The Duckworth Lewis Method*, released in 2009 by Neil Hannon, the songwriter behind the Divine Comedy, easily the funniest song concerns Warne's delivery to Gatting. The chorus of 'Jiggery Pokery' goes:

Jiggery pokery, trickery chokery, / How did he open me up? / Robbery! Muggery! Aussie skull-duggery! / Out for a buggering duck ... / What a delivery, / I might as well have been / Holding a child's balloon, / Jiggery pokery who is this nobody / Making me look a buffoon?

The song, with its air of joyful bewilderment, and its exalting in the confusion of a hapless victim, captures the spirit of the spinner rather beautifully.

Sometimes these spinners themselves can't help but be the butt of a joke. It was said of J. M. Barrie, a (very) part-time spinner who compiled possibly the greatest amateur cricket XI the world has seen – in terms of showbiz, that is, rather than competence – that he bowled so slowly that if he didn't like what he'd sent down he had time to go and fetch it back.

A wry smile spread across Mike Atherton's face when he recalled the time David Hughes, then captain of Lancashire, resorted to a bottle of oily calamine lotion, popular among spinners suffering from cut fingers following Benaud's chance discovery of it in New Zealand in the winter of 1956. Atherton, then a young turk fresh down from Cambridge, had conspired with a teammate to replace the contents of the bottle with soy sauce. Hughes was alerted to this only when, having applied the lotion, he wondered at the fishy smell on his fingers. Phil Tufnell was the butt of jokes throughout his playing days, something he milks now that he gets paid to embarrass himself on television. It was this spinner who, during an Ashes tour, heard an Australian in the crowd shout, 'Oi Tufnell, lend us your brain ... I'm building an idiot', which I should confess does rather counteract my suggestion that most spinners are super-smart.

But even the less smart ones are smart-arses, so that a discomfortingly high proportion of the greatest spinners are instinctive pranksters. Tufnell's wife went out one day to buy a pint of milk and never came back. This was a fortnight earlier. Goodness, said Simon Hughes, sorry to hear that. How are you coping? Fine, comes back the reply, I've been using the powdered stuff ...

The English spinner Roley Jenkins, playing once against Scotland, kept appealing desperately, only to be turned down time after time. 'I'm very sorry for those appeals, I forgot we were playing under Scottish law,' he said to the umpire. Still more appeals were turned down. He wandered up to the batsman, a Revd J. Aitchison. 'I understand you're a parson,' he said to him. Yes I am, came the reply. 'With your bloody luck,' Jenkins said, 'you'll soon be the Archbishop of Canterbury!' A little later the umpire tried to defuse the tension by asking how the bowler's spinning fingers were coping, to which Jenkins retorted with the instruction: 'Lend me the one you're not using!'

Jenkins was one of the legion of spinners who was the source of endless humour despite not making it at the very highest level. Two others among the English contingent of this species were Eric Hollies and Bryan 'Bomber' Wells. Hollies, the man whose googly denied Donald Bradman a career average of 100, once decided, towards the end of a day's play at Edgbaston, that he was getting tired. So he wandered off, but came back on a bike to bowl his last over. He had borrowed the groundsman's rusting machine, pedalled in from fine leg, deposited it near the stumps and told the umpire, 'Hang on to that till the end of the over.'

This was the man, after all, who told New Zealander Don Taylor that he needed a passport to enter Wales for the match against Glamorgan. Hollies convinced Taylor by keeping poker-faced, despite the protestations coming at him. And poor, naive Taylor was only told of this apparent requirement when the team were already on the coach, just miles from the Welsh border. Terrified, Taylor asked Hollies what to do. Thankfully, Hollies had just the solution. He told the overseas player to lie under a seat, hidden by the team kit, for the next twenty miles, until they were well into Wales. Taylor gratefully complied.

But few have done more to professionalise mischief, under the guise of spin bowling, than 'Bomber' Wells, the most eccentric of all professional cricketers in the 1950s and 1960s. His 998 first-class wickets are testament to the fact that he was a highly capable bowler. Strikingly overweight and unathletic – no impediment to such brilliant spinners as William Lillywhite and Warwick Armstrong – with his mannerisms he inspired imitation and affection in equal measure. He bowled off two steps if it was cold, one if it was hot and none at all if it was *really* hot. He once bowled an entire over while the clock in Worcester Cathedral was striking twelve. Derrick Bailey, 3rd Battalion, his Gloucestershire captain, was outraged. Claiming Wells was bringing the game into disrepute, he demanded he start his run from eight paces back. Wells did, but then bowled a ball of immaculate length having taken only a couple of paces at the end of his walk-up, as per usual. 'Sir Derrick went berserk,' he recalled years later. 'He dropped me for two matches, but it was worth it.'

Wells owed his county debut for Gloucestershire to the fact that another player, Sam Cook, had fallen on a packet of mints. He was completely uninterested in setting his field, leaving his captain to do it for him, and was possibly the lamest rabbit in the world, a total refusenik when it came to improving his batting. Bowling was what he wanted to think about. Once when playing Essex he encountered a young batsman who stepped away from the crease whenever he was about to bowl. So 'I ran all the way round the square, past mid-on, square leg, behind the 'keeper, back to mid-off, and I shouted, "Are you ready now?" And I bowled him first ball.'

All this made him one of the most popular players in cricket, with fans travelling hundreds of miles just for a sight of his usually very brief innings. Ultimately, for our purposes at least, the essential thing about Wells was that he was a spin bowler. The question of what came first – spin or clownishness – is redundant, because they were one and the same thing. In using a professional career as a spinner to facilitate his lifelong commitment to deviousness, mischief and practical jokes, Wells personified an essential component of the spinning spirit: a preparedness to find humour where others could not.

Not all the consequences of being clever are propitious where spinners are concerned. A vast number are, for example, neurotic and obsessive. Active minds tend towards neuroses more than those of dullards. A fine example concerns the English left-armer Tony Lock, that complex character forever remembered for denying Jim Laker all twenty wickets at Old Trafford in 1956. On the 1953–4 tour of the West Indies, Laker wandered up to Trevor Bailey and asked him, 'Are you sharing rooms with Bo [Lock's nickname, sometimes spelt 'Beau']?' Yes, said Bailey, at which Laker smiled, and wished him luck. Bailey was confused. Why the sarcasm? 'You'll find out in good time,' Laker said. Indeed he did, on the first night of the first Test:

That night we went to bed early hoping for a good night's rest. I had just dropped off, tired after a full day in the sun, when I was frightened to death by a piercing appeal for lbw. 'How's that?!' is not what you expect to hear in a bedroom in the middle of the night. There was Tony standing up in the middle of his bed, both arms held high with the sheet in front of him. I dared not speak. He held this pose for what seemed ages, and then dropped back, turned over and carried on sleeping. I did not know whether I should stay, or make a run for it, but it was some time before I got to sleep again.

When I told Tony about it the next morning, he denied it, of course. He simply did not know what he had done. I sought out Jim Laker at breakfast and told him about the night's happening. He simply curled up with the tears streaming down his face. He said: 'I knew it wouldn't be long before you found out' ...

... On another occasion he stood up in his bed clapping both hands. He was congratulating somebody on a great catch ...

The same tendencies gripped many others. 'Toey' Tayfield, easily the greatest spinner South Africa has produced, went through an elaborate ritual each time he returned to his mark, one demanded by his subservience to superstition. Jack Iverson, the mercurial Australian of the 1950s who later committed suicide – one of two bowlers in these pages to do so (the other being South African Aubrey Faulkner) – was remembered by one observer as follows:

My main memory of Jack is of him standing at the table in the dining room, spinning this ping pong ball incessantly with the fingers of his right hand. I don't remember him actually propelling it, but he was always spinning it, like a set of worry beads. It seemed almost an obsession with him.

What sort of a person spins things obsessively? What sort of a person wants nothing more, on seeing a sphere small enough to fit into one's palm, than to send it twenty-two yards while making it fizz and twirl and spit and zip? Who chooses to immerse himself in a culture and a competition wherein the route to the prize is circuitous rather than direct? Only someone with a playful and excitable imagination. It's impossible to devote time to spinning if you think of creativity as a chore, or spin as a tedious add-on to the rudimentary basics of the bowler's art. Only those predisposed to exult in the unknowable, to push the boundaries of the possible and to declare themselves a sworn enemy of the predictable would take up spin bowling seriously. Deception requires imagination, but it also necessitates empathy, the ability imaginatively to inhabit the lives of others. In part this means the ability to inhabit the mind of the batsman, and so calculate what he would least expect at any given moment.

If you speak to spinners who have played the game at the highest level, or read what they have said on their minority interest, one of the most striking things is the constant reference to other spinners, and the sense of their group identity. More than with any other form of cricketer, spin bowlers constitute a brotherhood through the ages, a tribe apart, a fraternity whose membership, once earned, is infinitely rewarding. There are subsets, of course, as in all tribes – off-spinners, leg-spinners and left-armers for a start – but seen as a whole, spin bowling has created its own version of what Islam calls the Ummah – the community of believers.

This is true of other aspects of the game: wicketkeepers exchange experiences on how to cope with certain conditions; fast bowlers teach each other the art of swing; but no other group has as strong a sense of itself as a discrete entity, or as collectivised an experience of persecution and vilification. Shorter boundaries, bigger bats and other proliferating impediments to a spinner's success, each one a two-fingered salute from officialdom, have combined to convince Twirlymen through the ages of a conspiracy against them by the authorities. It is precisely that sense of persecution that binds spinners together so tightly. It's consequently charming to be able to venture with confidence that, to a far greater degree than for most cricketers, spinners owe their careers to the generosity of other spinners.

Perhaps the most moving image is that of Sydney Barnes, the most complete of bowlers, and by then a dyspeptic old man, leading a blind Wilfred Rhodes – the greatest master of flight – around Lord's in his ninety-fifth year, Barnes acting as Rhodes's eyes and ears. O'Reilly watched Grimmett as a child, saw that he was named 'Grum' on the scoreboard, and allowed that nickname to stick to his small, socially nervous spin twin when they played together for Australia. They formed an intense bond, and O'Reilly counselled Grimmett through bouts of near-depression. He was extraordinarily generous with his own advice, telling Benaud the basics of leg-spin in a Scarborough hotel. Benaud was the recipient of considerable advice from other spinners – Bruce Dooland taught him the flipper; Doug Ring taught him the slider – and he, in turn, has been mentor to several generations of spin around the world, including, most profitably, Warne. Grimmett was inspired to bring new life to the dormant tradition of thumb-generated back-spinners – flippers – by a conversation with George Simpson-Hayward, an Englishman who was among the last of the lob bowlers. Barnes had learned the art of spin-swerve from his dear friend and Ashes rival Monty Noble. Tony Lock recommended Derek 'Deadly' Underwood to Kent after a special coaching session at a department store. Saqlain Mushtaq and Mushtaq Ahmed, both of them wronged by the politics of Pakistani selectors, have devoted themselves in retirement to coaching other spinners.

Warne profited immensely not only from Benaud but Terry Jenner and Bobby Simpson, who both bowled leg-spin for Australia, and numerous conversations with his contemporaries in the modern game, such as Mushtaq Ahmed (with whom he swapped knowledge of the flipper for knowledge of the googly) and Kumble. And then there was that evening with his close predecessor, Abdul Qadir. 'One of the most interesting nights of my life was at Qadir's house when we sat on the floor and flipped an orange to each other with different grips and different forms of spin and discussed tactics and how to sum up batsmen,' he said. 'That was an education and a very good night between two spinners.' It's a wonderful image: two spin-bowling greats, sitting on the floor in the sweltering heat of a Pakistan evening, needing nothing more than an orange to stimulate the sort of conversation that others would pay vast sums to hear, and each approaching the other with humility, knowing the thing about cricket, and especially about spin, is that you never stop learning.

There are exceptions, of course. Chris Schofield – who, despite a brief revival, never fulfilled the potential that led to his being selected as a leg-spinner against Zimbabwe in 2000, and indeed being awarded one of the ECB's first batch of a dozen contracts – was reportedly reluctant to approach Qadir during a net session with England in Melbourne in 1998. But he is unusual in this regard. Spin bowlers not only form a brotherhood, but tend to be exceptionally reliant on their true brothers.

Bowlers such as Kumble, Saqlain, Mendis, and Paul Adams of South Africa all started bowling spin after being encouraged by their brothers, whom they then bored for hours by insisting they let them try out their new techniques on them. My experience was exactly the same. My own brother taught me to bowl outside our house in Tooting.

'There is a great brotherhood among leg-spin bowlers,' says Warne. 'Spin bowling is an international language in itself and whenever two exponents get together we chat about our methods. It is no different from a couple of used car salesman bumping into each other – they will pass on a few tricks about deceiving customers, while we talk about deceiving batsmen.'

A wonderful story from the Perth Test of 2006 illustrates this solidarity. Monty Panesar, batting against Warne, got excited when he picked a couple of googlies correctly. He started shouting 'googly!' each time he thought he'd picked one. The Australian fielders ribbed their star bowler, knowing it would only egg him on. 'You're finished, Warney, Monty's sussed you out,' Ricky Ponting, the man who had beaten Warne to the captaincy, shouted. But at the end of the series Warne took the time to search out Panesar in the Sydney Cricket Ground, and speak to him for a prolonged period about spin. 'I was a little bit afraid to ask him,' Panesar told Brian Viner of the *Independent*. 'But Terry Jenner [Warne's mentor] was in there, and I know him a bit, so I said, "Do you think he'll talk to me?" We talked for about half an hour. He's a great, great man.'

It's this instant familiarity and banter that inspires many spinners to instinctively adopt the nicknames of other Twirlymen. Subhash Gupte, the great Indian leg-spinner, was called 'Fergie', after the West Indian Wilfred Ferguson. Some people called Laker 'Tiger', a nod to O'Reilly. I was called Mushy, a nod to Mushtaq Ahmed.

'Whenever you go to a dressing room and have a beer after the game, it's normally a fellow spinner you love to see and chat about things with,' says Daniel Vettori. 'I think there is a mutual appreciation – how everyone does his craft, how hard it can be sometimes and how funny other times. You will generally find that spinners will get together whenever they get an opportunity. Some share secrets, some don't.'

Warne's assertion that spin is an 'international language' is undoubtedly true, but there is a danger that it conceals another aspect of the great bowlers in the pages to follow, which is their susceptibility to national trends. There are no hard and fast rules that dictate why one country will produce a particular type of bowler, but national tendencies in relation to spin have causes that can be speculated on, if not isolated.

What are these tendencies? They are legion. The West Indies have yet to produce a great leg-spinner. South Africa, despite having a very similar climate to Australia, and similar soils, has produced hardly any spinners, while Australia has produced an endless stream. Pakistan has produced Qadir and the two Mushtaqs, but even with those greats there has been a tendency for Pakistanis to bowl swing – whereas, just across the border, Indians are famed for their production line of great spinners, even playing with four of them for a spell in the 1970s, a point of endless fascination to cricket fans and especially those such as the English who look on such possibilities longingly. Another, more inexplicable, national habit is the tendency of English left-armers to be completely bonkers.

Cricket writers have tried for a very long time to understand why this happens, and have generally flailed around unconvincingly. For what it is worth, I think it may be instructive to examine just one of those national tendencies, not necessarily because it can illuminate the others; rather, because it might show the limits of any explanation for them.

Why, after all, do Indians prefer to spin?

Anthropologists opine at length about the complex interplay between nature and culture in forging identities – an unscientific version of the old nature-nurture argument – and some aspiring Lévi-Strauss should probably devote his doctorate to resolving the interplay in so far as it relates to Indian spinners.

Nature first. A typically canny phrase of George Orwell's, from his moving essay 'A Hanging', refers to 'that bobbing gait of the Indian who never straightens his knees'. There is great wisdom here: Indians, especially in a time when vegetarianism was close to universal, and therefore height differences within the population were limited, are small and sinewy by nature. This fits badly with the requirements of extreme pace, and is better suited to the finger-manipulating demands of spin. The physique of the average Indian, therefore, recommends him to the pantheon of Twirlymen before that of great fast bowlers.

In addition to this, the Indian climate is doubly conducive to spin – first, because bowling fifteen overs a day in baking heat is certainly easier if you're not steaming in from just in front of the sight screen; and second, whether humid or dry, hot temperatures, when conjoined to fertile Indian soils, tend to create dustbowls, crumbling strips of earth that look, after tea on the second day, as if imported from Mars. Such wickets cause a spinning ball to grip and turn, albeit usually slowly; but they are little interested in igniting seam movement. They wear a new ball down quickly through heavy friction and come on to the bat slowly, giving the batsman plenty of time. What is more, the lack of cloud cover means conditions are rarely conducive to swing. Many an Indian medium-pacer would give his banana-shaped bat for just one chance to bowl on the first morning at Headingley.

As for culture, this may be more a matter for conjecture, but that is no obstacle to us. For several years now, social psychologists have been obsessed with the idea that members of a group 'catch' behaviour from each other. The theory was expounded at length in a brilliant book, published in 2009, called *Connected: The Surprising Power of Our Social Networks and How They Shape Our Lives*, by Nicholas Christakis and James Fowler. The authors devoted themselves to the analysis of the Framingham Heart Study, a pioneering medical experiment based in the Massachusetts town of Framingham. In 1948, thousands of townspeople signed up to a medical project that continues today. The administrators of the project kept detailed records of the associations, family relations and friendships that each of the contributors made. By looking at the study in detail, Christakis and Fowler could find out how a mostly self-contained group of people changed their behaviour according to the social environment – the culture – they lived in, and, specifically, the degree of correlation between the habits, norms and values of participants.

What they found was astonishing. If one particular person was found to be obese, the likelihood of their friend, their friend's friend and their friend's friend's friend being obese rose dramatically. The correlation was even more dramatic for smoking. And, according to the Framingham results, you are 45 per cent more likely to be happy if a friend became happy in the past six months.

All of which brings us back to the Indian mystery men. India has produced some great medium-pacers over the years – Kapil Dev was for a time the leading wicket-taker in Test matches – but the norm for most Indian kids playing cricket in the 1950s, 1960s, 1970s and even 1980s was to be surrounded by spin. It wasn't so much that bowlers were assumed to be spinners; rather they just tended to be, which meant their mates tended to be, too. This is the power of social norms: when a group of people behave in a particular way, entry to the group seems to be predicated on adopting that behaviour. India's bowling population is a very large group. That merely amplified the effect.

All this is compounded by two other cultural factors: first, the slowness of much of Indian life; and second, that basic intellectual curiosity which is the hallmark of Indian civilisation. India is a land where everybody is in a hurry but nothing seems to happen quickly. *Jaldi jaldi* – hurry! hurry! in Hindi – is a popular exhortation, but one usually met with inaction. Truly, India is the land of Ganesh, the elephant deity of Asia – beautiful, but lumbering, and occasionally frustratingly slow. At times, this is because Indians are so cerebral – I am, as you may have guessed, related by birth to this ancient argument – they want time to think through even the most basic things. Scholars of the game have therefore long said that a culture of brain over brawn must inevitably militate against raw pace. Indians, so this theory goes, would rather undo a batsman through calculation than knock his off-stump over via a bloody nose. And, as far as it goes, this theory may have some merit.

The trouble is, it needn't have been like this. As Mihir Bose told me: 'Had the Indians entered the Test arena in the 1920s, we would have been talking about the great Indian fast bowlers instead.' Indeed, during that decade, the outstanding bowling talents in India were medium and fast bowlers, not spinners. And, in a further delicious irony, as Bose notes, 'the hilarious thing is that in their first Test match at Lord's the Indians had huge trouble with two English spinners [Walter Robins and Freddie Brown] – they looked clueless against spin'.

Nevertheless, by the mid-fifties at least, Indians had become associated with spin. A culture had been created in which young bowlers would look horizontally at their peers, and vertically at their heroes, and noting everybody bowled spin, would try to imitate them.

More recently, Indians have had a more balanced production line, and though they have yet to produce a single bowler who can consistently hit, say, 93mph, they are not as reliant on spin as they used to be.

Is it possible to deduce from the above exactly why South Africans don't produce spinners, or why English left-armers are so often afflicted by what can only be described as a mild craziness? Possibly not, other than to fall back on the notion that nature and culture combine in their various measure to favour certain outcomes. I put the matter to the man who has probably had more thoughts relating to spin than any other man alive – Richie Benaud.

On the Indians, he said:

It has always been my view that India as a country has had good spin bowlers, occasionally bowlers have been better than that. I batted once against Chandrasekhar at Calcutta on E. W. Swanton's tour of 1964 and I thought he was a [great] bowler. I wasn't around when Bishen Bedi and Erapalli Prasanna were bowling but I know from watching them how good they were. There have been many others, including Anil Kumble.

I certainly think that the climate and the heat has had an effect on the fact that India tends to produce spinners rather than fast bowlers, though that has changed in recent times. Kapil Dev was the first really to bend his back and he was a wonderful bowler. It sometimes happened in my playing time that the medium-pacers were only there to remove the shine for the spin bowlers

And on the matter of why South Africa has produced so few spinners, despite the similarity of its climate to that of Australia:

It is true the climate in South Africa, or rather certain parts of South Africa, is similar to that in Australia, but they tend not to have too many Test match grounds where the temperature on each of the five days of a Test could be over the hundred mark, as has happened in Adelaide. In addition, the soil has always seemed to me to be different in South Africa, not quite as rock hard as in Australia and that has tended to produce proficient seam bowlers rather than spinners. The other thing is I think they still have an English touch about their cricket in that seam bowlers and finger-spin, rather than leg spin, has been their preferred way to go.

Within even this pithy answer is the combination of nature (soils, climate) and culture (favouring seam and finger-spin). It remains something of a puzzle why certain cricketing nations produce the types of bowlers they do, but if we take the relative cases of, first, India and Pakistan and, second, Australia and South Africa, we can isolate what is to a large degree common – climate – and what is to a large degree different – bowling culture. Perhaps then, the single most important influence is social norms.

Even that can't explain the curious case of the English left-armers. Let's look at just a few. We know Tufnell was a prankster capable of sudden perspicacity. Johnny Briggs, the great Lancashire slow left arm, who took more wickets for that club than any other bowler save Brian Statham, died at the age of thirty-nine after severe mental illness, which had caused him to be confined for prolonged spells in Cheadle Asylum. Keith Medlycott, a hugely promising left-arm spinner at Surrey, went on England's tour of the West Indies in 1989–90, but didn't play a Test. A popular cockney from Whitechapel, in the East End of London, he went to Sri Lanka with England 'A' the following winter when the yips struck:

the sudden, debilitating, spirit-crushing physiological failure bowlers endure when they just cannot bowl the ball to the batsman. Medlycott found himself coming in to bowl but, in the final moment, unable to release the ball. He'd lost it. He retired at twenty-six. Similarly, Michael Davies was another promising left-arm spinner at Northants, selected for an England 'A' tour having won his club's Young Player of the Year award. But he, too, lost his bowling completely, and the emergence of Panesar, when Jason Brown and Swann were already at the club, meant he was released at the age of twenty-four.

Perhaps the most telling example is that of Fred Swarbrook. In the 1970s, Swarbrook twirled his left-arm spinners with some success at Derby. He was a colourful character, something of a joker in the pack – his teammates once convinced a young journalist from London that he was the son of a Hungarian émigré, real name Ferenc Schwarzenberg – but the yips got to him. He could bowl in the nets, but out in the middle he was reduced to a quivering wreck. Eventually he went to a psychologist, who told him to carry a pebble in his pocket and rub it before coming in to bowl. When he sent the ball flying into the air, only for it to come back down and land on his head, his captain, the late, great Eddie Barlow, rightly sceptical of superstition, advanced an alternative remedy. 'Fred,' he said, 'have you thought about rubbing the ball and bowling the pebble instead?'

Other English left-armers have been extremely sensitive types who felt they were not shown enough love. Tony Lock, forever in the shadow of Laker, falls into this category; so too does Panesar, who is rare among cricketers in making little attempt to hide the distress and anxiety he feels when things are not going his way. Until Nasser Hussain, to his immense credit, got the best out of him, Ashley Giles was another spinner not fulfilling his potential, sensing as he was that his talents were not appreciated. And as Alan Hill put it in his excellent biography of Johnny Wardle, the brilliant 1950s bowler who could send down Chinamen at will, 'Reconciling the contradictions of Wardle's personality has been a formidable task. For those people who did not gain his trust he appeared to have enough chips on his shoulders to build a bonfire.' His clowning around 'masked his distress at the lack of appreciation of his talents ... he was devalued as a bowler and as the heir to Hedley Verity and Wilfred Rhodes [two other left-arm spinners]'.

This is the subtle mix of national and international characteristics that inform the spinning spirit. Those imbued with it, those who allow it to envelop them and devote their every spare thought – and possibly more – to the possibilities inspired by small balls, have a great many unique qualities. They are thinkers. They love to deceive, and to experiment. They laugh, and are laughed at. They feel the powerful tug of membership of an elite club, which also happens to be a minority endlessly discriminated against. They are tribal. They propagandise on their own behalf. They are especially sensitive to the qualities of other spinners their own country has produced.

But to the extent that it is possible to call on one quality above all others – after sheer physical skill – which spinners through the ages have made their own, it is stamina. Bloody-minded, two-finger-saluting, tireless, constant, persevering, dog-eared stamina. It's not just that, when facing adversity, the great spinners have risen to the occasion with all the aplomb of a Gordon Ramsay soufflé; it's more that, when a door has closed on them, they have time and time again unpicked the lock or barged their way through it rather than walk away.

We have already met William Clarke, one of the great spinners of his day, who said of bowling: 'At times it's enough to make you bite your thumbs to see your best balls pulled and sky-rocketed about – all luck – but you must console yourself with "Ah, that won't last long".' He was right. Asked what it takes to be a good spinner, Abdul Qadir answered: 'You need courage, above all.' Terry Jenner says of Warne: 'When he first played, he did not know how to defend himself. As he got better, he learned how to defend himself.' Rahul Dravid, the masterful Indian batsman, said of his dear friend Anil Kumble, 'He does not know what giving up means.' Wasim Akram said of Saqlain Mushtaq, the best off-spinner he's seen: 'He is as aggressive as a fast bowler, not afraid of getting hit, and has this total belief in himself.' The experience of spinners through the ages testifies to this fighting spirit.

Jim Laker's immature performance at Headingley in 1948, when Australia scored 404 in the fourth innings to win, was held against him for years. He took his 19-90 only years later, at the age of thirty-four; other bowlers would have quit years earlier. He had previously missed a trial for Essex because of a lacerated spinning figure, the bane of spinners every day of their playing lives. Benaud nearly quit because of the trauma caused by his cut fingers, before having the fortune to chance upon a solution. Atherton told me that Tim May, the best orthodox off-spinner he faced (counting Muralitharan as altogether different, and Saqlain Mushtaq as unorthodox on account of his doosra), often came on to bowl with barely healed skin, but would rip it on both his first two fingers by the third or fourth ball of his first over, wince a bit, and then bowl with cut fingers for a whole spell. It's often thought that blood only gets on cricket balls when a pace bowler hurts a batsman. In fact, it's usually when the calluses on a Twirlyman's fingers have yielded to the inevitable.

Bob Appleyard was ill, then had pleurisy, but kept on bowling, and managed to keep Jim Laker out of the side for a while. Clarrie Grimmett moved from one place to another, even after emigrating from New Zealand to Australia, so often was he rejected by selectors.

Wilfred Rhodes was turned down by Warwickshire before becoming a cricketing and statistical phenomenon. Hedley Verity had to wait until he was twenty-five before getting a breakthrough at county level, such was Rhodes's dominance; 'Tich' Freeman, the fabulous little English leg-spinner of the early twentieth century, joined Kent when it had three spinners – Colin Blythe, Frank Wooley and Douglas Carr. He served a long apprenticeship, before becoming a more successful spinner than all those three combined. Coaches at the highest level tried time and again to change Johnny Wardle's action; but he insisted on his own method, and came back stronger every time. Graeme Swann was in tears and on the verge of depression when constant arguments with Kepler Wessels at Northamptonshire reduced his bowling, and his cricket, to rubbish.

It's perhaps because of this that spinners tend to be better riper. Swann's own story confirms this: selected to tour with England when he was still immature, he had to hit rock-bottom before fulfilling his potential. The modern fad is to get bowlers into the Test arena while young – Paul Adams and Daniel Vettori (18), Mushtaq Ahmed, Saqlain Mushtaq and Anil Kumble (19), and Muttiah Muralitharan (20) were all very young when they first played for their countries – but most spinners reach their pomp in their mid-thirties. Shaun Udal, England's most recent off-spinner other than Swann, told me that he was bowling better than ever when he was thirty-six or thirty-seven, in part because he'd had nets sessions with Warne in which the Australian not only taught him the under-cutter (not a ball Warne, as a leg-spinner, bowled much himself), but because he asked Udal to fundamentally reappraise his approach. 'He asked me what I was trying to do as a bowler,' Udal told me, 'and got me to be far more attacking, to think harder about getting batsmen out. If he'd told me that a decade earlier it might have gone in through one ear and out through the other.'

Clarrie Grimmett only made his debut at thirty-three, and Arthur Mailey made his at thirty-five, but both were the better for it, and Warne was at his best not in 1993, but in 2005, when at the age of thirty-five he was the sort of Ashes colossus cricket will likely never again see. Importantly, whereas the 527 Test wickets he took before he was thirty-five came every ten overs, the 181 he took after passing 35 came every eight – and that despite his having a much more worn shoulder, back and wrist. By then, what he lacked in physiological youth he more than compensated for in wisdom.

I should confess that my own veneration of these wise old owls of cricket, and the stamina that allows them to prosper in the face of so much difficulty, is tied to my own shortcomings – the lack of stamina on my part, which meant my being dropped by a Surrey youth side, would prove fatal to long-cherished ambitions. And yet, surveying the history of mystery, it is impossible not to note that the courage of which Qadir speaks is one of the uniting virtues of the characters we shall now meet. Each of them had reputations that came on to bowl hours before they did themselves; and they owed that to the exuberance of their personas, and to their various personifications of the spinning spirit.

'With very few exceptions,' wrote Arthur Mailey, that tireless and masterful leg-spinner, 'the great spin bowlers of cricket were personalities and men of character – not always pleasant but invariably interesting. They may have lacked the charm and friendliness of their faster confederates; they may have been more temperamental and less self-disciplined; but there seemed to be an absence of orthodoxy about them and they were able to meander through life as individuals, not as civil servants.'

Interlude Two

OFF-BREAK

Grip **Batsman's Point of View**

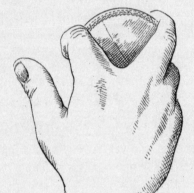

The first two fingers are splayed across the seam in the grip for the off-break. The thumb can rest on the seam, but by the time the ball is released most off-spinners keep its involvement to a minimum. The spin is imparted between the inside top knuckles of the first two fingers, with the index finger in particular straightening by the moment of release. The seam should spin along its own axis, which by now faces towards fine leg.

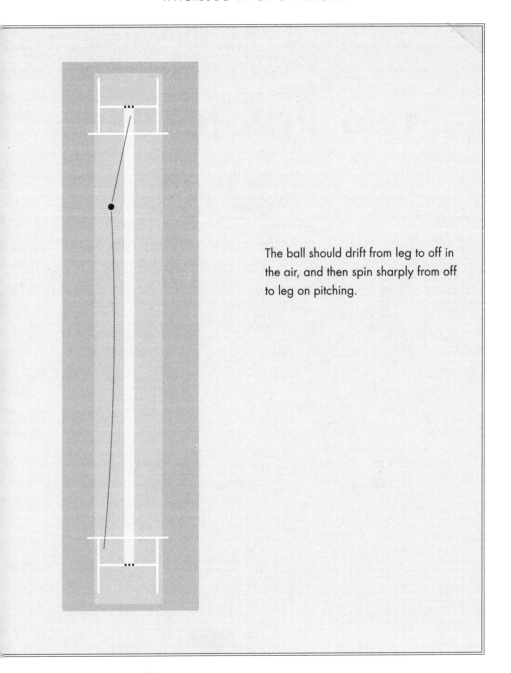

The ball should drift from leg to off in the air, and then spin sharply from off to leg on pitching.

Chapter Three

TWO DICHOTOMIES?

Unlike leg-spin, its older, more complex and more effective sibling, off-spin is a defensive form of bowling liable to be ineffective in all but the most helpful conditions. By making the ball naturally spin into the right-hander, and therefore into his comfort zone, the off-spinner lacks the basic advantage of the leg-spinner, who turns it away. And by relying chiefly on the first and second fingers, rather than a cocked wrist, the off-spinner lacks the levers of the leg-spinner (who is therefore likely to impart many more revolutions on the ball) and the variations, because most deliveries will emerge from out of the front of the hand. These elements have historically combined to make the off-spinner dramatically less successful at the highest levels of cricket, and recommend strongly that any young bowler with lofty ambitions who is disinclined to bowl fast should try, despite the inherent difficulties, to break the ball from leg instead. Off-spinning, or some subspecies of it, is after all the ultimate fate of almost all club cricketers of advancing age. And when did any of them conquer cricket's greatest summits?

The above paragraph could appear without much challenge in most modern or twentieth-century coaching manuals, and the vast majority of cricketers around the world, professional or amateur, probably espuse its basic arguments on a daily basis. That they are entirely and demonstrably false has been no impediment to the ubiquity of its central claims. They seem to gain currency even as the imperishable evidence both disproving them and, further, cogently arguing the opposite case, accumulates by the day. They have never been right, and never will be. Indeed, if the perniciousness of an idea can be calculated by multiplying its stupidity by its ubiquity, the received wisdom relating to off-spin must be among the most malicious in cricket. Why has it gone so long without substantial review?

Before answering that question, a brief survey of the swelling evidence supporting the off-spinner's case when resisting such abuse may be useful. The leading wicket-taker in Test cricket – a man with more than eight hundred wickets, and who will probably never be surpassed – is an off-spinner, albeit an unusual one with physical advantages that few other bowlers will have, namely Muttiah Muralitharan. Two other bowlers in that elite club who have taken more than three hundred Test wickets (putting Muralitharan's achievement into perspective) are conventional off-spinners – Harbhajan Singh and Lance Gibbs. Indeed, Gibbs, the first spinner to three hundred Test wickets, started out as a leg-spinner but dropped it for off-spin when he realised he could be more effective with the latter. The greatest performance in all first class cricket, never mind Test matches, was by that guileful son of Bradford, Jim Laker, who took nineteen Australian wickets at Old Trafford in 1956 spinning the ball sharply from around the wicket, on an uncovered wicket responsive to heavy overnight rain. The two most innovative bowlers of the modern game, a great and a future great who championed the doosra and the carrom ball respectively, are bowlers whose stock ball spins from off to leg, namely Saqlain Mushtaq and Ajantha Mendis. In the modern game, off-spinners, from Australia's Tim May to England's rejuvenated Graeme Swann, have been consistent match-winners, but in this respect are only continuing the tradition of historic greats, from the Australians Monty Noble and Hugh Trumble to that paragon of West Indian ingenuity, Sonny Ramadhin.

And yet the snobbery is sustained, intense and frequently personal. Ian Peebles, that great English leg-spinning hope of the 1930s, chided the 'uncomplicated cut of off-spin' as one of several 'enforced substitutes for the only craft of its kind [leg-spin]'. In his otherwise entertaining account of English cricket, Simon Hughes refers to 'off-spin, essentially a defensive form of bowling spinning into the body'. Brian Wilkins, in his magisterial work *Cricket: The Bowler's Art*, devotes ten pages solely to leg-spin, another thirteen to flipper-type deliveries (generally bowled by leg-spinners) – and five to off-spin. He even opens his chapter on off-spin with the assertion, curious for so sharply and soberly argued a book, that 'off-spin of slow to slow-medium pace can look vulnerable under pressure; more so than leg-spin'. Jim Laker was not selected to tour Australia until 1958 – 9, two years after his triumph at Old Trafford; until then the conventional wisdom had been that off-spinners couldn't take wickets Down Under. This voodoo logic cost him and like-minded souls hundreds of wickets to which they had rightful claim.

I bow to no one in my admiration for Gideon Haigh, arguably the finest cricket writer alive today, but when he says 'Off-spin is cricket's rubbish skill – something easy to do in a mediocre fashion, and the eternal preserve of the untalented. John Howard bowled off-spin – as indeed do I, and utter filth it is too', he performs the rare trick for him of revealing more about himself than about his subject matter. It's only some mitigation that he goes on immediately to say, 'That said, off-spin is supremely difficult to do excellently.'

Inzamam ul-Haq, old Potato Brain himself, once riled Brett Lee, the super-fast bowler, just as he was building up a huge head of steam, by politely enquiring if he would 'stop bowling off-spinners'. Even that sage of the game, the brilliant former Somerset captain Peter Roebuck, in an article lauding the return to significance of off-spin, can find time to write the following:

Although it is best to keep them in the dark when the topic is raised, finger spinners follow a dull profession. For all their toil, they basically run to the crease, roll over an arm, give the leather a little twist, land it on a length and cross fingers that nothing untoward ensues. They are not fast, do not turn the ball much, and are about as likely to pull a rabbit from a hat as Clem Atlee.

The myth of off-spin's ineffectuality is doubtless related to the fact that, as they age, club cricketers, that sturdy battalion whose enthusiasm remains the lifeblood of the sport, eventually succumb, like butter in a hot pan, to their inevitable fate. As bowlers no longer capable of even medium pace, and seeking to compensate with subtlety for what they, in their advancing years, lack in strength, they bring their fingers over the side of the ball during delivery and – hey presto! – have the eternal consolation of being off-spinners rather than mediocre slow-medium merchants. This damaging form of self-deception, practised with utter predictability around the world season after season, must be a chief source of the opprobrium unjustly heaped on off-spin.

And yet, if it doesn't seem unreasonable, I should propose a further possible explanation for the ubiquity of this invective. Even within off-spin, I contend, there is a dichotomy, between what I shall (crudely) call English off-spinners and subcontinent off-spinners. The former, moulded by the terrible experience of bowling on slow, lifeless wickets, the irresistible rise of limited-overs cricket, and three decades in which the English didn't think spin bowling an important part of their culture, have their personification in John Emburey, the former England captain. The latter, who benefit both from spicier wickets and encouragement from a young age, find their apogee in Erapalli Prasanna, and their extreme version in Muttiah Muralitharan. It is a pleasant curiosity of cricket that the greatest classical off-spinner of them all, Jim Laker, was an Englishman who, having profited from uncovered pitches, is much more at home in the second category. Similarly, Graham Swann and Tim May, the Australian who Atherton told me was the best orthodox off-spinner he ever faced, both profit from an approach to bowling that fits the Indian mould.

The English off-spinner is distinguished, above all, by his defensive approach and his failure to give the ball a ferocious rip. His priority is length and line, not twirl and twist. He is more concerned with metronomic accuracy and a low economy rate than with beating the batsman in the air and off the wicket. His action will convey a military precision and stiffness that seems too rigid for the serious spinner. Because he does not spin the ball fiercely – having grown up on wickets which discouraged him from really ripping it, since the spin and bounce off the pitch would be slow and consistent – he is forced to bowl a line tight on, or just outside off-stump. He may use the crease intelligently, and he has an effective arm ball and under-cutter, but looping the ball and inviting batsmen to drive through cover isn't his top priority. He'd rather grind them down with frustration.

How do we know all this? How do we know that players really obeyed this philosophy? And how do we know that Emburey, the boy from Peckham who stepped into the England captaincy after newspaper allegations brought about Gatting's temporary downfall, is the personification of this sensibility? Because, thankfully, Emburey told us so.

In that honest, anachronistic and classic text *Spinning in a Fast World*, Emburey describes how, when bowling on the pavements of Peckham in south London, he chanced upon his capacity to make the ball turn. He had always thought of himself as a medium-pacer, a speed he revisited when, on overseas tours, he would bowl slow seamers in the nets rather than give his England colleagues (and rivals on the county circuit) an insight into his variations. This is understandable, if slightly paranoid. We shall return to the specifics of Emburey's technique later, but for now some of the generic advice dished out in that book will serve our purpose, reflecting as it does a mentality common to what I have called the English off-spinner.

Emburey says that the off-spinner is a 'multi-purpose bowler in that he can be used effectively on all kinds of wickets. He can bowl defensively on "flat" wickets when the ball is not turning and try to lure the batsman into error, or he can attack when the conditions are more favourable.' The structure of that sentence suggests a preference for the former. He says his line and length are his 'greatest strength', and that when he first comes on his priority is forcing the batsman 'onto the defensive and giving him nothing to hit at all. That means bowling three or four overs of basic off-spin, not too flat but certainly without too much air.' As he was six-foot-two, accuracy was more important than aeration, which is partly why, although other off-spinners employ a top-spinner, Emburey didn't and doesn't. He also says 'unless you are very lucky ... the chances are the wicket won't be taking much turn at all'. Perhaps only an English off-spinner could be so gloomy. With such lifeless wickets to bowl on, that's to be expected.

Udal reinforced the message to me. 'The first thing I do when I come on is try to stay on. Get a few overs under the belt. Not get hit for too many boundaries. Settle into a rhythm and gain some confidence. Half the battle is convincing the captain he wasn't nuts to throw you the ball.'

The subcontinent off-spinner, by contrast, is an aggressor. He seeks to beat the batsman in the air before he beats him off the pitch, and knows he can only do so by spinning it fiercely from his first ball. The main distinction between him and his English counterpart, other than being one of attitude, is in the line he bowls. To the right hander he will frequently bowl a foot wide of off-stump, forcing the batsman to play against the spin (and ideally bowling him through the gate), or otherwise making him drag it a long way if he wishes to play with the spin. This was the basis on which Muralitharan took his sixteen wickets at the Oval in 1998. Turning the ball square, he was virtually unplayable, at times bowling so far wide of off-stump as to be suggesting that he was in no need of the cut strip.

To the left-hander, the English bowler would often stay over the wicket, trying occasionally to bowl him around his legs, but essentially bowling wicket to wicket (again). This was Emburey's favoured technique against the merciless Allan Border. But the Indian off-spinner will instinctively go round the wicket to the left-hander, angling into his off-stump and forcing him to play the ball turning away from him, hoping for an edge or an lbw with the one that goes straight on.

Of course, such a binary distinction is too reductive. But looking over the off-spinners England has produced in recent years, it's hard not to conclude that there is such a thing as an English off-spinner, and that he is defensive by nature. Aside from Emburey and Udal, bowlers such as Ray Illingworth, Jeremy Snape, Peter Such, Richard Dawson – remember him? – and Mike Watkinson, who admittedly batted and bowled medium pace, too, were all very similar, conditioned as they were on lifeless wickets. Robert Croft was slightly different, in being an adventurous spirit unafraid to try out all sorts of gimmicks, including stopping halfway through his action at the crease, only to bowl the ball, watch it bobble to safety, and hear his captain Nasser Hussain bellow his impression of the late, great South African Eddie Barlow from slip – I remember it as if it were yesterday, so condescending was the tone – 'Okay, Robbie, don't try everything at once.'

This, then, is a further dichotomy within spin bowling, between two types of off-spinner. The subcontinent bowler is likely to be more successful, and more watchable, than his English counterpart. It was with the latter in mind that Neville Cardus referred to the off-spinner as 'A craftsman in a great tradition'. He added 'a classic exponent of off-spin' was the exponent of 'the most classic of all kinds of bowling'.

Cardus died in 1975, just five years after the amendment to the laws of the game that, long overdue, said a batsman could be out leg-before wicket if he was hit outside the line of off-stump, provided he played no stroke and the ball was destined to hit his wicket. This came thirty-five years after the introduction of the rule that the batsman could be given out if the ball pitched outside the line of off-stump, though if it hit him outside that line he would then still survive. Both these rules made a significant impact on the fortunes of off-spinners, and it is worth bearing in mind, as we look at some of the greatest exponents, that these rule changes have given modern bowlers significant advantages that their forebears lacked.

That, plus the inexplicable surge in the number of left-handed batsman in cricket and the growing impact of Hawk-Eye technology on the game, may persuade some youngsters to reason as Lance Gibbs did, and bowl off-spin over its supposedly more exotic version. The presence of such masters as Saqlain, Swann, and – though he is much more of a wrist-spinner than an off-spinner – Muralitharan, will be a welcome aid to this process.

And yet, for all that, it is hard for me not to recall the influence that Warne had on my childhood self, and the impossibility, having seen him in action, of bowling anything but leg-breaks as a stock ball. If there has ever been a leg-spinner – or any wrist-spinner, for that matter – who was in his essentials a defensive bowler, I am yet to come across him. Off-spin needn't be defensive; indeed, my gripe is that far too many people who should have known better conceive of it as inevitably so. But the fact is there have been many off-spinners who preferred, initially at least but often long after, to be defensive. The same is simply not true of the leg-spinner.

Off-spinners, as the Interludes in this book show, are essentially reliant on getting their fingers to impart spin on the ball. Muralitharan is something of an exception: he uses his wrist more than his fingers. It's possible as an off-spinner to bring your arm over and not give the ball as much of a rip as you're capable of, instead just rolling your fingers down the side and hoping for some cut rather than spin. For leg-spinners, this is not really an option. Of course, some balls spin more than others, when all the levers are working in harmony and unison; but the basic action, which requires a cocked wrist to uncoil like a spring, and demands that the first three fingers coordinate the release of the ball, is anathema to defensiveness or passivity. It may also be what motivates Emburey to make the grand generalisation 'What I do know is that finger spinners possess far more control than leg-spinners.' That depends on who is doing the spinning. Warne possessed more control than almost every off-spinner save, perhaps, Laker and Hugh Tayfield in their pomp.

He also did something very few leg-spinners have done, which is bowl at leg-stump to the right-hander, and invite him to play against the spin, or across the line, as it is known. It was often said of Warne, early in his career, that he spun the ball so much he could afford to bowl a leg-stump line. This is not the full story. When Stuart MacGill was bowling so well for Australia at Test level, and even challenging a less than fully fit Warne for a place in the side, Warne's analysis was fascinating. He claimed that there was room to play two spinners in the side because MacGill was a different sort of leg-spinner. He bowled at middle-and-off-stump, and sometimes outside off-stump, to tempt the batsman into driving him, and also to set him up for the googly. MacGill, with his high, quick arm, had an excellent googly. Warne, on the other hand, bowled at leg-stump and encouraged batsmen to play through the leg-side. He didn't have such a great googly himself, and felt he was most dangerous when inviting batsmen to play against the spin. MacGill turned the ball at least as much as Warne, so it won't do to say Warne's leg-stump line was purely because of the degree of turn he got.

I expand later on the advantages of this approach, and the difficulties it poses to batsmen; for now it may be enough to note that this approach was fairly novel when the Australian started doing it – previous spinners, from Grimmett through to Benaud and Abdul Qadir, tended to vary from the middle-and-off-stump line to one just outside off-stump, when they would invite the right-hander to drive, often by leaving the cover area empty.

The leg-spinner, being an intrinsically attacking bowler, ought not to feel obliged to set overly attacking fields. He tends to feel no shame in putting a man back on the rope square of the wicket, whether leg-side or off, from the very outset, for protection against boundaries. To the right-hander, he should move his mid-off wide and his mid-on straight (the off-spinner should do the opposite), and if like Warne he turns it enough to make the leg-stump line viable, he should consider leaving mid-wicket vacant, to tempt the batsman into nudging the ball into that area, and potentially giving a leading edge.

Going round the wicket, Warne says, was a way of making sure that the leg-spinner's action was working. That was a theory Bobby Simpson, his early coach for Australia and a former part-time leggie himself, taught him. The other virtue of it was that, with the use of the bowler's footmarks outside the right-hander's leg-stump, it's possible to sow confusion, so long as you vary the spin enough to make the batsman know he can't get away with padding every ball away, safe in the knowledge he won't be given out leg-before. Jenner was responsible for the phrase 'Think high, spin up', by which is meant keep your arm high and remember you're sending the ball upwards, into the air, as well as towards the batsman. It's a useful reminder for the leg-spinner when his arm is sagging and he's dragging the ball down – often because he's coming to the end of a long spell. Leg-spinners have often had much lower arms than off-spinners; Grimmett, for example, was essentially round-arm. There is no prescription for how high the leg-spinner's arm should be, but it's a general rule that you have to beat the batsman in the air before you beat him off the wicket, and it's a good idea to make sure the ball spends some time above his eye level before coming down to land.

One of the most effective and satisfying dismissals a leg-spinner can achieve against the right-hander is by lulling him into a false sense of security, inviting him to hit some flighted deliveries, before deceiving him with the top-spinner. This ball, bowled with pure over-spin rather than any side-spin, looks for all the world like the delivery the batsman has just thumped to the boundary, but dips short and, far from coming off the middle of the bat, offers a catching opportunity to any number of fielders.

To the left-hander, the leg-spinner's task is much the same as the off-spinner's to the right-hander: throw it up outside off-stump and invite the drive against the spin. Sometimes this is more easily achieved from over the wicket, though it will depend on how much spin the wicket is taking. From over the wicket, the ball that doesn't spin and goes straight on, across the left-hander, can bring the slips into play.

Spinners of whatever hue should heed the maxim that it is better to be driven than pulled. The batsman who is pulling has plenty of time to play the ball, and so should have total control over the shot. The batsman who is driving has much less time to make contact with the ball after it has pitched. He is therefore additionally vulnerable to the vagaries of flight and pitch. A bowler's only excuse for bowling short is that the batsman is charging down the wicket, or he is bowling the flipper that skids on (or the under-cutter in the off-spinner's case). As Hedley Verity's son put it: 'My dad said: "The best length is the shortest you can bowl and still get them playing forward".' It is a recurring theme in the history of spin that the great bowlers have had an exceptional command of length. Spinners do not have the luxury afforded to fast bowlers, of calling a 'good length' an area covering the best part of two feet. For the spinner, it is probably half that, because, since the batsman has so much more time both to judge the initial length and to react to the ball's behaviour off the wicket, the margin of error is small.

The greatest spinners, far from running scared at this unavoidable requirement, have embraced it wholeheartedly. Time and again in the pages to follow, quotes from contemporaries of these greats, and wider analysis, land on the need for a brilliant command of length. We learn of W. G. Grace, an early exponent of leg-spin, that 'he held to the old-fashioned theory that length and straightness were the secret of good bowling'. Anil Kumble says of his own method: 'What I do is subtle. You try and beat them with length – actually, you beat them with pace because of the length.' And Bill O'Reilly, offering an appraisal of his dear friend and partner in destruction, Clarrie Grimmett, compared him favourably with Arthur Mailey on grounds of command of length:

> Grimmett never insisted on spin as his chief means of destruction. To him it was no more than an important adjunct to unerring length and tantalising direction. Grimmett seldom beat a batsman by spin alone. Mailey often did. I cannot remember Grimmett bowling a long-hop, whereas Mailey averaged one an over.

In their desire for the pitch and conditions, and the requirements of length, there is, then, much to unite these two basic dichotomies of spin. Left-armers who use the off-spinner's action are, of course, in effect leg-spinners, turning their stock delivery from leg to off and away from the right-hander. To them the arm ball (which carries straight on rather than turning off the pitch), delivered from over the wicket, is an invaluable weapon, especially if they can get it to swerve into the right-hander through the air. Few have done this better than New Zealand's current great, Daniel Vettori.

But beyond these two dichotomies, there are two other deliveries that rather conflate the categories, and show what a marvellously variable enterprise spin is. They both in their own way reflect the exoticism of mystery spin, and they have both caused commentators and pundits nearly as much trouble as batsmen.

After much experimenting, I have come to the conclusion that the doosra is essentially an hallucinogenic drug. It fills its user with the confidence of a world-beater, only for him to discover it is a temporary thrill with an immediate comedown and lasting side effects, all of them deleterious to personal wellbeing. Muralitharan aside, every single international bowler who has practised endlessly to master this delivery has rightfully had his action questioned, or has lost his stock ball altogether, or both. The saddest case is that of the bowler who everyone seems to think invented it.

Claimed by Saqlain Mushtaq when in fact bowled by Jack Potter – unless it was the carrom ball – decades earlier, this leg-break, bowled by the off-spinner, has gripped the cricketing imagination for much of the past fifteen years, and indeed tightened its grip considerably with Muralitharan's mastering of it. Endless orthodox finger-spinners have had it attributed to them when in fact they are bowling a different ball altogether. This misidentification has been especially acute if the bowler in question has been from the Indian subcontinent. Thus Harbhajan Singh's top-spinner is even today constantly labelled the doosra, and Rangana Herath's excellent carrom ball was for years similarly afflicted. Harbhajan has mostly dropped the doosra, knowing he is liable to be called for chucking; Herath's ball is an altogether different one, and he has never used the doosra in a match.

Expert opinion has it that the vast majority of bowlers simply do not have the requisite physiological dexterity to bowl it without blatantly throwing. 'The thing about the doosra,' Terry Jenner says, 'is that the people who have bowled it have normally had their actions questioned. Most of the guys don't have the flexibility to bowl that ball.' Jenner refuses to coach it, thinking it a certain way to destroy a fledgling career. Writing in the *Adelaide Review* in mid-2009, following a specially convened spin-bowling summit in Brisbane – that's what they get up to in Australia: they convene summits on spin bowling – Ashley Mallet, himself a Test match off-spinner for Australia, said:

> There was unanimous agreement that the off-spinner's 'other-one', the doosra, should not be coached in Australia. I have never seen anyone actually bowl the doosra. It has to be a chuck. Until such time as the ICC declares that all manner of chucking is legal in the game of cricket, I refuse to coach the doosra. All at the spin summit agreed.
>
> 'All' included leg-spinners Shane Warne, Stuart MacGill, Jim Higgs, Jenner and Peter Philpott, offies Gavin Robertson and Mallett, as well as Australian chairman of selectors Andrew Hilditch.

They are quite right to do so, and such is the prevailing mood in both the international and domestic arena that if a bowler does appear to be bowling doosras, he will almost certainly be submitted for consideration by the authorities. The most contentious current case – contentious largely because the Australians (who else?) contest his legality – is that of Saeed Ajmal, the Pakistani who has had considerable success in Twenty20 competitions. If Ajmal doesn't chuck the ball, Margaret Thatcher is a Trotskyist. No serious soul can doubt that Ajmal extends his arm quite considerably; the question nowadays is not *if* he does but *how much*. To the naked eye, it's quite possible that he regularly extends it less than 15 degrees; but what is to say that, on the odd occasion he really wants to get it to turn, he crosses that threshold and extends it from, say, 25 degrees? It is possible, but it's a brave umpire that calls no ball, given the ICC have cleared him. Ajmal's case is particularly irksome because his whole action, in which he bobs to the crease but then almost stops altogether, before springing out into a short delivery stride, is constructed around the need to bend and then straighten his arm.

But others have been damaged by it, too. It cost Saqlain Mushtaq at least five years of Test cricket, if (a big if) we disregard the eccentricities of Pakistani selectors. Shoaib Malik was reported not once but twice, and was never the same bowler again. Johan Botha, the South African briefly rated ninth best bowler in the international one-day rankings, was reported on his Test debut. He missed sixteen months of international cricket due to remedial action. Then he was tested at the University of Western Australia (UWA). His stock ball and arm ball and top-spinner and under-cutter clocked in with a straightening of the arm, but one that was less than 15 degrees. His doosra came in at 26.7 degrees. 'I was surprised that the doosra was a problem,' he said, 'because your elbow flexes less when you bowl it than with the other deliveries.' The evidence contradicted him. Intriguingly, the three umpires who initially referred him, Brian Jerling, Asoka da Silva and Rudi Koertzen – never far from controversy – submitted eighteen video clips to the ICC. But not a single one contained the doosra. Why? Because, Botha contends, he didn't bowl a single doosra on his Test debut, presumably fully aware of its contentiousness and of his reputation. If that is the case, it does suggest those three umpires were making the facts servant to their prejudices, rather than the other way round.

Vincent Barnes, Botha's bowling coach, offered what can only be called the Murali Defence. 'Johan's arms aren't straight when they hang by his sides. They are naturally bent at the elbow. He has a natural deformity.' Barnes also reported a curious observation from Bruce Elliott, the professor at UWA who conducted the tests, and who doubles up as the ICC's biomechanist: 'He said he had found that a lot of bowlers from the sub-continent could bowl the doosra legally, but not Caucasian bowlers.' And yet several bowlers from the subcontinent were reported, and rightly so. The only one who seems to have got away with it is Muralitharan, but he has been a special case for a long time.

The name of this delivery charmingly emerged from on-field banter: wicketkeeper Moin Khan called on Saqlain to bowl 'the other one' from behind the stumps. Tony Greig, vaguely conversant in languages other than English, recognised the word and put it to Saqlain in a post-match interview. The bowler confirmed its meaning, an act which initiated the spread of scurrilous gossip throughout the cricket world about the prospect of a genuine step-change, a paradigm shift, as scientists call it, in the whole art of spin bowling, one wherein off-spinners were expected to be able, with a minor but well-practised adjustment, to deliver leg-breaks – with an action indistinguishable from the off-break. This, it was widely thought, for a few years at least, would blur the distinction between off-spin and leg-spin forever. Everyone was at it. Alex Loudon, who was selected to tour for England but retired in 2007, aged twenty-seven, to pursue a career in business, was taught it by the son of Punjabi pop star, Gurdas Maan, while headboy at Eton. He never mastered it, and, though the premature halt to his career was caused by several other factors – including, chiefly, a dip in form when he left Kent for Warwickshire – his demise was not slowed down by his attempt to master this perilous delivery.

In any case, shouldn't the doosra be playable, just as the leg-spinner's googly, eventually, is playable, even if not always picked? In his wonderful autobiography, Steve Waugh, Australia's captain, explained his frustration at watching Saqlain take 6-46 in the Tasmania Test of 1999:

Fair enough, this is a special ball delivered with the skill of an illusionist, but it's also one we have talked about in detail and always have a plan to. We believe that Saqlain hardly ever turns his off-break, and that his stock ball is the mystery delivery that turns like a leg-break. To counter him, we believe that early on, until you've got accustomed to the difference in flight and bounce of this ball, you should play him as a leg-spinner and use your pad to neutralise the occasional off-break. However, for some reason we completely forgot about this strategy and paid the price, losing wicket after wicket to his 'freakish' skill.

All this is true of the bowler in possession of the carrom ball, a delivery which can be produced without chucking but which, unfortunately, seems to require the sort of finger strength reserved for exiles from Krypton. It turns like a leg-break, but, rather than the spin being imparted by the wrist, it is the work of the middle finger, which flicks the ball out as if it were a disc in Carom, the table-top board game of Indian origin.

Regardless of whether or not the bowler is being easily picked, adopting a prepared plan and sticking to it can usually ameliorate to some degree at least the potential hazards for the batsman of facing a bowler who spins it both ways. Such bowlers are a kind of synthesis of the possibilities represented by off-spin and leg-spin. They reveal the limitations of the binary distinction, just as the leg-spinners who bowl repeated googlies – Mushtaq Ahmed, say, or (his hero) Abdul Qadir – do, because, strictly speaking, if they keep bringing the ball back in from the off, they are off-spinners. But there is another type of bowler who, decades earlier, also challenged the notion that off-spin and leg-spin were as parallel lines, stretching to infinity but never making contact. The style of bowling was mastered by an underrated Englishman, Johnny Wardle, and slightly popularised by that amazing human being and West Indian, Sir Garfield Sobers. But one of its earliest progenitors hailed (slightly) from the land of the Qin Dynasty, not generally regarded as a vehicle for the evolution of Twirlymen.

Ellis 'Puss' Achong was the first man of Chinese origin to play Test cricket. Born in Belmont, Port of Spain, he was a good enough left-winger to play football for Trinidad and Tobago from 1919 to 1932. His slow left-arm orthodox bowling was also good enough to warrant his selection for the West Indies. Bowling to England's Walter Robins, himself a sometime wrist-spinner, in the Old Trafford Test of 1933, Achong kept spinning the ball away from the right-hander. But then he produced one that spun sharply the other way, to have Robins stumped. All the accounts suggest that this ball was delivered from the side of the hand through the orthodox leg-spinner's action: being left-handed, Achong's mystery ball came in to the right-hander. It is possible of course that he bowled an early, left-handed doosra, even that he flicked his fingers to bowl a carrom ball in the manner of Rangana Herath today; but that is not what those who saw it say. And when Robins trudged off, he said to Joe Hardstaff Senior, 'Fancy being bowled by a bloody Chinaman!', to which the great West Indian Learie Constantine retorted, 'Do you mean the bowler or the ball?'

But, in keeping with the argument of these pages, it is clear that the original Chinaman was not the original chinaman. Roy Kilner, one of the most charming men to play for England (he died at thirty-seven in 1928 after contracting enteric fever while coaching in India), bowled slow left-arm orthodox but laid claim to a wrist-spinner that came in from the off. When he died, the crowd lining the streets of Wombwell, near Barnsley, exceeded 100,000, it is estimated. Maurice Leyland, a powerful left-handed batsman for England and Yorkshire, was known as a slow left-arm orthodox bowler. But his *Wisden* obituary, which sympathised with the difficulty of his getting much bowling when Yorkshire at that time boasted Wilfred Rhodes, and then Hedley Verity, read:

According to Bill Bowes [the Yorkshire bowler and legend], Maurice claimed he was responsible for the term 'Chinaman'. Because his chances of bowling were few, he began bowling the occasional left-hander's off-break instead of the normal and natural leg-break. Whenever two batsmen were difficult to shift or something different was wanted someone in the Yorkshire team would say, 'Put on Maurice to bowl some of those Chinese things'. Roy Kilner explained, 'It's foreign stuff and you can't call it anything else'.

Whether Leyland really did adopt the term before Achong's dismissal of Robins in 1933 is doubtful, but he was certainly bowling the ball in the 1920s. And yet we know it was bowled even before then: Charlie 'Buck' Llewellyn, the first man born of white and black parents to play cricket for South Africa, bowled Chinamen at the start of the twentieth century, having taken extensive advice from the quartet of googly bowlers (especially Reggie Schwarz) his country produced in imitation of Bernard Bosanquet. Born in Maritzburg, now Pietermaritzburg, he eventually played for Hampshire, a journey made more recently by Kevin Pietersen, so it's possible to speculate that the man who has popularised switch-hitting batting was merely following the man who popularised a 'leggie-in-the-mirror' type of bowling.

Llewellyn's daughter responded angrily to the publication of a biography of him by Patrick Allen in 1976, seeing the assertion that he was of mixed race as inflammatory, and declaring that both her parents and grandparents were of 'pure British stock'. Allen wasn't alone in presuming that Llewellyn was mixed race. In *Overthrows: A Book of Cricket*, J. M. Kilburn noted that Llewellyn 'was dark-eyed and dark-skinned and South Africans called him coloured'.

Another bowler who might have been described like that, and who also defies simple categorisation between the two dichotomies, is Paul Adams. It's a welcome sign of how far that country has come that Llewellyn should be explicitly associated with a modern bowler who South Africans do call coloured, but for whom it is neither compliment nor insult, but purely the fact of the matter. Possibly more than any other bowler in these pages, including Jack Iverson, Paul Adams is the duck-billed platypus of the history of mystery, so easily does he claim membership of several categories that usually remain distinct. He has the following attributes. He is left-handed and spins the ball away from the right-hander. But, rather than do this in the orthodox fashion, he employs wrist-spin. To employ left-handed wrist-spin to move the ball away from the right-hander (something the Australian Michael Bevan was known to do), he bowls left-handed googlies as his stock. So – a wrist-spinning left-armer, who employs the wrist-spinner's wrong'un to achieve just the effect that left-arm orthodox bowlers produce.

Still with me? It gets better. Rather than bowl his left-handed googlies using the grip and release of conventional googly bowlers, Adams's grip has the thumb and middle finger running along the seam, nearly joining up to meet. He seems not to involve his fingers much in the imposition of spin, but a quick snap of the wrist, cocked just enough to make sure that when it uncoils the spin is towards slip, does achieve considerable revolutions. Kumble occasionally released his slower googly in the same way, and Adams is capable of getting one to go straight on, like a top-spinner, and another to come into the right-hander, by changing the position of his wrist at the moment of release. Most of his spin comes from that sudden burst of kinetic energy that must inevitably result from the madness of his delivery stride.

I have studied Adams's action closely for the best part of fifteen years and I am afraid that the only way I can explain why he would adopt such a method is that this is a conspiracy. Adams is in cahoots with the organisers of London's 2012 Olympic Games: his entire career has been devoted to readying people for that unspeakably horrific logo, which is now here to stay, and which seems a clear imitation of his body shape at the moment of release. Head spearing into the earth, front leg braced and back leg arching skyward like a proud swan, so supple must his torso be that no ballerina could reasonably view a spell of his without collapsing with the agony of envy.

The action took its toll on his small body, and he eventually lost both spin and accuracy, which wasn't very good for someone who always bowled a four-ball in the over anyway. Adams, just like so many of the other distinguished spinners, learned to bowl with a brother. Noel and he played together in Grassy Park, a Cape suburb, and in their backyard with a tennis ball that had the pelt scraped off. They discovered that his natural but unorthodox style could generate both sharp spin and swerve in the air. When Eddie Barlow chanced upon him, Adams and his brother had no language to describe what he did; they simply talked of his in-spinner and out-spinner.

Adams concealed the ball naturally, knowing that his action meant the batsman wouldn't see it until the moment before it left his hand. But eventually he became easier to read, and the emergence of Nicky Boje as a credible, orthodox left-arm spinning alternative, together with Adams's dip in form, made it hard to deny that his place in the side owed more to political pressure for non-white players than the quality of his spin.

Since retiring at thirty-one, Adams has turned down the chance to become a national selector, focusing on commentary instead. But his contribution to the game, and to the history of spin bowling in particular, is assured because he defied convention and combined so many different traditions in a single bowler. We cannot reasonably call him a Chinaman bowler, even though that term now refers to any left-arm spinner who employs the wrist-spinning method. That would be to elide the essential and marvellous fact that he bowled a googly – and an unorthodox, thumb-and-middle-finger one at that – for his stock ball. Maybe we could test the limits of political correctness and see how far South Africa really has come by declaring this Cape-coloured mystery spinner to be the pioneer of his own style of spin, importantly distinct from Chinamen. Capemen bowlers: left-arm spinners whose stock ball is the wrong'un, which leaves the right-hander. How they bowl that wrong'un we'll leave to them.

Whether Capemen or Chinamen, these exponents of left-handed legerdemain achieve what the purveyors of the doosra and the carrom ball achieved. They show up the binary distinction of cricketing imagination, between off-spin and leg-spin, to be both needlessly and tediously reductive. In fact, whether a bowler has one that goes the other way or not, we must reconsider, and then recalibrate, the mindset that sees those two dichotomies as imperial overlords of spin. They are simply its aging parents – and parents eventually pass away, to be replaced by a new generation.

The New York Yankees baseball player Yogi Berra said when you come to a fork in the road, take it. The latest generation of spinners, conscious of the great dangers in practising deliveries such as the doosra, should at least think of how they can call on other, seemingly rival, traditions and make them friends rather than enemies. And those of us who care about spin should celebrate the limits of the two dichotomy approach. When we see the fork in the road, we should take it.

Interlude Three

TOP-SPINNER

Grip   *Batsman's Point of View*

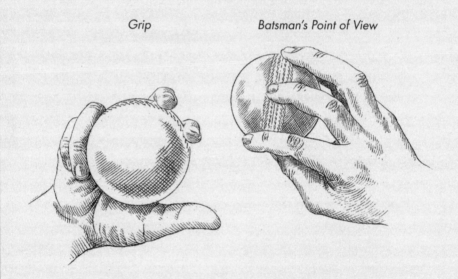

The grip for the top-spinner is the same as that for the leg-break. The tops of the first two fingers are across the seam. The spin is imparted by the third finger, which straightens from a bent position. On the bowler entering the delivery stride, the back of the hand starts off facing the sky. As the arm comes round, the wrist unfurls in an anti-clockwise direction, or from right to left, but not as far as with the leg-break. This time, at the moment of release the back of the hand points towards third man, so that the seam is positioned straight down the pitch. The seam should be spinning along its own axis – straight on and towards the batsman.

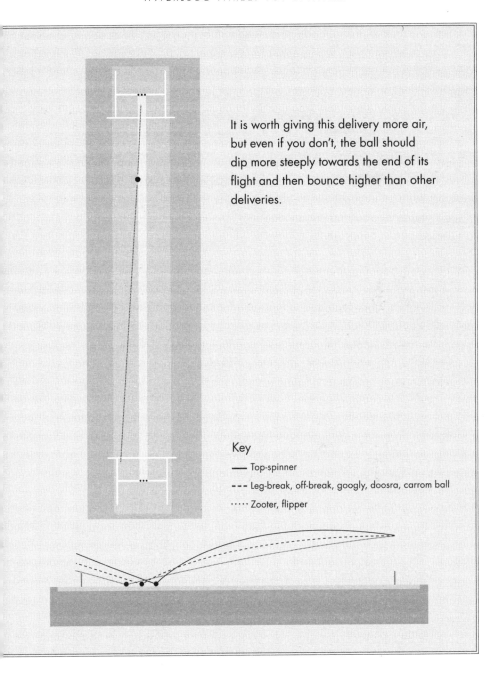

It is worth giving this delivery more air, but even if you don't, the ball should dip more steeply towards the end of its flight and then bounce higher than other deliveries.

Key

— Top-spinner

--- Leg-break, off-break, googly, doosra, carrom ball

····· Zooter, flipper

Chapter Four

SWIFT PIONEERS

The limits of approaching spin bowling as two basic dichotomies are illuminated by the rich contribution of the Swift Pioneers.

It is an oddity of cricket in its present condition that so few spinners bowl at medium pace, although there are encouraging signs of this changing because of the Twenty20 revolution. For now, conventional wisdom suggests that, if told such and such a bowler was a spinner, one would surmise that he was either an off-break or a leg-break bowler, hopefully with a few variations, and one might then politely enquire as to whether he were right- or left-handed. Very few people would think of him as likely to be a medium-pace bowler, or possibly a slow-medium-pace bowler, who spun the ball both ways off the pitch – not cutting it, as fast bowlers do, by landing the ball on an angled seam, but spinning it, getting the wrist and the fingers involved in the action – and consequently achieving pronounced swerve in the air.

And yet, in the last decades of the Victorian era, there arose in England and then Australia bowlers who were genuinely medium pace – at a guess, bowling just above, and just below, 70mph – who imparted spin on the ball and could make it go both ways. Three stood out in England

– W. G. Grace, A. G. Steel and George Lohmann – and a further three stood out in Australia – F. R. Spofforth, Monty Noble and Hugh Trumble. Each in his own way pre-empted the rise of the greatest bowler in the era that immediately followed: Sydney Barnes, a fast spinner, was the most complete bowler of all time. Of more recent spinners, there are those, from Tiger O'Reilly to Bhagwat Chandrasekhar and Derek Underwood, who bowled at medium pace; but very few successful spinners of the present day ape that method. And yet, to the likes of Grace and Lohmann it seemed perfectly natural that they should combine medium pace with what was, at times, prodigious spin. They would also bowl the occasional much slower ball, and so try to deceive the batsman in flight; but their basic method was to repeatedly drop the ball on a nagging length and line, and turn it the width of the bat in either direction. This method was simple and successful in equal measure.

Before turning to it, however, it may be instructive briefly to attend to another bowler, not hugely distinguished at the highest level, but who also employed the medium-pace-cum-spin method with grand efficacy. Lacking in true greatness, what makes him interesting is, again, his utility in debunking a commonly held myth about the history of spin.

Walter Mead probably wasn't the father of the flipper – at least not in the sense of being the first to bowl that magic delivery. But, with a grip very much his own, his claim to have been wronged by history is credible. It is very widely believed that Clarrie Grimmett, the brilliant little Australian who became a world-beater in the 1930s, invented the flipper. Though he had the decency never to make that claim himself, countless others have done it for him. For now, let's examine Mead's claim on the flipper – a back-spinning ball of huge advantage to the leg-spinner, delivered from underneath the wrist with a clicking action that incorporates the thumb, and which hangs in the air before skidding in from the off. In other words, the reverse of the conventional leg-break, whose top-spin component causes it to dip in the air, and whose side-spin component causes it to break from leg to off, and away from the right-hander.

Deep within the recesses of that infinitely charming book *Great Bowlers and Fielders: Their Methods at a Glance*, by George Beldam and C. B. Fry, originally published in 1906, is a description of Mead which makes explicit not only his right to be both a medium-pace bowler and a spinner, but also his claim on the flipper. His employment of this ball makes him the missing link between the thumb-generated under-armers of William Lillywhite's day and the flipper merchants of Australia, from Grimmett to Bruce Dooland and Richie Benaud, a full century later, themselves predecessors of the latest bowlers to experiment with the delivery, such as Anil Kumble and Shane Warne.

Known as 'the Essex Treasurer', Mead's bulbous eyes emerged from under heavy eyelids and were planted on a wide, rectangular face. They sat above a thick, proud moustache. His forefinger was 'long, strong, sinuous', and his run-up started with the ball 'muffled' beneath his diaphragm. He played only once for England, against Australia at Lord's in 1899 (53-24-91-1), but *Wisden* considered him 'in his day one of the most notable of slow-medium right-arm bowlers'. It went on: 'With an easy delivery and remarkable command of length, he possessed exceptional powers of spin and could make the ball turn on the best of pitches. While generally employing the off-break, he sent down an occasional leg-break with good effect.' Of how many modern-day bowlers, even those only worthy of a single Test, could it be said they were slow-medium in pace, spun the ball both ways and had exceptional accuracy to boot? To put it another way, of which present-day bowler, if any, might we be moved to write, as Fry did of Mead: 'A medium-pace bowler of the highest class, full of life, very accurate in length, rather deceptive in flight, and able to break the ball both from leg and from off'?

The brilliant, grainy pictures reproduced by Beldam and Fry show that Mead had two grips. One was basically the conventional leg-break grip, involving the first three fingers with the thumb initially on, too. This was for his leg-break, sent down the orthodox way, which left the pitch with a 'curious, upward curl'. The other grip was altogether different. Fry writes of Mead having:

> ... A very curious grip for his off-break; the ball sits in a kind of cup made with the thumb and second finger and the first finger is hooped around over the top of the ball; the first finger aided by a quick twist of the wrist manages to put a great amount of spin on the ball.

Mead wasn't very good at concealing the difference between the two grips, since, according to Fry:

> It is easy to detect whether he is bowling the off- or the leg-break because when he is going to use the latter he changes the ball in his hand at the last moment and arranges his grip with very obvious care. Needless to say, the batsman, although he knows what is coming, is not thereby relieved of all difficulty.

Not for Mead, then, the attempts at disguise used by later flipper bowlers, such as Dooland, who concealed his hand until just before delivery, or Paul Adams who did the same more recently. But this grip, with the ball sitting in a cup made by the thumb and middle finger, seems to me to be almost unique in the history of spin. Other bowlers with unorthodox grips, such as the bent middle-finger grip used most notoriously by Jack Iverson and, before and after him, Warwick Armstrong and Johnny Gleeson respectively, propel leg-breaks off the middle finger. Mead seemed to bowl a delivery from underneath the hand with a clicking action – but, rather than click his fingers using thumb and middle finger, he used his thumb and index finger. Almost certainly there have been a few other bowlers over the course of the game's history who did this, and one of them was Monty Noble, of whom more presently. But no others that I or, dare I say it, most cricket historians, have yet come across.

The picture is muddied further by the fact that many people writing about Mead in later years surmised that his unorthodox delivery, bowled with an unusual grip and coming in from the off, must have made him one of the first to bowl the googly. Alas, it's not the first, or last, time that the googly, as with the flipper, has been subject to confusion. H. S. Altham, one of the great players-turned-writers of the game, thought that Mead bowled the googly, or Bosie, before Bernard Bosanquet lent his name to it. But from Fry's analysis, for which we must now be immensely grateful, we can surmise that Mead almost certainly did not bowl the googly. How do we know? Well, first, there is no reference to a looping off-break delivered from the back of the hand, which is what the googly is. And, second, there is the following description from Fry of the ball Mead bowled from under his wrist, with that unusual grip of his:

> The batsman cannot easily get to the pitch of the ball and yet has very little time to watch the ball from the pitch if he plays back. Some bowlers who commanded a good off-break on sticky wickets are fairly easy to hit with a certain amount of pull in the stroke, but Mead's bowling comes off the pitch in a way that baulks the success of the pulled drive.

If it sounds and smells like the flipper, and if it is bowled, and behaves, like the flipper, there is a decent chance that Walter Mead was more than capable of bowling, and frequently did bowl, what we today, and Clarrie Grimmett years before us, would have called the flipper. Whether Mead's was the first flipper we'll never know. But we can be confident Grimmett's wasn't. And we can be confident, too, that very few (if any) bowlers of the flipper have emulated Mead's method of deploying the index rather than middle finger.

Moreover, the flipper was probably bowled by Grace, too. This only adds to the delightful and reasonable claim that the rotund doctor from Gloucestershire was the most complete player the game has ever produced. Never mind that this bearded, bulky, boisterous man, a kind of Victorian Brian Blessed, who in his youth had been a champion hurdler and runner, 'a good shot and a skilful fisherman' (according to E. W. Swanton), dominated the game for four decades and has long been the closest thing we have to a personification of it. Never mind that he was one of the greatest batsmen, and one of the greatest bowlers. Never mind all that – the wonderful thing about Grace, certainly in terms of his claim on these pages, is that, although he started out as a round-arm medium-pacer, in later years he combined this medium pace with guile and spin. And, what is more, he had two favoured deliveries: first, the over-the-wrist orthodox leg-break, of which he was the foremost early exponent; and, second, the under-the-wrist, thumb-generated, skidding off-break. It's true: half a century before Grimmett used it in a match, WG was bowling the flipper.

For evidence, we need only return to Fry, who said of him, 'he could put drag spin on it [the ball] by turning his hand the reverse way and cutting under the ball'. This gives us a picture not of the under-cutter, as bowled by off-spinners such as Graeme Swann and Shaun Udal, but, rather, of a flipper, with the seam upright and his hand behind the ball – that is, the flipper as occasionally bowled by Benaud. This would suffice, but in addition we have Fry's assertion that this delivery 'looks a great deal simpler than it is. A spectator watching from the side of the ground can easily see the length of the ball, but the batsman is often deceived by the flight.' This testifies to the flipper's ability, because of the back-spin on it, to hover and hang in the air, rather than dip as balls with top-spin (over-spin) do.

The story of WG's life has been amply told (and best of all, in my view, in Simon Rae's magisterial *W. G. Grace – A Life*). He was one of the defining characters of late-Victorian England, a man who could be insufferably pompous and unpardonably rude, but also hugely generous with his time and wisdom. His bowling has not suffered for a lack of analysis either, though perhaps with good reason it has generally been considered secondary to his batting. One of the reasons for this is the suggestion that his style of bowling would have been less successful in modern times. He took many of his wickets with leg-before decisions while coming from around the wicket. In those days, batsmen could be given out leg-before to balls that pitched outside leg-stump, which modern players can't. Given the forceful nature of Grace's personality, many an umpire may have felt his welfare imperilled were he to turn the doctor down.

Grace's obituary in *The Times* provides an engaging and contemporary account of the efficacy of his method:

No-one else placed his field as he did. To the spectator nobody looked an uglier or a much worse bowler, but to the batsman he was very difficult. He was slow, with a most ungainly action, but he could bowl on either side of the wicket, did not object to being hit, and he soon found out the weak points of an opponent. What made his bowling difficult was his length and direction. The ball dropped down from a great height and frequently looked like a half-volley until the batsman tried to hit it, then it was found to be a good length. He had a long arm and often bowled round the wicket, so that his ball looked to the batsman a beauty to hit to leg; the batsman tried to do so, but misjudged the length and missed it and was astonished to find himself given out leg-before wicket. He used to have a deep square leg and many a time used he to get batsmen out by bowling for catches.

The idea that he was 'bowling for catches', especially via a leg-side field, suggests parallels with methods used in Twenty20 today. The passage refers to his 'later years' as a bowler: in his twenties he bowled with less spin and more pace. In his prime he combined the two.

So, too, did many of his contemporaries. As the legalisation of over-arm bowling in 1864 receded into memory, several slow-medium-pacers emerged who experimented with spin. William Buttress, of Cambridgeshire, then one of the most successful counties, bowled over-arm leg-breaks at medium pace well enough to be considered the father of leg-break bowling by H. S. Altham. We know from previous chapters that this view should immediately be amended to say he might have been the father of the *over-arm* leg-break, rather than the leg-break *per se*, but even then we should remain sceptical. Alas, his penchant for ale, which united him with spinners ranging from William Clarke to Phil Tufnell, caused death from alcoholism at forty-one in 1866.

That year marked the eighth birthday of A. G. Steel, reckoned by many of his contemporaries to be second only to WG as the finest all-rounder of his day, and in later life a President of the MCC and a barrister in Liverpool. But whereas WG focused more on spin towards the end of his exceptionally long career, Steel's attention moved away from his bowling, and towards batting. This was a shame in many ways, not least because it was his quick leg-breaks and off-breaks as a young man that led *Wisden* to assert that he was the finest player ever to come out of Marlborough College. Indeed, in 1915, *Wisden* contained the following:

The late Mr. W. J. Ford, who was a master at Marlborough in Steel's time, and an excellent judge of the game, has left it on record that Steel was never a better bowler than during his last year at school. Mr. Ford describes his bowling, that his regular pace was slow, almost slow medium, so it was never easy to get out and take him on the full pitch, and considering he was perpetually breaking the ball both ways, in which respect he was practically the pioneer of slow bowlers, he kept his length with remarkable accuracy, over-pitching rather than under-pitching the ball. Mr. Ford adds that he never knew a bowler more difficult to drive than Steel, for among other gifts he could send a ball up at a great pace ... As may be gathered from Mr. Ford's criticism, Steel's bowling perhaps owed its success to a certain trickiness, with the usual result that as batsmen found his tricks out, so did he become rather less effective.

This reference to 'a certain trickiness' is an early indication of the spectre of mystery that can hang from a bowler, so that his reputation precedes him. It conjures up the sense of an unknown and even unknowable danger. This is compounded by the unverified and unverifiable reports that Steel sent down a googly in the very first Test match, a claim which certainly complicates the usual tale of it having been invented by Bernard Bosanquet years later.

Though it might be a stretch to say it made him 'practically the pioneer of slow bowlers', certainly Steel's 'trickiness' made him deeply influential, and entrenches him in the tradition of great spinning medium-pacers around this time. Altham, clearly borrowing from *Wisden*, said Steel was:

... slow, yet fast enough to make jumping out to him a matter of great difficulty, he could alter it [his chosen delivery] at will, and had quite a fast ball in reserve. He was a master of the short half-volley, the slow bowler's best length ball, and he could spin the ball either way, though favouring the leg-break.

By the short half-volley we must assume this is the ball that the batsman thinks is there for the drive, but, because of the element of top-spin on the delivery, in fact isn't, leaving him vulnerable to mistime his shot, and so bring the slip region or short cover point into play. The master of this method in the modern day is Shane Warne, who deceived hundreds of batsmen with his 'short half-volley' during his career.

It's in a description of another medium-pace spinner, possibly the best England produced aside from Barnes, that Altham's admiration really takes off. I am connected with the subject George Alfred Lohmann, though obviously not because this blue-eyed, blond-haired son of a stockbroker was among the finest looking specimens ever to play the game. Rather, Lohmann learned to play the game on Wandsworth Common in south London, about one hundred metres, at its south-western tip, from where I learned to play the game, though Sinjuns CC in the 1990s was nothing much like the Church Institute for whom Lohmann played in the 1880s. But, just as I did, he saved his pocket money, and packed his sandwiches, to fund trips to the Oval. He met with rather more success than me, not least when suddenly called on to bowl in front of the Hon. Robert Grimston, a noted amateur player.

Before he died of tuberculosis at the age of thirty-six in Matjiesfontein, in the Klein Karoo region of South African (he emigrated there in 1897), Lohmann was so brilliant a bowler that he acquired a better strike rate, and lower average, than any Test bowler since or before. In those two senses, his 112 wickets in eighteen Tests, at a stunning 10.75, may never be surpassed. Which explains Altham's excitement:

We have the testimony of both WG and C. B. Fry that Lohmann was the best medium-paced bowler they had ever met, a combined verdict, it will be noticed, that embraces half a century. In an age still wedded to the formalism of length, he was the first English bowler really to master the revolutionary lessons of [the Australian, F. R.] Spofforth, and to make length the handmaid of variety in pace and spin and flight. He was on the slow side of medium; he could break the ball back as he chose from the off, could bowl a leg-break at will, and always had in reserve the ball that looked like spinning but went straight on. But subtlety of flight was his greatest asset; with his very high delivery he was always dipping short of what the batsman expected; he could suck him out with his held back slow ball, or get him driving at the half-volley, which somehow 'swam' into a yorker.

Altham, as a veritable cricket nut, might ungraciously be described as prone to hyperbole – though, if hyperbole is good enough for Nyren, it's good enough for the rest of us. But I defy anyone to apply this masterfully crafted prose to a modern bowler and claim a comfortable fit. Just like in Fry's descriptions of Mead, and in Mr W. J. Ford's analysis of Steel, so Altham saw in Lohmann – who, incidentally, was one of the game's first truly outstanding close fielders – a completeness of skill, and a rainbow of competences, which make even the best modern bowlers curiously monotonous by comparison. The insistence on his insistence of length – 'handmaid of variety in pace and spin and flight' – is a recurring theme among great spin bowlers, strikingly reminiscent, for example, of Tiger O'Reilly's suggestion that his dear friend Grimmett was above all a bowler of immaculate length.

Ralph Barker's similarly admiring account adds to our impression of Lohmann as an unusually complete master of his art:

Lohmann was never fast, and was always slower than Spofforth; he bowled mostly at medium pace, but like Spofforth could send in a faster ball. He believed that to be effective a bowler should concentrate on four basic skills: length, break, lift from the pitch and a deceptive delivery. The last of these skills he regarded as the most important of all, since length was something that a batsman got used to, break and lift were becoming harder to achieve on the improving wickets of the time, and a bowler was eventually thrown back on his resources of deception.

This recalls Nasser Hussain's perennial (and justified) complaint during his tenure as England captain: when pitches go flat, on the subcontinent, in the Caribbean, in South Africa and Down Under, a captain's aching need is for raw pace or a bit of mystery. (A bit of Lohmann might have come in handy, too.) WG's description of Lohmann's magic was typical, in combining abrasiveness with a kind of reluctant but irrepressible generosity: 'It is simply ludicrous to watch batsman after batsman walk into the trap. After the trick was done one could not help saying "What an absurdly simple ball to have been bowled by!" – but all the same it was a triumph of the bowler's art.' WG, having employed a similar combination of medium pace and spin to Lohmann, would have appreciated his skill and variety.

All of these medium-paced spinners profited from the increase to six-ball overs (of which Lohmann was particularly fond) in 1902 – up from five, having been four until 1889 – because it gave them a longer go at doing over the batsmen. In Australia, they missed out the five ball over altogether, bowling six balls an over from 1891. Perhaps this, together with the exchange of ideas and borrowing of methods facilitated by the first Ashes tours, in part explains why some of the other great medium-pace spinners were Australian.

So while most of these bowlers were English, a group of Australians used their own brand of swift mystery to prove to the English that the 'colonials' should be taken seriously. They were the first of many, of course, to do this: the bulk of the history of cricket is a sequence of imperial inversions, in which the English are humiliated at various times by those who have formerly been their subjects. Three stand out: Monty Noble, Hugh Trumble, and 'the Demon' Spofforth.

Ah yes, 'the Demon'. Frederick Robert Spofforth was to many minds first and foremost among bowlers: no player had, by dint of his bowling alone, previously caused as much fear as he did. He was among the first international bowling legends. Generally credited with making over-arm bowling fashionable in England after touring in 1882, he had started out as an under-arm bowler as a boy, but converted when he realised the additional options available to him with the arm coming over the shoulder. With his sunken eyes, hooked nose and classy quiff perched across a six-foot-three frame, and a swaggering nine pace run-up inviting batsmen to engage with each handsome feature, Spofforth bamboozled many of his victims with what George Giffen, the great Australian all-rounder, could only describe as sheer 'devilry'.

Legend veritably oozed from him. One tale – impossible to verify – has it that in 1881 he rode a horse four hundred miles to play a minor game in Australia, then took all twenty wickets, each one of them clean-bowled. One of the earliest bowlers to terrify batsmen with pace, he was generally keen on speed, running 100 metres in 10.2 seconds in 1881, a record for New South Wales (though in a time when stopwatches relied on the human eye). He was inspired to take up cricket by watching George 'Tear'em' Tarrant, who he saw bowling for George Parr's visiting Englishmen in 1863–4. It was Spofforth, of course, whose rampaging through fourteen English batsmen at the Oval in 1882, including 7-44 in the second innings as they were bowled out for seventy-seven chasing just eighty-five, led to the mock obituary of English cricket in the *Sporting Times* whence The Ashes emerged. He had issued one of the most celebrated of sporting clarion calls in the dressing room before the Australians took to the field. 'This thing can be done,' he said.

Like Grimmett in his scientific approach to the game, Spofforth examined the finest detail of opposing batsmen's techniques. He was rightly regarded as a principled man, and might have played in the first ever Test in Melbourne had he not refused to because his friend Billy Murdoch, the wicketkeeper, was ungraciously dropped. Such obstinacy led to frequent brushes with controversy, such as when he used unusually pronounced spikes on his shoes, which opponents claimed were for the benefit (via footmarks) of whichever of his countrymen were bowling at the other end. Lancashire's Dick Barlow once had the temerity to raise this issue with 'the Demon'. He soon found himself floored by a left jab.

Much like countless other bowlers since his time, including Sir Richard Hadlee, he slowed down from tearaway to thoughtful artisan as his career progressed. And he did so by learning to bowl a carefully controlled range of spin and swerve, to compensate for what he lost in pace. Spofforth was obsessed with the behaviour of the ball in the air. Just as Barnes two decades later cocked his wrist back at the point of delivery to accentuate the swerve, which was always in the opposite direction to the turn, so Spofforth seemed capable of making the ball move one way in the air, and then the other off the pitch. This he achieved through spin rather than conventional swing or seam. It's worth pointing out what 'swerve' meant to Spofforth's contemporaries – and what I mean by it – is movement in the air caused by spin. The more familiar term today, used constantly when explaining the behaviour of Warne's leg-break, for example, is 'drift'. I'll use the two interchangeably: but the key is that they are different from conventional swing, which is created by air moving at different speeds around a ball with one rough side and one smooth side.

Spofforth reckoned he had three types of swerve, and with it three types of spin: in-swerve (for the leg-break); out-swerve (for the off-break); and something he called 'vertical spin'. The archives are not altogether clear as to whether this was achieved through back-spin or over-spin, and the fact that he is alleged to have had a separate ball, one which dropped short of the length predicted by the batsman, muddies the picture further. Was this other delivery a 'short half-volley', of the kind Altham detected in Steele – that is, an orthodox top-spinner? If it wasn't, could it have been simply a slower ball, sent on a higher trajectory? If it was the latter, does that leave Spofforth's 'vertical' swerve delivery as one achieved with back-spin? If so, that suddenly opens the delicious prospect that he, too, was an early sender of flippers to opponents. On this latter calculation he would have four deliveries: the leg-break (with in-swerve); the off-break (with out-swerve); the slower ball, dropping short of the predicted length; and the flipper, his 'vertical' swerve achieved through back-spin. There's huge conjecture in all this, of course, but then we are talking about a period for which conjecture is necessary.

Just as Warwick Armstrong, the monumental Australian we meet at greater length in the next chapter, acquired vast wealth after his playing days, so Spofforth turned to business, becoming director of his father-in-law's firm, Star Tea Company, in England, and acquiring a mini fortune. So attractive to him was the prospect of acquiring wealth that he abandoned Test cricket altogether in 1886, when not far from the peak of his powers, to migrate to England.

This deprived him of the opportunity of playing under a distinguished Australian captain, though one who sits behind Benaud, Armstrong and Steve Waugh at least in contending for the title of that country's best. As an all-rounder, though, it's thankfully still fashionable to say that Monty Noble was the best Australian cricketer there has been (Bradman, alas, didn't bowl too well). All-round talent was something he had in abundance, because before his death (which prompted a stand at the Sydney Cricket Ground being named after him) Noble was one of the finest writers the game has produced, as well as a distinguished broadcaster, dentist, banker and manufacturers' agent.

Wonderfully poised at the crease, he had an elegant backlift, quick feet and a very good eye, making him a formidable batsman. Standing over six feet tall, he used his long legs to get to the pitch of the ball and drive graciously, helping him on the way to seven double centuries in an exceptional career. But if the Australians were forced to choose a specialism for him, they would have taken his bowling, and that, too, even before he took 7-17 and 6-60 in the second Test against England at Melbourne in 1901–2.

Noble is a marvellous case study in bowling, and for several reasons. First, he fits essentially with the premier bowlers of this period in being what to the modern eye is a conflation of categories: spin at medium pace. Second, he employed a grip that, aside from Mead, was hardly in use anywhere before or since, with the ball spun between thumb and index finger. And third, he had that same propensity for swerve in the air that Spofforth had, but in greater measure; indeed, no bowler's swerve in the air caused as much terror to batsmen, except for Barnes's. Which is rather apt, because Noble and Barnes were mates, and spoke extensively about how to achieve this swerve.

The phenomenal Barnes occupies a slightly later period in the game to Noble, so is reserved for spin bowling's First Flourish. But he and Noble shared many basic characteristics: theirs was an artistically, and practically, reciprocal relationship. Noble varied his pace according to the conditions, from slow to medium and even medium-fast, and took the out-swerving off-break as his stock delivery. He had a well-concealed quicker ball, and turned the ball sharply at times – *Wisden* recorded his ability for 'astonishing break-back' – but at other times aimed at the stumps and hurried it through, much like Sonny Ramadhin half a century later. He came in off a long run-up and, just like Peter Such for England in the 1990s, seemed to take forever to get to the crease. His grip, in using the index rather than the middle finger to impart spin along with the thumb, seemed to sacrifice a strong lever for a weaker one, but it is testament to the strength of his digits that he spun it sharply nevertheless.

In a sign that the best bowlers learn and borrow not just from each other, but from other sports, Noble acquired and practised the grip after speaking to American baseball stars who were touring Australia to promote their game. Theirs was a sport in which it was essential to master swerve: pitchers didn't have the option of beating hitters with turn off the ground. Noble learned how they delivered a curve ball, and worked tirelessly to emulate it.

And, much to the chagrin of his countrymen, he was generous with his new discovery. He spoke to George Hirst, the brilliant left-armer and Yorkshire all-rounder, described by Lord Hawke as the greatest county cricketer of all time, and soon Hirst had mastered it. But it was in conversations with Barnes, then touring Australia with England, that Noble's passing on of trade secrets had its greatest effect.

In one of those glorious meetings of Twirlymen minds, where the thread between generations of spinners is most robust, and the line of continuity most straight, Barnes recorded how he

… asked Noble if he would care to tell me how he managed to bring the ball back against the swerve. He said it was possible to put two poles down the wicket, one ten or eleven yards from the bowling crease and another one five or six yards from the batsman, and to bowl a ball outside the first pole and make it swing to the off-side of the other pole and then nip back and hit the wickets. That's how I learned to spin a ball and make it swing. It is also possible to bowl in between these two poles, pitch the ball outside leg-stump and hit the wicket. I spent hours trying all this out in the nets.

Barnes conflates 'swing' with spin-induced swerve, as we'll see in the next chapter. This habit of his, which he kept up for decades, becomes less defensible when noting that *Wisden*, in naming Noble a Cricketer of the Year in 1900, was typically sensitive to the distinction:

As a bowler [Noble] has plenty of spin and varies his pace well, though not with so little perceptible change of action as [fast bowler Henry] Howell. A good deal had been said about his ability to make the ball swerve in the flight, and there can be no doubt that this peculiarity in his bowling puzzled many of our batsmen, especially during the early part of the tour.

So here, again, we have the picture of Noble as a bowler far more dextrous in his methods, far more rounded in his skills, and far more malleable in his abilities, than most of those playing today. He bowled at medium pace, denying the batsman time. He could also bowl slowly, giving the batsman more time than he desired, and so beating him in the air. He bamboozled and 'puzzled' batsmen with these subtle variations, all of them reliant on an approach to the crease that indicated the ball would be given an almighty rip. In this respect, he was a man of his time, a Swift Pioneer who accommodated half a modern coaching manual in his method.

Though it came over a year after the hagiography in *Wisden*, it was only really after those thirteen wickets in Melbourne that Noble was considered a bowler of the first rank in his era. He partly owed that reputation, and, indeed, many of his wickets, to the man bowling at the other end, with whom he briefly formed the most devastating spin partnership since the legalisation of over-arm bowling, and certainly until the South African googly merchants started bowling in tandem a few years later.

Hugh Trumble was the first man to take two hat-tricks in Test cricket (both at Melbourne, his home ground). On a separate occasion, that game in 1901–2, he and Noble became the first men in the history of the game to take all twenty Test wickets between them, Trumble finishing with seven of them. This feat has been achieved only six times in Test history, most notoriously by those fellow members of the Twirlymen brotherhood, Jim Laker and Tony Lock, in the Old Trafford Test of 1956.

Well over six foot tall, Trumble bowled brisk off-spinners that could be unplayable on a sticky wicket, extracting uneven bounce from his very high arm. It must be said that he had a striking resemblance to Spofforth, and, by extension, Dennis Lillee, and not just because each sported a moustache, though Trumble's sticking-out ears distinguished him, even from a great distance. Here, too, was a bowler who slowed down and acquired spin over the course of his career, eventually combining them effectively enough to be Wisden Cricketer of the Year in 1897. On his first tour of England, in 1893, 'his high delivery medium pace bowling struck English batsmen as lacking both sting and variety'; by the time he returned for the third time in 1896–7, 'Trumble convinced Englishmen he was entitled to rank among the great bowlers of Australia', a bowler whose 'strength lay in the combination of spin and extreme accuracy of pitch'.

This, added to a brisk medium pace, made for a wicked brew. It was one common to the legion of world-beating bowlers who emerged in the decades after the legalisation of over-arm bowling in 1864. And though their distilled wisdom was personified in the man who dominated the era immediately following their own, Sydney Barnes, they were genuinely distinct from the vast majority of great spinners of the twentieth and now twenty-first centuries, in correctly thinking spin and medium pace were compatible. It's true that some more modern bowlers have pushed it through quickly but they were exceptions to the rule, and none of them was as skilful in deploying that brilliant but too often overlooked weapon, spin-swerve (drift). The great medium-pacers of the late Victorian period, English and Australian, approached the crease with a spectrum of deliveries available to them, and a liberal mindset, open to experimentation. With the closure of their careers, cricket therefore didn't lose something invaluable, but began to forget it: a wonderful method of bowling that even today begs for resurrection. Yet just as one artform was being lost, another was bursting into life. It was called the googly.

Interlude Four

GOOGLY
(OR WRONG'UN, OR BOSIE)

Grip   *Batsman's Point of View*

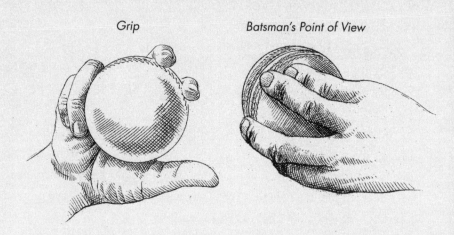

The grip for the googly is the same as that for the top-spinner and leg-break. The tops of the first two fingers are across the seam. The spin is imparted by the third finger, which straightens from a bent position. On entering the delivery stride, the back of the hand starts off facing the sky. As the arm comes round, the wrist is bent further inwards than for the leg-break and top-spinner. This time, at the moment of release the back of the hand points towards the batsman and will end up facing the ground. The seam should be spinning along its own axis, which is now pointing towards fine leg.

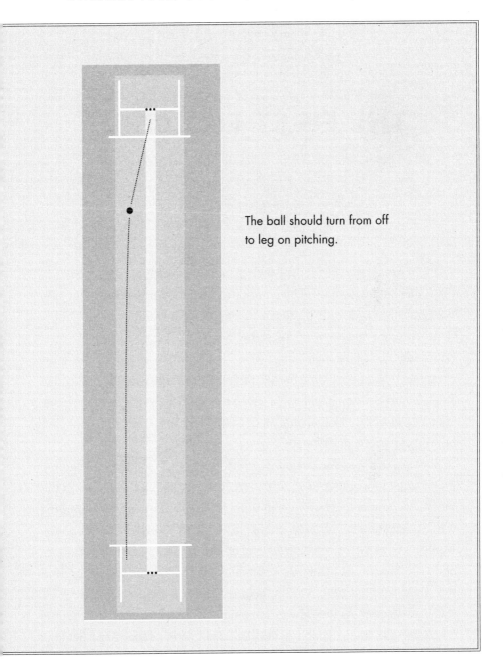

The ball should turn from off to leg on pitching.

Chapter Five

THE FIRST FLOURISH

The first great flourish of spin bowling had two principal characteristics. First, like the eras that followed and immediately preceded it, its spin bowlers were aware of themselves as part of a tradition, and sought to learn from the wisdom of those before them, and pass on their knowledge to future Twirlymen. The First Flourish produced the most complete bowler of all time in the crabby, cranky and usually unplayable Englishman Sydney Barnes. He owed a huge debt to his predecessors, specifically Monty Noble, and, as became clear in the previous chapter, he was conscious of that debt.

Second, this was the period in which the googly suddenly became a major force in world cricket, and then, just as suddenly, found itself the victim of a smear campaign from those whose welfare (and livelihoods) it most threatened – namely, confused batsmen. Bowlers emerged who would use it as their stock ball; several others used it as a deadly variation; and so effective was their deployment of it that terror spread around the world through news cables, hearsay and the tortured memories of touring batsmen. As the Edwardian era matured, and before the ruinous pity of world war, a monumental backlash took shape. This devious delivery seemed an affront to English decency and manners, against the spirit of the game and, just as with the round-armers seven decades previously, googly bowlers incurred the wrath of fellow professionals, most of them playing the victim card, and laying the special pleading on pretty thick. The googly was blamed for all manner of ills, from the occasional failure of leading batsmen, to the loss of a spirit of fair play and heightened disrespect for long-established practices, in cricket and beyond, throughout the Empire.

Twenty-two years after he allegedly bowled the first googly in Australia, dislodging the brilliant Victor Trumper along the way, the man credited (wrongly) with inventing this delivery wrote an article in the *Morning Post*, reproduced in *Wisden*, reflecting on the impact his supposed invention had on the game. He submitted the headline for the piece himself. It was: 'The Scapegoat of Cricket'.

Confidence came easily to Bernard James Tindal Bosanquet, and with good reason. Tall and debonair, he was popular at Eton, a hugely talented sportsman and coached so well by Maurice Read and William Brockwell, two Surrey players, that when he played against Harrow for the first time in 1896 he scored 120. Just four years later, and by this time completing his studies at Oxford, having obtained a Blue, he represented the University at hammer throwing (1899 and 1900) and billiards (1898 and 1900). But it was for the fruits of his cocksure experimentation when playing twisti-twosti, a pastime where the object is to spin the ball past your opponent, who is sitting at the other end of a table, that he would achieve lasting renown.

Bosanquet, who shared the names 'Bernard' and 'Bosanquet' (in that order) with one of Victorian England's most brilliant political theorists, twenty-nine years his senior, and whose son Reginald was a distinguished toupee-sporting ITN news reader, did *not* invent the googly. As I said in the introduction, human history might be rectilinear, but the history of ideas certainly is not: there is no such thing as an original idea. This is especially true of spin bowling, where all patents are fraudulent.

The Surrey captain K. J. Keys once wrote a letter to Jack Hobbs suggesting a Mr H. V. Page of Oxford and Gloucestershire was bowling genuine googlies in 1885, though, curiously, only in between wickets and never actually at the batsman. A. G. Steel, whom we met in the previous chapter, and reckoned in his day to be a potential successor to W. G. Grace, probably sent down a googly when he bowled in the first ever Test match, in England in 1880. The Australian George 'Joey' Palmer was recorded in *Wisden* as an off-break bowler, but reports that some of his deliveries came from the back of the hand convinced many that he bowled a genuine googly.

Bosanquet himself reckoned that Nottinghamshire's William Attewell (better known as 'Dick'), a pioneer of off-theory – bowling outside off-stump to a packed off-side field – sent down googlies. He suspected the same of 'Rockley' Wilson, who was educated at Rugby and of similar age to Bosanquet. Wilson was eventually Master of Winchester for forty years, where his pupils included Douglas Jardine, England's captain through the Bodyline series of 1932–33. When a journalist enquired about England's chances under his old student just after England had set sail for Australia, Wilson replied with stunning perspicacity: 'He might well win us the Ashes. But he might lose us Dominion.'

Despite all this, Bosanquet is widely credited with having invented this delivery, which he said was motivated by a desire to avoid bowling fast on hot afternoons. His claim to have done so is aided by the fact that he passed it on to friends who had great success with it (particularly South Africans – see below), and that for many years it was called a 'Bosie' in his honour. The Australians called it a wrong'un – a term long in use

Down Under to refer to felons and homosexuals (a double whammy when applied to Oscar Wilde's paramour, Lord Alfred Douglas, known as Bosie). The word 'googly' itself is of unknown provenance, though it was used in Australia to denote a high, looping ball that confused the batsman, making him all goggle-eyed. It's possible that 'googly' emerged as a variant. Tom Horan, the Irish-born Australian batsman who wrote under the pen name 'Felix' in *The Australasian*, suggested rather implausibly that since 'goo' was a baby-like sound, and 'guile' was what this delivery contained, a conjunction of the two conveyed the relative status of batsman and bowler when it was delivered. Even less plausibly, as Frith has written, some suggested that it was of Maori origin, and coined on the 1902–3 tour of New Zealand led by Lord Hawke. It may have gained traction in England because the word 'googler', used to indicate some unspecified type of bowling, was in common use around 1898–9.

Having discovered that, by cocking his wrist at twisti-twosti, he could make the ball deviate from left to right instead of from right to left, Bosanquet made the inevitable graduation to a cricket ball. This happened, he said, 'about 1897'. And yet, in a letter to *The Times* in 1956, his brother revealed discussing flicking a tennis ball across the uncovered slate of a billiards table from around 1892 (the family weren't short of cash). For several years later, Bosanquet would flick a hard rubber ball to the end of his garden, asking his cousin Louise to retrieve it.

Nevertheless, it was the twisti-twosti experiments that launched his supposed invention on to an unsuspecting world. Soon he was the 'star turn' in the nets at Oxford, amusing onlookers by making visiting batsmen look silly. Here again there is the influence of a certain braggadocio, or at least extreme self-assurance, in Bosanquet, which gave him the pioneering spirit and disregard for risk common to all great inventors, never mind Twirlymen. He was a crowd-pleaser and, at times, a rascal. 'It was not unfair, only immoral,' he said of his new delivery, knowing that would wind up all the batsmen already cheesed off with him. On the 1903–4 tour of Australia, because he wore bright jumpers the crowd at the SCG would call him 'Elsie'. Even in 1908 he was brandishing this swashbuckling spirit, hitting an astonishing (if scarcely believeable) twenty-five-minute century for Uxbridge against the MCC. It's a disposition that we know much about from that brilliant article he wrote in the *Morning Post*, reproduced in *Wisden*. Bosanquet's own testimony remains the best account of the emerging phenomenon:

> It took any amount of perseverance, but for a year or two the results were more than worth it, for in addition to adding to the merriment of the cricketing world, I found that batsmen who used to grin at the sight of me and grasp their bat firmly by the long handle began to show a marked preference for the other end!.

Bosanquet first deployed the delivery in a match against Leicestershire at Lord's in July 1900, perhaps in a small measure of desperation, because the left-handed Sam Coe was on ninety-eight. Bosanquet cocked his wrist, sent his googly down and had Coe stumped. It was bad enough for the batsman to fall on ninety-eight, but what must have really irked him was that the ball bounced four times. Such a delivery would of course be called a no-ball today. 'This small beginning marked the start of what came to be termed a revolution in bowling ...' he wrote.

And yet, as with all revolutions, there were those who saw chicanery afoot, and who opposed the new arrangement. Indeed, the googly was seen in many quarters as just not cricket, a deceitful attempt by the bowler to bend the rules to his advantage. That there was no mention in the laws of the degree to which the wrist could be cocked at the point of delivery did not matter: this was out of order. Among the most influential dissenters was Arthur Shrewsbury, the greatest batsman of his age, who muttered that this delivery 'wasn't fair', and resolved to play Bosanquet as an orthodox off-break bowler. The mercurial A. C. MacLaren, who as captain was later a huge influence on players, including Barnes, said in 1907: 'If this sort of bowling becomes general, I'm packing my bag for good and aye, and what's more, goodbye to all style and attractiveness in batting.' That's scapegoating all right, as Bosanquet knew.

Poor old googly! It has been subjected to ridicule, abuse, contempt, incredulity, and survived them all. Deficiencies existing at the present day are attributed to the influence of the googly. If the standard of bowling falls off it is because too many cricketers devote their time to trying to master it … If batsmen display a marked inability to hit the ball on the off-side or anywhere in front of the wicket and stand in apologetic attitudes before the wicket, it is said that the googly has made it impossible for them to attempt the old aggressive attitude and make the scoring strokes.

But, after all, what is the googly? It is merely a ball with an ordinary break produced by an extra-ordinary method. It is not difficult to detect, and, once detected, there is no reason why it should not be treated as an ordinary break-back. However, it is not for me to defend it. If I appear too much in the role of the proud parent I ask forgiveness.

Bosanquet's career at the highest level was an inconsistent affair. He was only selected for the 1903–4 tour, some said, because 'Plum' Warner, later the Grand Old Man of English cricket and then on the selection committee, owed a favour to his Oxford and Middlesex 'pet'.

The selection was reported as scandalous in many papers. It seemed exactly that when, in a match against Victoria, Harry Graham marched out to cover point to make contact with one particularly errant delivery. And yet, against the brilliant New South Wales hero Victor Trumper, he sent down two leg-breaks, which were played with ease into the covers, before 'with a silent prayer' sending over a googly – which some claim was the first ever bowled in Australia (impossible to prove) – and knocking back Trumper's middle stump. The batsman smiled at the bowler, shook his head, and said, 'That was too good for me, son.' Only the googly Eric Hollies employed in Bradman's last Test, which deprived the Don of a career average of 100, is more celebrated of all wrong'uns. It was this delivery to Trumper that inspired one Australian newspaper to say: 'He is the worst length bowler in England and yet he is the only bowler the Australians fear.'

He took part in six tours in all, including the great Ranjitsinhji's team of 1899, but played in a total of only seven Tests. In 1904, *Wisden* once reported that he bowled a 'wretched length'; another time, it described how 'The home side indeed were quite demoralised by Bosanquet who, although making the ball turn, bowled in the first innings in very erratic fashion'. His match figures in that game were 14-190. He bowled Australia out at Sydney in 1904 to regain the Ashes, and in 1905 took 8-107 in the first return Test at Trent Bridge. He did little bowling in the following two Tests at Lord's and Headingley, and was then dropped, never to return. Benaud says, 'that he could have had such a short career … seems to me one of the more remarkable happenings in the history of the game'. Ever the showman, he would conceal the ball for as long as possible, and to add to the mystique around his method made a great play of pretending his success in dismissing a batsman was owed to something other than his deception

– the pitch, the weather, a ball that wasn't truly spherical, or such like. But Bosie's legacy has long outlived him. In that glorious thread linking spin bowlers who span several generations, the strength of Bosie's connection to his successors was particularly strong. In the first Test at Sydney in 1903, when R. E. Foster scored a scintillating 287 not out on debut, and Bosanquet managed 3-152 on his own debut, two of the enthralled fans included future masters of the googly. Herbert 'Ranji' Hordern, was watching in the members' stand. And Arthur Mailey, a poor little boy rich with ambition, was watching with the other common folk on the Hill. He would go on to be an outstanding wrist-spinner for Australia.

If the reaction of Arthur Shrewsbury and A. C. MacLaren to Bosanquet's weird off-break seems over-sensitive to us now, more than a century having passed since its public ventilation, consider the following (measured, sober, impartial) analysis of the emergence of googlies by R. E. Foster, the man who made his debut for England on the same day as Bosanquet, and acquired immortality via the pub quiz in remaining the only man to have captained England at both cricket and football:

Personally I think it will deteriorate batting. For this kind of bowling is a very great invention, and it is possible it may completely alter cricket, and no one who has not played against it can realise the difference it makes to a batsman and his shots. It must again be reiterated that this type of bowling is practically in its infancy, and if persevered with, as it surely will be, must improve and become more difficult to deal with. Now a batsman, when he goes in, may receive a ball which either breaks from the off, perhaps from the leg, or again may come straight through very quickly. If he survives half-a-dozen overs he ought to be getting set, but such bowling never allows the batsman to get really set, because he can never make or go for his accustomed shots.

Of course, it is a huge compliment to Bosanquet and his like that a player of Foster's stature should regard the googly as 'a very great invention', but what is arresting about this analysis, other than the fear it conveys, is the fact that googly bowling is seen as a coherent, mischievous whole. Foster doesn't dismiss all wrist-spin bowling; nor does he dismiss the variation to basic leg-spin bowling introduced by Bosanquet. Rather, by 'this kind of bowling' he dismisses those bowlers who spread fear by repeated use of the googly. Presumably he would not have made such a complaint had he been facing orthodox leg-spin alone, given that there was a lot of it around at the time. That he was moved to speak out in such terms is symptomatic of the distress this allegedly new delivery was causing batsmen.

The specific catalyst for Foster's complaint was the emergence in South Africa of the first great spin-bowling quartet. It was one of only two to conquer the summits of Test cricket. And the remarkable thing is its key members had no qualms about using Bosanquet's recent creation as their stock ball.

For a few years at the start of the twentieth century, this quartet dominated batsmen on the matting pitches of South Africa. The matting took sharp spin, but its secondary virtue was a propensity to make the ball bounce steeply because of the hardness of the surface. As a result it was no surprise to see a batsman negotiate a ball of a good length at chest height; and many a batsman who played a forward defensive ended up with a bloody nose, the ball smacking him in the face. And yet there were local variations, too, always discussed at length in advance of games and incorporated into bowling tactics. The mat at Cape Town was laid down on turf, and therefore not too quick; the mat at Johannesburg was over thick red dust, so that the ball would skid through. At Durban, where something called superfine yellow gravel was under the mat, the wicket would be fast and true.

Bosanquet's secret had slipped out primarily through Reggie Schwarz, a student of St Paul's School and Cambridge. Schwarz, of Silesian ancestry, was strikingly handsome and, according to *Wisden*, in possession of 'a particularly attractive voice'. Bosanquet invited Schwarz on a tour of America in 1901, where they became close and forged a bond that would solidify when they were both at Middlesex. Schwarz in fact represented England at rugby, but took up South African nationality to play for his adopted country at the end of 1901, having been invited by the financier and diamond tycoon Sir Abe Bailey, for whom he worked as secretary. When selected as a batsman and medium-pace bowler to tour England in 1904, Schwarz came across his old pal at the very first game of the tour. Bosanquet took nine wickets on that occasion, and was soon immersed in conversation with Schwarz. By the time of the fourth match of that tour, Schwarz had abandoned medium pace for googlies, and picked up 5-27 in the second innings. By the end of the tour, having boarded the ship in South Africa without expecting to bowl very much, he led the bowling averages with 65 wickets at 18.26.

A charming edition of the *Sydney Mail*, from 23 November 1910, related this tale while looking ahead to the series South Africa were shortly to play against Australia. The article, a double-page spread, had the heading 'The Springbok meets the Kangaroo: Exciting Match in Sydney'. Schwarz and Aubrey Faulkner (see below) were two of the three players picked out for special profiles. (The other was David Nourse, the prolific batsman.) For a flavour of the way international rumour about the googly spread in that heady era of globalisation, part of the profile of Schwarz is unbeatable:

By practising assiduously on the Wanderers' ground [in Johannesburg] he mastered the art of bowling the 'googlie' [sic], having learned the 'grip' by watching Bosanquet. He first bowled 'this stuff' in a match of importance against Oxford University for the South Africans. Remarkable to relate, he did not know how to place his field, for when asked by his captain (F. Mitchell) 'how he would have them', he answered 'Oh I don't know; just scatter yourselves'. They did, and Schwarz also proceeded in the 'scattering business', as he clean-bowled five of his opponents for 27 runs, besides bowling three with no balls. What a remarkable debut – probably unique – as regards no-balls.

The use of inverted commas around certain words offers an insight into how mystery is packaged, and the flagrant disinterest in field placing is a bold precursor of 'Bomber' Wells. Clearly, there is a bit of spin, in the public relations sense, here: the tale about fielding may be apocryphal, and the *Sydney Mail* is drumming up a sense that there is an element of fluke or illegality in his magic new delivery. It adds that 'it has been said that since 1907 Schwarz has lost his deadliness as a bowler, but his bowling against South Australia proved otherwise'. All in all, an effective little hype machine, and tabloid journalism, 1910-style.

As the newspaper also reported, Schwarz abandoned the leg-break altogether because he felt it interfered with his rhythm (as did Lance Gibbs sixty years later.) So Schwarz bowled mostly googlies with the occasional top-spinner when he uncocked his wrist slightly, and also an orthodox off-break, all landed on a nuisance of a length. In a vivid description of his method for *Wisden* in 1908, Foster opined that Schwarz made the ball come in from the off anywhere between six and eighteen inches, and though sluggish through the air had pace off the wicket – a lethal combination, speaking volumes about his technique, which must have imparted sharp spin. Foster also thought that batsmen should have scored more off his bowling, playing him as an orthodox off-break bowler who could be manipulated for twos and threes.

As Major Schwarz, he eventually served with distinction in the Great War, and was awarded a Military Cross after having been wounded twice. He came to Europe for service in France after winning plaudits in the campaign in German South Africa. But having survived the Armistice, he contracted influenza and died at forty-three.

The *Times* obituary was gushing about the man who did most to invigorate South Africa on the national stage. 'He had the great gift of absolute modesty and self-effacement,' the Thunderer said. 'No one meeting him casually would ever have guessed the renown he had won in the world of sport. Quiet, almost retiring, in manner; without the least trace of side; and with a peculiarly attractive voice and way of speaking, Schwarz impelled and commanded the affection even of acquaintances.'

The least of the four bowlers was Gordon White, though as one of South Africa's premier batsmen he might have been forgiven. Like Schwarz, he was an international in another sport, though his sideshow was football rather than rugby. On the celebrated 1907 tour to England, where South Africa were led by the brilliant wicketkeeper Percy Sherwell – who reckoned he could pick most of the variations sent down by his quartet – White took 56 wickets at 14.73, though not nearly as many as Schwarz's amazing 137 at 11.7. That he finished with the less impressive nine wickets from the 17 Tests in which he played is more a reflection of the merits of his teammates than a commentary on his own deficiencies. Indeed, Jack Hobbs reckoned he was the hardest of the four to pick, not least because, since he seemed to bowl the top-spinner as his stock delivery, anything that turned either way – and he could turn it in both directions – came as a surprise to the batsman. White, like Schwarz, served during the Great War, but he died a month before his teammate from wounds received in Gaza. He was 36.

Of the remaining two there has been a long argument about which was better, but that this debate has been led by South Africans themselves might indicate that it is really born of shame at the country's failure to produce more than half a dozen quality Test match spinners in the century following their retirements. There ought not to be much doubt that Ernie Vogler was the best of the four.

Foster said in 1908 that Vogler must be 'the greatest bowler playing cricket in either hemisphere at the present time', and certainly he was feted everywhere he went. Like Garfield Sobers years later, he would switch effortlessly between medium pace and spin. With a new ball in his hand, he would bowl fast off-breaks, getting the ball to swerve away in the air much as Sydney Barnes did. Then, with the ball five or six overs old, he would shorten his run-up, and from the very first ball after this adjustment assiduously land the most beautiful leg-break on a length. This, his stock ball, turned anywhere between two or three inches and eighteen inches (that is, prodigiously), but he thought nothing of sending over a googly once every other over. So difficult was this to pick from his fast arm that one victim after another fell bowled or leg-before, preparing to cut the ball pitched outside off. His googly generally didn't turn as sharply – around three to four inches – but was loaded with top-spin, and therefore dipped violently.

He also had two straight balls, according to *Wisden*'s obituary, which added that he was 'a bowler of infinite resource': a fast arm ball on a length, directed at the stumps; and a slow, looping yorker, which seemed 'more to quiver than swing in the air'. If that sounds an inoffensive delivery, it should be noted that it twice accounted for no less than C. B. Fry in the 1907 series. Foster wrote: 'He has rather a hesitating run up to the wicket, but in the last few steps never gets out of his stride. The ball is well concealed from the batsman before delivery, and the flight and variation of pace are very deceptive indeed.' All of which caused Sherwell to say that, of the quartet, Vogler was the hardest to pick.

He was the hardest to pick in other ways, too. Born in Swartwater, Cape Province, he was raised in Durban, played for Natal, and settled in Pretoria. Mature at twenty-eight, he was accepted on to the ground staff of the MCC, and boarded the ship with the intention of graduating into the Middlesex first XI. But though he bowled impressively and offered exciting variation from the medium-pacers then dominating the county circuit, Vogler was prevented from playing for Middlesex. The problem wasn't competence; rather, his crime was being a 'colonial'. What with Albert Trott and Frank Tarrant – two Australians – already representing British dependencies, there would be no room for Vogler.

Instead, he signed up with Sir Abe Bailey , and returned home. On the 1907 tour he took 119 wickets at under 16, while scoring 723 runs at 21. His 36 wickets were crucial in securing the 1909–10 series against England. Vogler, who today is sometimes referred to as Bert, but was earnestly called Ernest by Bosanquet, had other distinctions too. He was the only one of the quartet to take ten wickets in an innings, the first time that was achieved in South African first-class cricket. He took 6-12 and 10-26 for Eastern Province against Griqualand West at Johannesburg in 1906–7. In one day.

He was also the second man able to boast of a king pair in Test cricket – that is, when batting he was out first ball in both innings. Despite this, he was a useful batsman. Indeed, he is one of only three number elevens to top-score in his team's innings in Test cricket, when he made sixty-two not out against England at Cape Town in 1905–6, passing 'Tip' Snooke's sixty. (The other two were Fred Spofforth, who scored fifty against England at Melbourne in 1884–5, and Asif Masood of Pakistan, who hit thirty against the West Indies at Lahore in 1974–5).

Vogler's relationship with Sir Abe Bailey, his benefactor and one of the most influential public figures in South Africa, turned sour, however. David Frith got hold of an extraordinary letter written by Vogler to Clem Hill, the Australian captain, written after the Australian tour of 1910–11:

Just a line to ask you to do me a great favour. As you know I am out here under contract with Sir A. Bailey, and my agreement does not expire until Sept next, but since last March he has refused payments so I am taking it to court, as the amount is £475. I have already issued summons, and he is defending the case. His defence I believe is that I was drinking heavy in Australia. Now I would esteem it a great favour if you would give me a letter to show that this was not the case during any matches we played against you when I was playing and it would assist my case greatly if you could get some of the players who were playing for you to endorse what you say in your letter.

Whether or not Hill replied, Vogler was by then in terminal decline as a bowler. Batsmen began to work him out, but weariness from the dispute with Sir Abe cost him his confidence, and without that he was a mere shadow of the man who inspired awe in the likes of Foster. Yet he easily outlived the other members of the quartet, dying in 1946, aged sixty-nine, in Pietermaritzburg (birthplace of Kevin Pietersen and, in a former incarnation, Charles Llewellyn, one of the first Chinamen).

The last of the quartet, Aubrey Faulkner, was one of the game's finest all-rounders, in the league just below Sobers, Botham and Grace. The aforementioned article in the *Sydney Mail* refers to him as 'the champion all-rounder of the visiting team', though it casts doubt over whether, given the presence of Monty Noble, Warwick Armstrong, George Hirst and Wilfred Rhodes, he really can be called the 'best all-round player in the world'. The wonderful cricket writer A. A. Thompson summarised it well when he said Faulkner 'seemed to be able to do everything he wished and to do it serenely ... Over a period of years [he] was almost in a position to toss up in any given game, whether he wished to be regarded as South Africa's most brilliant batsman or most deadly bowler.'

Quite apart from that, he was as complex and psychologically fascinating a player as the game has seen, with a penchant for intense hard work and an aching sense of injustice and virtue. He was another great spinner-soldier. He, too, served in the Great War, spending time in Salonika, Egypt and Palestine, helped to capture Jerusalem, caught a bad case of malaria which was to affect him for the rest of his life, was awarded the Order of the Nile and, in 1918, the Distinguished Service Order. His first marriage failed, but with rugged features, brooding eyes and a sturdy deportment (he weighed over 200lb), he never lost his reputation as one of the game's first sex symbols and remarried in 1928.

A teetotaller and non-smoker, as a child he once beat up his father for hitting his mother. (That his father was an alcoholic explains his own attitude to booze). After retiring, he became the most influential and sought-after coach in the game. He started as games master at St Piran's Preparatory School in Maidenhead, then created the first cricket school in London out of converted garages in Richmond and Walham

Green, near Fulham. He did it his own way, using unfashionable methods, and gained global fame and respect. Among the dozens of future stars to flock to his door was Ian Peebles, England's great leg-spinning hope of the 1930s. Although Peebles eventually succumbed to googly disease, he worked for a time as Faulkner's secretary. Among his descriptions of Faulkner was the assertion that he was 'lusty and highly-sexed'.

His devotion to his pupils was unconditional. If a young player turned up late, and Faulkner's right arm was hurting from being the only coach on a particular day, he would bowl for hours more with his left, still landing the ball on an immaculate length and making it spin. Yet despite the turnover of pupils, he struggled to make a living. His wife was forced to help out with secretarial work to keep the school open. Eventually, overwhelmed by the demands he had placed on himself, Faulkner lost the war with his own demons. Leaving a note saying 'I'm off to another world, via the bat room', he turned on the gas tap in a small store room of his cricket school. Only forty-eight, he died in the bosom of an institution whose benefit to the game long outlasted him, leaving his wife an estate worth less than £300. But before that sombre day, he had brought something magical to cricket, and not least when sending down his googlies.

Wisden's obituary put it thus:

One of the earliest exponents of the googly, he differed from other bowlers of that type because of his ability to send down quite a fast ball, almost a yorker, and when at his best, with faultless length, skill in turning the ball either way and a puzzling variation of flight he proved too much for some of the world's greatest batsmen.

'Dick' Lilley, the Warwickshire and England wicketkeeper, paid Faulkner one of the most sublime compliments ever given to a bowler when he said his deliveries were 'Briggs through the air, Richardson off the pitch' – references to Johnny Briggs, the brilliant left-arm spinner from Lancashire who seemed to make the ball hang forever, and Tom Richardson, the Surrey quick who was the fastest (and possibly greatest) of his day. Faulkner's first striking performance with the ball in a Test was his 6-17 at Headingley, in the 1907 series, though the 15-99 by England slow left-armer Colin Blythe meant it was in vain. His all-round efforts in the home series against England in 1909–10, and against Australia the following year, secured his reputation. After the war, he played for South Africa in a one-off game in 1924 though he was completely out of sorts, shortly before devoting himself to coaching and the project that ended with his early death.

The question that lingers is why it was four South Africans who took the baton passed on by Bosanquet. It is curious that his delivery found little traction in English county cricket. Not until Tich Freeman and then Peebles (who, incidentally, was a Scot), turned up in the 1930s, did England produce another wrist-spinner of distinction. Certainly the archives are reticent about the notion of an outbreak of googly bowling in England. Except, that is, for the extraordinary little tale of D. W. Carr.

England fans will recall the recent bizarre episode of Darren Pattinson. A former roof-tiler who made his first-class debut in Australia, Pattinson had taken 29 wickets at just over 20 for Nottinghamshire in the summer of 2008. He had already been in England's thirty-man squad for the ICC Champions Trophy, but made little impression. Called up as cover for James Anderson ahead of the Headingley Test against South Africa, he was as shocked as the selectors – never mind fans, most of whom had never heard of him – when an injury to Ryan Sidebottom meant that he would play. It seemed extraordinary: Graham Gooch called it 'one of the most leftfield decisions I've ever seen'; Ian Botham pronounced it 'the most illogical, pathetic, and diabolical piece of selecting I've seen'; Geoffrey Boycott lambasted the selectors, too, saying 'wild hunches are no way to build a cricket team'. Pattinson bowled respectably, 2-95 from thirty overs with one difficult chance off his own bowling going to ground, as South Africa scored 522. He was subsequently, and harshly, dropped, making his name a byword for selector's eccentricity, notwithstanding his younger brother James's selection for Australia.

One of the most revealing of all comments about the matter came, typically, from Christopher Martin-Jenkins, who said his selection was 'the biggest rabbit-out-of-the-hat' for ninety-nine years. He meant that very precisely, as you'd expect. It had been 99 years since the biggest shock selection of them all.

'Douglas Ward Carr, the now famous slow-bowler', began Wisden's Cricketer of the Year essay in 1910, '... Whatever he may do in the future, Mr Carr can boast of a record which is absolutely unique in the history of cricket.' That is, he was offered a trial at Kent in May, at the ripe age of thirty-seven, and by August he had made his Test debut – his one and only appearance – after causing a sensation around the country. Ambling through life as an unexceptional medium-pacer, Carr was so taken by all the talk of this new off-break, the googly, that he had a go at it himself. With two games to play of the 1909 Ashes series, and with England 2-1 up, the selectors thought he should have a go in national uniform too.

At that point he had played only three first-class matches, none of them in the Championship, and, having only ever played in the Home Counties, he was unfamiliar to most spectators. Nevertheless, as Martin Williamson argues: 'The decision was not as desperate a gamble as it might seem. England had been looking for a match-winning googly bowler ever since the success of South Africa's quartet a few years earlier, and Carr fitted the bill. As the summer progressed, his name was increasingly promoted by the newspapers despite his lack of experience.'

Born in Cranbrook, Kent, and educated at Sutton Valence and then Brasenose College, Oxford, Carr damaged his knee when playing football at university, restricting his capacity to play cricket. He was a schoolmaster for years in Kent, playing decent but unexceptional club cricket, until intoxicated by the sight of the South African googly merchants. The rest is history. As he told *Wisden* in 1909:

I was always a leg-break bowler of sorts, but often used to bowl medium-fast stuff. I started trying to acquire the googly about four years ago, and practised hard all that winter and the following spring, only to find that directly I had got the off-spin I lost the old leg-break entirely – in fact for that season I hardly made the ball turn at all either way. In the following year I got a bit better, and in August 1908 I really got the thing going, and met with some success in club cricket.

This process happens often in cricket, of course, in reverse as well: Saqlain Mushtaq got so good at his doosra that he lost his off-break, a travesty that hastened his departure from the Test arena. Many bowlers find that there is a new method of delivering the ball – bowling off-breaks, for example – which sits comfortably with their physiques. When they go back to the old way – bowling leg-breaks, say – they suddenly find the years of toil erased from their muscle memory.

For Carr, it led to a first-class debut against Oxford University in 1909, where he took 5-65 in the first innings, opening the bowling. *The*

Times, not employing a particularly expansive vocabulary, thought he 'hardly troubled the batsmen' and felt his googly was 'hardly hard to spot'; but word of mouth has a strange capacity for amplification, and soon enough Carr was bowling against the Australians. A. C. MacLaren, the newspapers said, kept him on too long, and though he took five wickets in the first innings, his match figures of 7-282 weren't enough to keep him in the side. He played on for Kent, but the commitments of work, and the onset of war, meant that straight after completing his debut he disappeared altogether, never to be seen again.

Or not, as the case may be, because in 1929 he did make a return of sorts, albeit in fiction. Carr was to a great extent the inspiration for Tom Spedegue. Mature readers may recall that wondrous short story by Sir Arthur Conan Doyle, 'Spedegue's Dropper', detailing the travails of Spedegue, the asthmatic schoolmaster with a weak heart who bowled heaven-touching lobs in the New Forest, over a rope linking two fifty-foot trees. He was plucked from the obscurity of village cricket to defeat Australia in a deciding Ashes Test, and was carried off the field on his teammates' shoulders, before retiring from the game on doctor's orders.

Carr, the real Spedegue, was plucked from club rather than village cricket, and died in a nursing home in 1950, without much fanfare in the obituary pages. But, during a few short weeks in 1909 he had been the depository of all hope for a sporting nation.

Since Carr was incapable of touring South Africa the following winter, this torch of spinning hope soon passed to other Englishmen, still trying to fill the shoes of Bosanquet. It briefly fell to a man who was a very strange sight at the crease, as he employed a method which was thought to have faded from the first-class game.

George Hayward Thomas Simpson-Hayward was the last of the lobsters. Educated at Malvern College and Cambridge, where he achieved a Blue in both football and cricket, he had a handsome, rugged frame, albeit far more slender than that other lobster decades earlier, William Clarke. Long after the legalisation of over-arm bowling, and at a time when some bowlers were beginning to generate considerable pace, Simpson-Hayward, as if deposited by a Tardis, looked completely incongruous among his peers. True, there had been others: D. L. A. Jephson of Surrey often bowled under-arm at the other end to Tom Richardson, a great of his day, and took three-hundred wickets for his county and a celebrated 6-21 for the Gentlemen against the Players in 1899. Jephson believed lobs should be used only 'medicinally' – that is, when other options have failed – and such was his crouching action that he became the subject of the only horizontal *Spy* cartoon, called 'The Lobster'. Walter Humphreys of Sussex, meanwhile, took 150 wickets at an average of 17 in 1893, and is thought to have been the last lobster picked for a county side purely on his bowling. He did go on an England tour, aged forty-five and with silver hair, but rather than being given a game he was put in charge of Christmas celebrations while the team was in Australia. He said he rode a tricycle to keep fit for his bowling.

The only lobster to play for England in this period, and ever since, was Simpson-Hayward. A Worcestershire player, he was taken on a tour of South Africa for experimental reasons and proved a sensation, taking to the matting wickets with all the glee of one of the South African googly quartet. In the first of his five Test matches in 1909–10, he took 6-43. He was a fabulously arresting sight; the label 'lobster' is a little misleading, because, far from sending the ball moonwards, Simpson-Hayward's swift arm pushed it through at a reasonable pace. 'He seldom flighted the ball like the ordinary lob bowler and did not often use spin from leg', said *Wisden* – with the implication that he did have a leg-break in him. Just like Lamborn, the mysterious 'Little Farmer' whose first name has been lost to history and who may have bowled the first off-break over a century earlier, he used his thumb to impart sharp off-spin. He seemed to have two off-breaks: one basic delivery with plenty of top-spin, and another where he 'flicked' the ball 'as we have all seen many a wrathful billiard-player do when returning the white from a most unexpected pocket – it spins and spins and breaks sharply from the off, and it sometimes hits the wicket'. This reference to billiards is a glorious invocation of Warne's later tantalising spinsters on a billiard table while at the Australian Academy. For now, let's be assured that to send the ball down on a twenty-two-yard strip employing this method he must have had fantastically strong digits – stronger even, perhaps, than those Ajantha Mendis and Rangana Herath use for their carrom ball today.

One of the greatest achievements of Simpson-Hayward's career would not become apparent until many years later, when a conversation he had with Grimmett was decisive in generating the rediscovery of the flipper by that great Australian – a delivery which has flummoxed countless batsmen since. Like that of many of his contemporaries, Simpson-Hayward's own career at the top level might have been longer had it not been for the intermittent but regular appearance in an England shirt of Sydney Barnes, who seemed to do the job of several bowlers at once.

Glorious to think there was an age in which the sight of a lobster at one end, and the most skilful of all bowlers at the other, would not have been mere fantasy. That they were both spinners only adds to the charm of it all. Much like Simpson-Hayward, Sydney Barnes is in a sense a player who belonged both to another era and to no era. He was of another time, yet timeless. He could easily have counted, for example, among the Swift Pioneers of the previous chapter. John Arlott wrote that Barnes was 'a right-arm fast-medium bowler with the accuracy, spin and resource of a slow bowler, whose high delivery gave him a lift off the pitch that rapped the knuckles of the unwary and forced even the best batsmen to play him at an awkward height'. He appears to us now as a treasured exhibit from an era that has long passed, and the best ambassador for an approach to bowling that modern coaches would respond to with cries of 'heresy!', so insistent was it on the broadest possible range of skills.

To look at the pictures we have of him is to observe a peculiar late-Victorian authenticity. His gaunt features, sunken eyes, forcefully protruding jaw and (initially at least) drooping moustache suggest an uncompromising schoolmaster. This impression is furthered by the stiffness of his back, always rod-straight. The only surviving cine film of him was shot from long-range nearly a hundred years ago; later, when he was almost eighty, he showed his action to a cameraman, and even then his arm was close to the vertical. Such qualities combine to give him an air of stern authority, which he carried on to the pitch with brutal and prolonged efficacy. Of him more than any other bowler could we forgive (and repeat) that abused cliché: he was the most complete bowler that ever lived. The truth of that view justifies its ubiquity. Though unconventional by modern standards, and though he bounded in off a long, kangaroo-like run-up, he was above all a spinner, a Twirlyman, one of us.

And a cantankerous rascal to boot. Rarely, if ever, was it said of Barnes that he was gregarious or amicable. This was the man who, when he took forty-nine wickets in a series on the South Africa tour of 1913–14, still a record for a Test series, did so while bunking the fifth Test, in protest at the decision of tour organisers not to pay his wife's hotel bill. That, I think, is my definition of true heroism, and I trust his wife thanked him for it, though we have no evidence either way.

In his first match for the Players against the Gentlemen at Lord's, he bowled one over before sulking off, claiming lack of fitness. Many of his teammates suspected he was lying; they were certainly unimpressed.

Later, when he was playing for Lancashire, he was unhappy with his salary of £3 a week during the summer and £1 a week in the winter. He felt, given that he was doing all the bowling and taking all the wickets, he should be paid better. In any case, he could get better money (£8) playing in the Lancashire and Bradford League, and by playing less cricket would have time for a lucrative sideline in copying and engrossing legal documents (he had exquisite handwriting, just like Grimmett). Lancashire were understandably frustrated at his refusal to sign a new contract. The board said he would not be allowed to play in a match against Nottinghamshire, but Barnes turned up anyway, and got changed and ready as usual in the dressing room. It was an openly provocative gesture. When A. C. MacLaren – the man who had vented his fury at the outbreak of googly bowling, and who had personally catapulted Barnes from the lower leagues to Test cricket – walked out with his side, Barnes followed him, as if part of the team. It led to a great commotion and a scene on the team balcony. MacLaren had to call Barnes off the pitch, demanding that he recant, a plea to which the star bowler succumbed with immense reluctance. *Wisden* that year was unequivocal: 'temperament is a great thing but in it Barnes has always been deficient'.

Barnes consistently claimed that his demands for more money were born of pragmatism rather than pride. In this he was much like William Clarke six decades before, and Bishen Bedi six decades later. Not that he was short of self-esteem, however, claiming late in life that the only bowler he ever saw who might have been more skilled was the fast Englishman Tom Richardson. He laughed off the notion that Tiger O'Reilly was a better spinner. Asked which batsman had caused him most trouble he responded: 'Victor Trumper.' Asked who next, he responded: 'No one else ever troubled me.' Once, after passing the outside edge of two tail-enders again and again, he muttered at the end of the over, 'They aren't batting well enough to get out.' That's where the popular commentator's quip of today comes from. His robust views made him many enemies, not least when he later played for Warwickshire, where his teammates were infuriated by his superior salary. But his undeniable brilliance with the ball meant that demand for him was relentless. The air of majesty and mystery about him is to some degree a function of his being, as John Arlott put it, 'perhaps the least seen of all the great players'. During thirty-five years of cricket, he played only two full seasons and six County Championship games. But he acquired career statistics that are extraordinary.

In his twenty-seven Tests between 1901 and 1914 he took 189 wickets at 16.43, and a wicket every seven overs. In seven Tests against South Africa, he took six ten-wicket match hauls, including 17-159 in the second Test at Johannesburg in 1913–14. This included his forty-nine-wicket haul in that series.

For Staffordshire he took 1,432 wickets at eight runs each over twenty-two seasons. This included 14-23 against Cheshire in 1909, and 16-93 in a single day against Northumberland. He is the only player ever to be selected for England while playing league rather than county cricket, and he went on playing at first-class level until he was fifty-seven, taking 76 wickets at 8.21 in his penultimate year. He would go on making a living from league cricket until he was sixty-seven. Playing for Staffordshire at that age, he took such figures as 6-32 and 4-12 against Great Chell, 5-22 against Caverswall, and 5-43 against Leek. In all cricket he took 6,229 wickets at 8.33, warranting his position at the top of the ICC all-time bowlers' rankings. Every league club that paid for his services won its competition, a remarkable distinction. He took five wickets in five balls in a league match, and four in four balls four times. He got through so many overs, and was so effective with the ball in his hand, that captains would tell him not to bat in the nets in case of injury.

His most celebrated feat came in the second Test at Melbourne in the 1911–12 Ashes, where he took five wickets for six runs as Australia slumped to 11-4 and then 38-6. It may have been the finest spell of bowling the game has seen. His field had only three men on the leg-side: short square leg, mid-on and fine leg.

He accomplished all this while combining prodigious spin with severe pace. The dazzling county player Jack Meyer insisted Barnes was faster than Alec Bedser, which, though likely to be an exaggeration, is indicative of prevailing opinion. C. B. Fry thought that 'in the matter of pace he may be regarded either as a fast or a fast-medium bowler. He certainly bowled faster some days than others; and on his fastest day he was certainly distinctly fast.' He owed his early (and formidable) reputation to being thought of as a young tearaway. And yet he also spun the ball. Not rolling or cutting his fingers across the seam and down the side of the ball, but spinning fiercely, with a conventional leg-spinner's grip for his stock ball, which went away from the right-hander, and an off-spinner's grip for the one that turned in. Barnes himself recognised that it was this feature – genuine spin at pace – that marked him out from his contemporaries, most of whom knew him simply as the greatest bowler ever. In a letter to Jack Fingleton, the Australian batsman who later became a journalist, he wrote:

I thought I was at a disadvantage in having to spin the ball when I could see bowlers doing the same [making the ball swing] simply by placing the ball in their hand and letting go; but I soon learned that the advantage was with me, because by spinning the ball, if the wicket would take spin, the ball would come back against the swing

... I may say I did not bowl a ball but that I had to spin, and that is, to my way of thinking, the reason for what success I attained.

This is one of the most important paragraphs written in the history of bowling. It explains the method that caused the greatest bowler of his day to be just that, and it is a formula for some future great to deploy at his will – and, in so doing, resurrect a method that was unjustly buried with Barnes, albeit that a few later spinners (O'Reilly, Chandrasekhar, Underwood) flirted with an inferior version of it. By 'the ball would come back against the swing', Barnes means it would go one way in the air and then the other after pitching. The passage shows that even the master bowler himself fails to distinguish between swing and swerve, but it is clear what he means. If the seam is revolving on its own axis, and not scrambled, a bowler may achieve drift. Shane Warne's ball to Mike Gatting in 1993 drifted from off to leg before spinning back, with the seam pointing towards second slip as the ball made its way down to the batsman. Swerve, in this sense, is simply drift speeded up. It is a wonderful curiosity of the laws of physics that, if properly released, a spinning ball will drift and swerve in the air in the direction opposite to ground spin. This distinguishes it from the swing achieved by fast bowlers, where the ball hoops in the air and then continues in the same direction after pitching.

What Barnes realised was that, by changing the axis on which the ball spins, a bowler can have a considerable impact on the amount of swerve achieved. In his day, the seam was less pronounced than it is today, but what marked him out technically from almost all our other Twirlymen is how much his deliveries curved in the air. Spofforth and Noble, and to some extent Hirst, got huge swerve, but Barnes probably got more. His best ball, which at most times was his stock ball, was the fast leg-spinner, delivered from wide on the crease, swerving into leg-stump and spinning away to the off. Countless batsmen were dumbfounded by it.

His other ball was the fast off-break. The 1902 *Wisden* claimed that he didn't possess an off-break, but in fact he had discussed it at length with Monty Noble in Australia the previous winter, copying his practice technique of putting two poles down on the pitch, and swerving it between them before spinning it back the other way. He spun the off-break between his first and second finger, as a conventional off-spinner would, and his proficiency at this variation later drew comparison with Sonny Ramadhin. With this delivery, too, he achieved pronounced swerve in the direction opposite to the ground spin (that is, from leg to off). How did he do it?

The most intriguing aspect of Barnes's delivery stride, of which we have excellent illustrated evidence, is the degree to which his wrist is bent back, so that the palm is facing the batsman. Barnes released both his fast, in-swerving leg-break and his fast, out-swerving off-break from this position. The axis of the ball is tipped back in comparison to a normal leg-break bowler, though the direction of motion for the wrist is similar: anti-clockwise for the leg-break, and clockwise for the off-break. From the images we have of him, this suggests that, at the point of delivery, Barnes gave the impression of screwing or unscrewing a lightbulb above, and slightly in front of, his head. Unscrewing for the leg-break; screwing tight for the off-break.

One of the major advantages of this is the disguise: with the wrist starting and finishing in very similar position for both deliveries, the batsman will struggle even in good light to decipher which is which. Fry recorded that 'he made the ball go first one way and then the other without betraying any difference in his delivery'. Barnes himself said:

'I want to drive home that the whole run-up, action and follow through should be the same [for both deliveries]. The arm should stay at the same height and come over in the same way.' That the uncoiling of the wrist which marks the orthodox leg-spinner's release is abandoned altogether was another useful tool of deception. Barnes by this method emerges as a master of disguise.

There is a pace at which a bowler maximises the potential for turn, depending on the pitch. It also varies from bowler to bowler (England's Graeme Swann can make the ball grip even when he's bowling quite briskly – that is, over 60mph. This is to his credit: it proves he gives it a significant tweak). This optimal pace is usually between 50 and 60mph, slow enough to allow the side-spin imparted on the ball to grip the pitch, and take it off in a direction different from the initial line of travel. Barnes was much quicker than this, probably around 70mph. He achieved turn, but not of the sort that marks out a Warne or a Stuart MacGill. Given his pace, which undermined the capacity of his deliveries to grip the wicket and so spin off in a sideways direction, it suited him to sacrifice a little in terms of turn, by tilting back the axis of the ball in his wrist. This might make it less likely for the seam to hit the pitch, but the associated benefit in accentuated swerve more than compensated. Like a mosquito homing in on a target, his attention never wavered and the combination was as injurious to the victim as the nastiest bite.

Even as late as 1928, the West Indians agreed with the view first expressed by Noble and Clem Hill twenty-one years earlier, that 'Barnes is the best bowler in the world at the present day'. He was forever adjusting his field, to the immense irritation of his team captain and the crowd: in one Ashes match, they started hollering at him to get on with it, to which he responded by throwing the ball down, folding his arms and staying at his mark until they'd shut up.

He was a tall man (six foot one), and of such a powerful build that there was some speculation as to whether a deformity in his wrist was behind the power of propulsion he achieved. Batsmen struggled to pick him from the hand, and consequently to identify the best way to play him. Herbie Taylor, the South African, was the only batsman who ever came close to working Barnes out, aside from Trumper. He said he looked at a spot a yard above Barnes's head as his arm came over, which sounds a superstitious and unconvincing explanation, but then he had some success playing him only off the back foot. Yet even he was eventually so stuck in the crease that he became a constant candidate for leg-before.

It is humbling to think Barnes could terrify top-class batsmen for close to four decades. His fitness must have been immense, and owed a great deal to a simple, natural action (he claimed only ever to have had three hours of coaching). It was this action, the culmination of a bounding run-up that got shorter with the years, and in which the ball would be transferred from left to right hand two strides from the crease, that is evoked in those grainy images. Ralph Barker, leaning heavily on 'Plum' Warner, gave a description of Barnes's elegance, which is testimony to the fact that we may never see his like again:

Tall, lean and upright, he had a bouncy run-up of moderate length, beginning with a few short steps, then accelerating into big, swinging strides that developed into leaps before he delivered the ball. As he leapt into his last stride, the ball held out waist high, he began the unusually long, loose, circular swing of the arm from which he got most of his pace. He did not put much body weight into his action, nor did he get any significant power from the bend of his back. But he made full use of the impetus he gathered in his run-up to the wicket, his actual delivery was a model of co-ordination, and his arm was as high as it could possibly be.

And yet, if some thoughtful young bowler could exhume from Barnes's grave that distinctive approach to bowling – genuine spin and swerve at medium pace – another star could appear in the bowlers' firmament, a bowler whose range of skills covered the whole of the bowling waterfront.

Even Barnes, for all that he had an exceptional command of the ball, lacked a googly. Doubtless it wouldn't have chimed with his method, placing a strain on his shoulder that would have threatened the longevity of his career, and been easy to detect, while his off-break and leg-break were at times impossible to tell apart. So it is incredible to think that, despite the international reputation of Bosanquet, the awe inspired by the South African quartet, and even the sensation stirred up by Douglas Carr, the googly might have died out soon after it was born, a victim, perhaps, of the relentless scapegoating to which it was subjected.

It's almost conceivable that, had it not been for the South African quartet, Bosanquet's Bosie would have lain dormant for years, waiting for a Grimmett or a Subhash Gupte to chance upon it, and lay down another false patent. Yet one of the chief reasons we can say with confidence that the googly probably *would* have survived is because of the presence at that 1903 Sydney Test of two particularly intrigued spectators, a magician named Mailey, and a Houdini called Hordern.

Of very few spinners who played in only two Test series could it be said that they had as sensational an impact as Dr Herbert Vivian Hordern. Nicknamed 'Ranji' because of an alleged (but in fact very faint) resemblance to the great Ranjitsinhji, Hordern took eight wickets, including a second-innings 5-66, against South Africa in 1910–11. A year later, in a series against England, he took thirty-two wickets, including 12-135 in the first Test and 10-161 in the last. Gambolling in off a long run-up, and bowling leg-breaks and googlies at medium pace, he ensured Bosanquet's allegedly new delivery became frequent spectator viewing in Australia, regularly sending one down each over.

It was said that he massaged his fingers as he walked down the street. He was conscious that his livelihood depended on them. His habit seemed to pay off: the commentator Johnnie Moyes, who later watched Mailey, O'Reilly and Grimmett, rated Hordern the finest googly bowler he had ever seen.

[He] was without doubt an amazing bowler. He took a long run, brought his arm right over, was a length as well as a spin bowler, and of medium pace. He didn't seem to be flighting the ball, yet did so, as the batsman discovered when he tried to move down the pitch to him. That wasn't easy as Hordern was slightly faster through the air, but the temptation was there, as I found to my cost in Victor Trumper's benefit game, only to hear Sammy Carter say, 'Got you, son' … Sometimes you could see the tip of the little finger sticking up skyward like a periscope of a submarine, but only if you were concentrating on it. If you did see it, you recognised the approaching 'bosie'.

Born into an upper-middle-class merchant family, he was two generations down the line from Anthony Hordern, whose Anthony Hordern & Sons was established in 1823 as the largest department store in Sydney, a kind of antipodean Debenhams. The young Hordern's scholarly ambitions took him to the University of Pennsylvania, whence he qualified as a dentist (just as Monty Noble had done). He toured constantly. Once, in Jamaica, he woke to find five boys inspecting his right hand, trying to work out how it had managed to spin out so many locals the previous day. It was on the MCC's tour of America in 1907 that he met Reggie Schwarz, during a fixture in Philadelphia. Hordern discussed his having seen Bosanquet at Sydney in 1903, and the two men talked for hours about, among other things, the efficacy of that Englishman's famed delivery. Hordern had already been working on the googly, but now added the top-spinner to his repertoire. Being a kind of halfway house between the googly and the leg-spinner, this latter delivery came easily to him.

He briefly went AWOL on the south coast of Australia after returning from war, before reacquainting himself with the dentistry profession, and taking time out to write a book whose title referred simultaneously to his favourite pastime and the source of his chief claim on cricketing glory. He called it *Googlies*.

In tone and style the book bears a pleasant resemblance to Arthur Alfred Mailey's autobiographical contribution to sporting literature, *10-66 and All That*, which must be among the most charming books ever written about the game, and takes its title from the figures he achieved against Gloucestershire in 1921. Mailey describes in the book how he learned of his selection for Australia from a discarded newspaper while cleaning a water meter under a coolabah tree next to a chicken coop. He was so overwhelmed with emotion, he said, that he couldn't remember whether or not he had reconnected the water meter – and, indeed, whether or not the old lady whose needs it served ever had clean water again.

Mailey's was one of the more remarkable spinning biographies. Born in a Sydney slum with (like Faulkner) an alcoholic father, he lived in a two-room shack on a sandhill, with a photograph of Victor Trumper on the wall. His experience of poverty, and the effect it had on his bowling, was exactly that of the English spinner Roley Jenkins, who once said, 'I bowled like a millionaire even though my childhood was so poor that knives and forks were like jewellery.'

Practising the googly at home with an orange, just as Warne and Qadir would do in the latter's living room, Mailey took a battered cricket ball everywhere he went as a child, constantly obsessing over spinning permutations. He stitched trouser seams, collected empty bottles and sold newspapers – including the *Sydney Mail* – to earn a living and gave up cricket for a year to go fishing with his mother and disabled brother. He later lost two other brothers in the war. But long before that conflict enveloped the game everywhere, he had chanced on a source of income that would massively aid his later success as a spinner. He relates the tale in his autobiography:

At sixteen I was given the opportunity to become a glassblower. A galvanised iron shed in which a furnace melted glass to a light amber liquid was my next workroom. On a summer day the heat was intense. Even without the furnace the unprotected shed registered 110 degrees [F] in the shade. The floor was of roughly laid bricks which often burnt holes in my hobnailed blucher boots. This was hell all right, but it held at least three virtues. I became the youngest bottle blower in the State at a wage of £3 a week – half as much as an MP received in those days. It allowed me to buy decent clothes and pay the fee to join an art class. And, much more important perhaps, the continual spinning of the four-foot pipe which held the molten glass gave me fingers of great strength and toughness.

When bowling, my fingers never became calloused, worn or tired, and this, I feel, was responsible for the fact that I never met a bowler who could spin the ball more viciously than I, even if my direction or length were faulty. 'Chuck' Fleetwood-Smith might have been an exception.

Continual blowing expanded and strengthened my lungs and later enabled me to bowl for hours without showing much sign of fatigue. Thinking back, I feel that greater use could have been made of my lung power when appealing, but as it was I seemed to get along on what was described by [writer] Neville Cardus as a 'somewhat apologetic whimper'.

Indeed, at the Oval in 1926, umpire Frank Chester thought Mailey had Jack Hobbs plum in front while on nought. But he couldn't give the batsman out because the bowler didn't appeal. Hobbs went on to make a hundred.

By then, Mailey was established as one of the premier spin bowlers in the game. He visited England under Warwick Armstrong in 1921, having entered the Test arena at the age of thirty-five, taking 146 wickets at 19.61, and then again under Herbie Collins in 1926, when he took 141 wickets at 18.7. He was capable of bowling long spells despite a slender frame. And yet for such a potent wicket-taker he seemed at times to possess a flagrant disregard for length. It wasn't his job to bowl maidens, he said – that's what medium-pacers were for. Mailey used this approach to justify his costliness, which was a constant feature of his bowling. In the 1920–21 series he went for over a hundred runs in six of the eight innings (and 95 and 89 in the others). When he was smashed for a world record 4-362 off 64 overs while playing for New South Wales against Victoria in 1926–7 (the innings closed on 1,107), Mailey made light of it: 'It was rather a pity Ellis was run out at 1,107,' he said. 'I was just striking a length … My figures would have been a lot better if some cove in a tweed coat had held a couple of catches in the shilling enclosure.'

These runs were justified in pursuit of wickets, he said, which, after all, was what he was paid for. In his early days he took many of them with huge googlies, but just as Peter May would later reduce Sonny Ramadhin to the brink of tears by padding away balls pitched outside the off-stump but turning in, so batsmen facing Mailey cottoned on to this means of exploiting what was then an ineffective lbw law. This proved a nuisance (though Mailey continued to use the ball as a variation) but he made his main weapon a leg-break spun so sharply as to merit the common opinion that he turned the ball more than any other bowler until then. Peebles thought he knew why:

The enormous spin was the product of an ideal leg-break bowler's action. Mailey ran a few springy paces at an angle to the wicket, curled his wrist up in the region of his hip-pocket, and flipped the ball out with nicely co-ordinated movement of arm, wrist and fingers. He was a dangerous bowler in the air as well as off the pitch, for the fast-revolving ball dropped steeply at the end of its flight. The batsman who made any misjudgement of length was in poor case to combat the sharp break in either direction.

Mailey recommends himself to us through his having further slowed down, and given the ball yet more air, over the course of his career. This is despite complaints from captains about the number of runs he was conceding. Probably the other reason his poor economy was tolerated was because he was one of the most popular players the game has seen. Decades before television replays made players cautious of such things, he boasted of using underhand methods in order to aid his team, and bowlers in particular – who, after all, were the workhorses of the game. He would shake hands with wicketkeeper Bert Oldfield – overtly or covertly, depending on the sensibilities of the opposition – in order to acquire some of the bird lime that wicketkeepers in those days rubbed on their gloves to improve grip. And he boasted of using resin on his fingers to improve their grip on the lacquered part of the ball. When English fast bowler Johnny Douglas confronted him on the matter, he retorted that fast bowlers tended to have worn thumbnails, so assiduously did they try to raise the seam of the ball. His action was no different. And anyway:

I accepted these standardised rules [i.e. other laws of the game] because I had come into cricket with them, but when the crazy idea of disallowing the bowler to use resin to allow a better grip of the ball, and a law forbidding the lifting of the seam, blew in, I bade goodbye to this form of freedom and became a rebel. Although it was against the law, I must break down and confess that I always carried powdered resin in my pocket and when the umpire wasn't looking, lifted the seam for [teammates] Jack Gregory and Ted McDonald. And I am as unashamed as a Yorkshireman who appeals for lbw off a ball which pitched two feet outside the leg stump.

Typically, Mailey managed to inject, into a confession of his own serial illegality as a player, a dig at those pesky Poms with broad accents. And, clearly, the strength of character he forged in those Sydney slums never left him.

He was believably known as the best spin bowler in the 1920s, the Jazz Age in America and the age of Evelyn Waugh's bright young things in Britain. Mailey co-opted himself into this inter-war exuberance, finding himself the toast of London's dinner-party set thanks to the fame he acquired as a cartoonist. A favourite pastime, it now proved lucrative: he was paid £20 a week – then a major signing for Fleet Street – and had a wonderful reputation, owed in part to his sketches in the *Referee* and the *Sportsman*, where he operated under the pen name of – what else? – 'Bosey'.

In later life he became something of an Australian national treasure, not least for his writing, and settled to a life of oil painting, sailing and running a butcher's shop in Sydney, the city of his birth. The sign above the shop window said it all: 'I used to bowl tripe; then I wrote it; now I sell it'.

Mailey was certainly a better bowler than a fellow Australian leg-spinner of the same era, but whereas the fairy tale element of Mailey's career stemmed from the rags-to-riches narrative of his life, the magic of the life and career of Warwick Windridge Armstrong was different: he was born to be a national hero. Of the legion of players who became national heroes in Australia, and emblems for that country's evolving sense of itself – Spofforth, Bradman, Benaud, Lillee, Border, Warne and Steve Waugh come to mind – none could match Armstrong for the fullness with which he personified his era. And it was greatly to his advantage that flesh is not something he lacked.

'The Big Ship', as he was known, is commonly and correctly considered a contender for being the fattest man ever to play Test cricket. The label may be derived from his having previously been known as 'the Leviathan of Cricket', at a time when the world's biggest ocean liner was being redeployed in the Atlantic as the troopship *Leviathan*. As Gideon Haigh points out, however, contemporaries emphasised the fact that he was big over the fact that he was fat. By the end of his career he weighed 140kg and remained six foot three. The *Watchman* said that 'to see him bend to pick up the ball' was like observing 'a mountain in labour'. Neville Cardus, ever ready with the hyperbole, found a verbose way of stating the obvious:

Armstrong – how well the name befits his composition! ... He is elemental, of the soil, the sun and wind – no product of the academies. Nature has by herself fashioned him – he has grown on the cricket field, like the grass.

He might have added that even his middle name – Windridge – conjured up a further sense of primal power. Armstrong made no apology for being huge. He would have thought risible the recent tale of Samit Patel, the England limited-overs all-rounder, who, on being told he needed to lose weight, instructed his mother to use less oil in her cooking. (It didn't do the trick: Patel, dismissed as 'unfit, fat and lazy' by Kevin Pietersen, took a fitness test in January 2010, only to be told he was still too plump.) And yet, for all that, Armstrong started his career almost half as heavy as when he finished. Before playing Test cricket, he was briefly an Aussie Rules footballer for South Melbourne, where he was recorded as weighing 84kg. As a young cricketer he was equipped with inquisitive eyes, arched eyebrows, a broad, searching nose and a special batting talent. The result was that his girth expanded in proportion to his stature in the game, reaching a fitting apogee when, upon retirement, his rotundity was unmatched in the international game. He smoked, at times heavily, and had a penchant for whisky which in later years he translated into a commercial career with whisky company Distillers, making a fortune along the way. He once scored a century at Melbourne after downing several glasses, claiming it was good for the malaria he had contracted. He would box and play football on the Melbourne Cricket

Ground in winter, so as to stay dextrous, if not fit. He was irresistibly similar in deportment and temperament to W. G. Grace, but the mark he made on the game was ultimately, as with Grace, down to the force of his character. His defenders would call him deeply principled; his opponents would squeal that he was truculent and incorrigibly self-satisfied.

Such was his nature that when Armstrong took a firm stand on an issue, few got in his way. This made him an effective reformer. He campaigned for timeless Tests, claiming that was the only way to avoid boring draws (a shaky argument, but one that at least had the merit of considering the paying public). Even before the First World War, he claimed that tour itineraries were getting too heavy, and players therefore risked burnout. He would have thought today's money-spinning schedules farcical.

He was one of six players who refused to tour England in 1912 because he thought the Australian Cricket Board weren't paying players enough. This earned him the enduring respect of many teammates. On the field, he displayed a similar sureness of mind. When Frank Woolley walked in to make his debut, in the Oval Test of 1909, Armstrong made an absurd play of lumbering up to the wicket, bowling looseners to vaguely perplexed fielders and holding up play for fifteen minutes, as the crowd's boos grew ever louder. The laws about time-wasting were changed as a result. He made a lifelong enemy of Jack Hobbs by venting his displeasure when the England man stood his ground during a hit-wicket appeal. At Trent Bridge in May 1905 he refused to bowl until the crowd calmed down (a counter-productive strategy), and at Old Trafford sixteen years later did the same thing, sitting on the cut strip until the crowd stopped jeering.

By the time his career was over, he had become (as he would remain) one of the most brilliant Australian captains of all time, competing with Benaud and Steve Waugh for that title, having enacted an uncompromising and at times brutal philosophy of winning at all costs. This he did while dominating opposition with a rare degree of consistency and longevity. On tours of England in 1902, 1905, 1909 and 1921 he scored nearly 6,000 runs and took 443 wickets at 16.45. On the 1909 trip he scored 303 not out against Somerset at Bath, and 2,002 runs in all, with 130 wickets at 17.6, to boot. After the war he led Australia to eight successive victories against England, an Ashes record.

One of the more celebrated stories to hang from his reputation was provided by Mailey, who employed a hack's licence in exaggerating it in his autobiography. A newspaper blew across the outfield and in front of Armstrong during the fifth Test at the Oval in 1921. Asked later why he picked it up, Armstrong said it was 'to find out whom Australia were playing'. Alas, the story is apocryphal: it was a leaflet with photographs of the players in that game, which captured his attention briefly.

There are two respects in which Armstrong's contribution to spin bowling, generally overlooked by biographers, is decisive. First, his grip; second, his preference for going around the wicket.

Surviving film of Armstrong in 1905 shows a wondrously elegant bowler, with high action and considerable poise, moving through the crease in rhythmic fashion. Yet to understand more fully the enduring significance of Armstrong in the history of spin, as opposed to the history of cricket more broadly, it is necessary to take a closer look at a photograph of the Australian in that magical book to which we must return, and not for the last time, *Great Bowlers and Fielders*, by Beldam and Fry.

Armstrong is described as having: 'An uncommon grip for a leg-break bowler. Apparently the second finger, curled under the ball against the seam, is the one that takes the purchase when the hand is turned' – and the pictures bear this out. It does indeed seem that Armstrong, who had a huge, windmilling delivery stride in which his left arm was rod straight and high, bowled leg-breaks off his middle finger (as opposed to the third finger, as orthodox leg-break bowlers do today). This suggests that he pre-empted, by five decades, the unusual method said to have been patented by the mercurial mystery man Jack Iverson, and copied a decade later by his fellow Australian Johnny Gleeson. Their grip, often referred to as the Iverson grip, or the Iverson–Gleeson grip, ought now to be amended to the ungainly Armstrong–Iverson–Gleeson grip, undermining another false patent in the history of spin. All three shared the unusual habit of bowling a leg-break off the middle rather than the third finger. (Curiously enough, 'Tich' Freeman also used his middle rather than third finger as the spinning lever, but his hands were so small that he was far more dependent on a supple wrist.) There were, however, crucial distinctions between their methods: the photographs show that Armstrong kept his index finger on the ball, using that as a supporting mechanism for the thumb and middle finger; Iverson, as the celebrated pictures of his grip show, kept the index finger well out of it. So too did Gleeson.

The other difference between Armstrong and his fellow countrymen and successors is that he didn't bother with the googly. Iverson used this as a stock ball, and Gleeson certainly bowled it, too, though he added an off-break later on as well, in part to save his shoulder. For Armstrong, a top-spinner and subtle variations of pace sufficed. Like W. G. Grace, the player whose likeness to him inevitably draws the most commentary, Armstrong took many of his wickets by making it terribly difficult for umpires to say no.

His lack of a googly can't be explained by reference to the fact that he went round the wicket. After all, a googly to the right-hander from around the wicket can be mightily useful – Hollies's googly to Bradman, the one that cost him a career average of 100, was delivered from around the wicket. And a googly spinning away from the left-hander could be a priceless weapon: Mushtaq Ahmed bamboozled hundreds of left-handers with his googly from round the wicket. Rather, Armstrong seems to have considered the googly, by then in common use, superfluous, and something of a distraction. He was a relentlessly accurate bowler, and knew that he could get wickets by plugging away at an awkward length and line. Often, though, the leg-stump line was used as a defensive measure. In Tests against England in 1905 and 1921 – years when the laws surrounding wides were more lax – Armstrong bowled wide of leg-stump with a 2-7 or 3-6 field – that is, packing the leg-side. In one game, after he'd earned figures of 52-24-67-1, he prompted the remark that such bowling 'shows what dull stalemate play such tactics can produce'.

In bowling his leg-spin from around the wicket, Armstrong was again reminiscent of Grace, who was one of the first of the over-arm era to do so, and another Australian, Kent-born Willy Cooper, who similarly took many of his wickets leg-before. Len Braund, a brilliant English all-rounder, was another to bowl leg-breaks from around the wicket.

What united many of these bowlers beyond the basic angle of their delivery was that they could use it both to be very attacking and very defensive. In the days before a batsman could be given out leg-before to a delivery that pitched outside the line of the leg-stump, balls directed at the wicket could be difficult to get away. At the same time, balls wide of leg-stump could be hard to score off, particularly if the leg-side was packed. Benaud's 6-70 to win the Test from around the wicket at Old Trafford in 1963, his finest hour with the ball in hand, took advantage of rough created by bowlers' footmarks. Benaud bowled plenty of over-spinners to bring his leg-slips into play.

So, too, albeit from over the wicket, did England's finest wrist-spinner since Bosanquet, a man whose top-spinner may have brought him a quarter of his wickets, many of them taken via catches on the leg-side. The first thing to understand about Alfred Percy 'Tich' Freeman – other than that his nickname was owed to his standing a mere five foot two – is that probably no bowler has been so prolific over so long a period. The records that attach to his name include some that are scarcely believable. There is some dispute over the exact figures, but even allowing for a hefty margin of error, reading them elicits a sharp intake of breath. The only bowler to run him close is a contemporary, Wilfred Rhodes.

Freeman is the only man ever to have taken more than three hundred wickets in a season, and it's close to certain that record will never be broken. His 304 wickets in 1928 included 69 catches and 52 stumpings from Les Ames, possibly the finest 'keeper to spin ever, though Australia's Ian Healy might have something to say about that. (The following year, Ames stumped 64 of his 100 victims when keeping for Freeman.) Freeman's almost absurd record of five-wicket hauls – 386! – is a full ninety-nine ahead of the next man, Rhodes. His 140 ten-wicket match hauls is double that of the next man, Charlie Parker. Only Rhodes has taken more than his 3,776 first class wickets, at the tidy average of 18.42 – and Freeman took his in around half the time. For six seasons between 1928 and 1933 (inclusive) he averaged 250 wickets a season, at a time when the next most prolific bowler took around sixty. He took seventeen wickets in a match twice (1922 and 1932) and ten wickets in an innings three times – 1929, 1930 and 1931. He took nine wickets in an innings five times, including 9-11 at Hove in 1922. This statistical colossus would have taken plenty more had it not been for the intervention of the First World War, which coincided with the first four years of his professional career.

Nicknamed 'the Little Master' seven decades before Sachin Tendulkar stole it from him, Freeman overcame the disadvantage of having a small hand and stubby fingers to spin the ball vigorously. Loop came naturally to him; because his arm was low at the point of delivery, the ball went up and above the batsman's eye line before it came down, making his flight tantalising and deceptive. Indeed, Freeman's whole career is best understood as the enactment of devotion to that old, still useful, maxim: you must beat the batsman in the air before you beat him off the pitch. Frank Woolley, one of the great all-rounders and a colleague of Freeman's at Kent, who bowled slow left arm, could pick Freeman's googly (though most batsmen couldn't) and encouraged him to use it more sparingly. Part of its effectiveness as a weapon stemmed from the fact that he had such a supple wrist. Just like Subhash Gupte, Freeman could cock or uncock it so quickly that batsmen barely had time to tell what he was up to. This was fortunate, since Freeman's hands were so small that, in the combination of wrist action and finger snapping all leg-spinner's employ, he was far more dependent than most on working the wrist, as William Lillywhite put it. It was partly because his hands were so small that he used his middle rather than third finger to impart revolutions on the ball. As he gripped it, his second, third and little finger were bunched up together.

Woolley also helped Freeman to develop the essentials of his technique, which involved imparting mostly over-spin rather than side-spin. Certainly he could turn the ball, but he didn't bother with sharp turn, focusing instead on the virtue of an immaculate length. In this regard he seems irresistibly similar to Grimmett, a titan of the era that followed, who was also a small man and, at least according to Tiger O'Reilly, a flight and length bowler first and foremost. Both also had in common a shiny, bald head, though Grimmett kept his covered, and both played first-class cricket well into their forties. Freeman was distinguished by the pronounced downward bend in his big nose, so that Horace Walpole's assertion about George II – that he bowed so low the tip of his hooked nose swept the dust from the floor – is apposite here too.

Freeman would pull up his trousers before coming in to bowl, off a short run-up, around five paces, just like Lance Gibbs. His short delivery stride – always helpful in getting some extra loop – prompted Peebles to observe that he looked 'like a spring snapping'. As he readied himself to plant the front foot on the crease, Freeman's leading arm, his left, came high across his body, and with the palm facing heaven, and fingers and thumb bunched in close proximity, he looked for all the world like he was making an offering to the spin bowling gods with each ball he sent down.

For a while he teamed up with C. S. 'Father' Marriott, to form one of the most effective leg-break combinations ever seen in county cricket. The real mystery about this mystery man, however, was why he fared so badly at international level. Though for well over a decade he was the dominant bowler in English county cricket, along with Rhodes, he was never picked to play against Australia in England. The majority of his wickets on the county circuit were taken against tail-enders, critics said. I have a right to bowl at them if they're batting because I dismissed the whole of the top order, Freeman retorted. In twelve Tests he took a respectable 66 wickets at 25.86, and he had a decent tour of South Africa in 1927–8, but a fleet of lesser leg-spinners were preferred – Walter Robins, Ian Peebles, Dick Tyldesley, even Marriott on one occasion, when he took 5-37 and 6-59 in his only Test. None of them prospered as Freeman's record suggested he might have done, given a more substantial opportunity. Yet the lingering feeling was that batsmen prepared to come down the wicket to him could exploit the predictability of his pace and flight – which is just what the Australians did to him. Intriguingly, he was dropped after the third Test on the Ashes tour of 1925; in the final Test of that series, on a helpful wicket in Sydney, Grimmett himself made his debut, taking eleven wickets. One wonders how Freeman's confidence in an England shirt might have been boosted had he been given the chance to bowl on that track. Of course, had he failed to do well, Grimmett's success would only have shown him up further.

Possibly the major reason that Freeman took so long to break into the national side, and then played only sporadically, was that England already had a distinguished, flighty spinner who turned the ball from leg to off. That was Wilfred Rhodes, the man with whom Freeman seems numerically and historically wedded, and another statistical colossus, not least when his monumental batting efforts are considered, too.

There is a long heritage of great spin bowlers keeping out nearly great bowlers, much to the latter's chagrin (and sometimes to the former's, too). Stuart MacGill might have been considered a great if only Warne hadn't been around. Srinivasan Venkataraghavan would have played more if it hadn't been for the quality of Erapalli Prasanna. So, too, with Freeman and Rhodes.

With penetrating hazel-green eyes, pursed lip and narrow brush moustache, Rhodes was described as 'Yorkshire cricket personified' by Neville Cardus. He was probably England's greatest all-rounder, beginning his Test career at number eleven and eventually opening alongside Jack Hobbs (with whom he once put on 323), batting in every position along the way. He was the only man whose Test career spanned thirty years (1899–1929), the only man to bowl competitively at both WG and Bradman, and the oldest man to play Test cricket (he was fifty-two years and 165 days old when capped against the West Indies on 3 April 1930). Over his career he scored 39,802 runs and took 4,187 wickets, well ahead of Freeman in second place. In sixteen seasons he did the double of 100 wickets and 1,000 runs.

Christopher Martin-Jenkins makes the bold claim that 'Rhodes the bowler was the greatest-ever exponent of flight', citing the laudatory portrait left by Altham: 'An action of balanced economy but beautiful rhythm was the basis for supreme control of both length and direction; he could turn the ball on wickets that gave no help, and on those that did its bite and lift were deadly.' He didn't have room for Cardus, who strengthens the case: 'Flight was his secret. Flight and the curving line, now higher, now lower, tempting, inimical; every ball like every other ball, yet somehow unlike; each over in collusion with the others, part of a plot.' Here, again, is the emphasis on length, and the recognition that he spun the ball enough to be dangerous even on unresponsive surfaces, while giving the batsman nothing to hit. It's a measure of his nagging, relentless accuracy that Victor Trumper, the great Australian, was moved to say, 'For God's sake Wilfred, give me a rest' (or, by a common variation, 'Please, Wilfred, give me some peace!'). He favoured going around the wicket to the right-hander, attacking their off-stump and forcing them to play, and liked to leave segments between cover and mid-off empty, to encourage the drive. Few modern captains have the confidence, never mind the wherewithal, to let the slow left-armers begin a spell with such a field.

Rhodes was the latest in a list of great Yorkshire left-arm spinners, though he and Hedley Verity, who excelled in the 1930s, were a class above their predecessors Edmund Peate and Bobby Peel. Johnny Wardle, also a Yorkshireman but capable of bowling Chinamen, too, was in the rank in between. Rhodes had initially played in Scotland before having a trial with Warwickshire. Whoever it was there that rejected him doubtless felt the shame of that decision accumulate for decades after. He only got into the Yorkshire side because Stanley Jackson, a senior player at the county, couldn't decide between Rhodes and one Albert Cordingley, and settled the matter by tossing a coin, which fell in Rhodes's favour.

He later coached at Harrow and went blind in old age, but continued attending cricket matches, depending on his ears and even his nose to deduce the intricacies of the action he couldn't see. By this charming process he continued to wield significant influence in the game for close to seven decades. Ultimately, though, his authority was a product of the exceptional, and exceptionally long, career he had, in particular, the period of his Test career, which in spanning thirty years coincided pleasantly with the beginning and end of this, spin bowling's First Flourish. It was an age in which the googly, an allegedly new delivery, entered the scene, and was instantly vilified as a threat to civilisation by batsmen in England and beyond – not a light charge to make in the years before and after the Great War. Blamed for many a batsman's failure, the googly nearly died in its infancy, but a thread linking it to those wonderful South Africans, and by extension to the Antipodes, kept it alive. What with the emergence of one of the great slow left arms, and the phenomenon of bowling skill that was Sydney Barnes, this was not a bad time for the spectator interested in spin. And though war would soon intervene – fatally so, in the case of Hedley Verity – as cricket entered the 1930s, a decade dominated by the bat, and particularly that of Bradman, spin bowling was varied, strong and ambitious. For two great Australians, and one heroic Yorkshireman, that would be enough to be getting on with.

Interlude Five

FLIPPER

Grip

Batsman's Point of View

 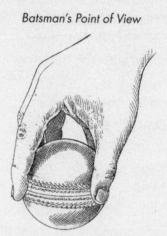

The best way to get the hang of this delivery is to snap your fingers a few times. That means clicking the thumb and middle finger. Now put the ball in between your thumb and middle finger, and do the same thing again. You should be able to snap the ball out between these two levers. Resting your index finger on the seam will feel natural, but the spin is imparted more between the thumb and middle finger. On entering the delivery stride, the palm is over the ball, with the back of the hand facing the sky and the seam forming an equator around the ball. As the arm comes round, those two fingers snap, and the ball is released like a flying saucer heading towards the batsman. The seam should be spinning on its own axis, so that it doesn't make contact with the ground on pitching.

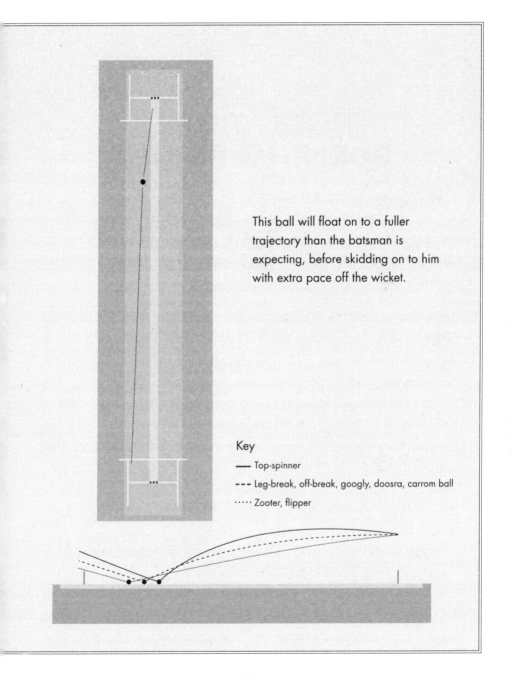

This ball will float on to a fuller trajectory than the batsman is expecting, before skidding on to him with extra pace off the wicket.

Key

—— Top-spinner

--- Leg-break, off-break, googly, doosra, carrom ball

····· Zooter, flipper

Chapter Six

TIGER, TIGER, BURNING BRIGHT

'He was a medium-pace bowler,' wrote the Don in 1930, '[who] could make the ball turn both ways, but never achieved any outstanding success on turf wickets.' Eighteen years later, after captaining him for Australia, this assertion had been amended: by now, Tiger O'Reilly was the finest bowler Bradman had ever seen. Writing his obituary in the 1993 *Wisden*, Gideon Haigh, whose judgement on these matters can be trusted, described him as 'probably the greatest spin bowler the game has produced'. At the time of O'Reilly's passing the previous autumn, Shane Warne had performed unexceptionally in only four Tests, so that Haigh's claim would not have immediately met with much challenge by those who saw O'Reilly in action.

Bradman and O'Reilly were always on mildly acrimonious terms until the latter's death in 1992. Pointedly, even when saying O'Reilly was the best bowler he'd seen, the Don added that Clarrie Grimmett was the best spinner he'd seen – implying that O'Reilly, who probably bowled his stock ball at around 65mph, which is significantly quicker than most leg-spinners, about the pace of the Swift Pioneers in fact, was a medium-pacer first and foremost. Bradman knew how much this irked O'Reilly, as it did other swift Twirlymen (Barnes and Underwood come to mind) who take exception to the suggestion that they cut the ball rather than spin it. Most people would say the blame for the fractiousness between two of the game's greatest players, were it divisible in any way other than 50/50, should lie chiefly with Bradman. Their characters clashed. As Patrick Kidd put it: 'Bradman was tee-total, conservative and meticulous to the point of obsession, while O'Reilly had the exuberance and *joie de vivre* you would expect from an Irish expat.'

He certainly did, and, together with his dear friend Grimmett, formed probably the greatest spin-bowling partnership cricket has known. Within it, O'Reilly was the better bowler – just – albeit they were starkly different in their methods. But such was the extrovert nature of Tiger that he shone through the era in a way no other bowler did, causing batsmen sleepless nights and earning him the label of the best bowler in the world. Which he was, in a period light on top-class off-spin, heavy-on outstanding batsmen and flat pitches, but also containing Hedley Verity, a bowler and a man of the first rank. Together with his mentor, Rhodes, and Bishen Bedi, Verity had one of the finest slow left arms the game has seen.

The best introduction to this intensely religious Yorkshireman lies in the account of his death, as relayed in *Wisden*, when, as Captain Verity of the Green Howards, he was severely wounded in the battle at Catania plain in Sicily in 1943:

The objective was a ridge with strong points and pillboxes. Behind a creeping barrage Verity led his company forward 700 yards. When the barrage ceased, they went on another 300 yards and neared the ridge, in darkness. As the men advanced, through corn two feet high, tracer-bullets swept into them. Then they wriggled through the corn, Verity encouraging them with 'Keep going, keep going.' The moon was at their back, and the enemy used mortar-fire, Very lights and fire-bombs, setting the corn alight. The strongest point appeared to be a farm-house, to the left of the ridge; so Verity sent one platoon round to take the farm-house, while the other gave covering fire. The enemy fire increased, and, as they crept forward, Verity was hit in the chest. 'Keep going', he said, 'and get them out of that farm-house.' When it was decided to withdraw, they last saw Verity lying on the ground, in front of the burning corn, his head supported by his batman.

Captured by the Germans following the gunfire, Verity was taken to a military hospital at Caserta, near Naples, on the Italian mainland. He died after a second operation.

With hindsight, to begin your final sentence with the words 'Keep going' speaks of a character fit for service to greater causes than spin bowling, and those words were the guiding principle of a Yorkshireman whose perseverance inspired immense affection and goodwill everywhere he went. In that long line of Yorkshire slow left arms – Peate, Peel, Rhodes, Verity, Wardle – his sacrifice robbed him of the chance to justify his ranking as first among them. Rhodes's longevity denied Verity the opportunity to play for Yorkshire until he was twenty-five, but as with so many of the great spinners, the stamina he showed in waiting for a breakthrough would pay dividends later. Monty Panesar, today no longer England's first-choice spinner, should draw inspiration from his story.

Verity had taken up cricket after leaving Yeadon and Guiseley Secondary School and moving to Rawdon, where he played for the local club and his father, also called Hedley, was a coal supplier. Before being called up, he had done enough to suggest that he could compete with Rhodes and Bedi for the status of the finest slow left arm there has ever been. Verity didn't always take kindly to comparison with Rhodes. 'Both of us are left-handed and like taking wickets,' Verity said, 'let's leave it at that.' Although Leonard Crawley, the county player who pioneered pinch hitting in the 1920s and 1930s, thought Rhodes the much better bowler, saying he was 'far and away the best left-hand bowler I ever played. Compared to Verity his bowling was like a glass of fizz with a cup of cat's piss.' Years later, when finally retiring, Rhodes is said to have bowed out with the approving words: 'He'll do', referring to Verity, and out of deference Verity named his first son after Rhodes. (However, by naming his second son Hedley, he created a third Hedley Verity in three generations.)

Like Ashley Giles years later, he started as a medium-pace bowler but changed his method when he realised he was able to give the ball a considerable tweak. This course of action had been recommended to him by George Herbert Hirst, another great Yorkshireman. Verity often bowled at just short of medium pace, but he also varied his pace distinctly according to the wicket. Broadly, there were two models. On wet or disintegrating wickets he slowed down and gave the ball plenty of air, knowing he could rely on variation in the wicket. On dry, flat wickets, he pushed it through briskly at the right-hander's middle-and-off pegs, and took many of his wickets with a quicker, in-swerving yorker, not dissimilar to the brilliant, in-swerving delivery with which Daniel Vettori now snares many an unsuspecting victim. Verity would bowl this delivery, described by teammate Bill Bowes as an arm ball, approximately sixteen times a season, 'and it would give him sixteen wickets'. Most contemporary reports suggest there was a pronounced in-swerve, despite *Wisden*'s contention in 1932 that 'Happily, he has avoided the fetish of the swerve'. The second of these two models – the brisk, flattish spinner who speared it in and made the batsman play every ball – made Verity very much the forerunner of Derek Underwood.

The philosophy of length Verity brought to his art was outlined by his son Douglas, at a memorial game at Hove in September 2009:

My dad said: 'The best length is the shortest you can bowl and still get them playing forwards.' With slow bowling particularly, you set your field and try to get them driving at you. Then you try to deceive them with flight or a change of pace or spin.

Here the influence of Rhodes can be detected, and it's a fair bet that Bedi bowled according to that, too. Pictures of Verity clutching the ball in his hand suggest his grip was slightly unconventional, in that, rather than splaying his first and second fingers across the seam, his middle finger appeared equidistant from both the first (index) finger and the third finger. This suggested he achieved some of his turn with a quick flick of the wrist. He was a bowler who, in Martin-Jenkins's glorious phrase, had an 'easy, springing run-up to the wicket [that] suggested a cat preparing for the kill' – this feline reference being a touch kinder than Crawley's. Verity's penchant for remarkable figures was extraordinary, even bearing in mind he came shortly after Freeman and Rhodes. By the time his career was cut short at thirty-four (then a spinner's prime), he had taken 1,956 first-class wickets at an outstanding average of 14.9, with 164 5-fers and fifty-four match hauls of ten wickets or more.

This included the best figures ever recorded in a first-class match, 19.4-16-10-10 against Nottinghamshire at Headingley, just yards from where he was born, and 7-9 from six overs in his last first-class game, at Hove in 1939. Eight years earlier he had taken 10-36 against Warwickshire at Headingley on his birthday. Yet his most celebrated feat came in an England shirt, when his fourteen wickets in a single day, on a drying pitch at Lord's, secured England's only Ashes victory there in the twentieth century. He averaged 185 wickets a season, and took over 200 in 1935, 1936, and 1937. Don't let the feats of Freeman and Rhodes cause you to think that this is anything less than exceptional.

Moreover, let it not be forgotten that it was Verity – not Harold Larwood – whom Don Bradman most feared during the Bodyline tour. 'I could never claim to have completely fathomed Hedley's strategy,' the Don wrote years later, 'for it was never static or mechanical.' Verity – not Larwood – topped the tour averages, with 44 wickets at under 16, and he was the only player from the Bodyline series to tour India with Jardine the following winter.

But Verity belonged to a generation of Yorkshireman – Sergeant Len Hutton, Captain Herbert Sutcliffe, Lieutenant Norman Yardley – for whom cricket would be a precursor to great sacrifices – in Verity's case, the ultimate one. After taking that 7-9 in 1939, he remarked while walking off the pitch, 'I wonder if I'll bowl again.' It is a salutary reminder that few careers, in this era or the one immediately preceding it, were untouched by the horrors of world war. Indeed, some of the spinners who would excel after the Second World War were conditioned by their service: the enigmatic Jack Iverson learned his unorthodox grip while on service in Papua New Guinea. For most spinners in the first half of the century, however, war either cut their life short brutally, as with Verity, or denied them several prime years of their careers. It was the exceptional good fortune of Clarrie Grimmett that he began to excel only when he was already in his thirties and so caught the bulk of the inter-war era. He made his debut in 1925, but before we get to that year it will prove instructive to rewind slightly. One of the most important factors in the way Grimmett's career developed is that it nearly didn't at all.

It was back in 1905 that the shy little boy at Mount Cook Boy's School in Wellington was bowling in the nets. Even then, aged thirteen, he was strikingly diminutive, being dismissed as a midget (with some justification), a point of concern to his watching headmaster, a man named Hempelman.

Partly because of his small physique, the boy, who could bowl extremely briskly for his age, also tired quickly. On one occasion, when asked to bowl just one more over in the nets lest he exhaust himself ahead of a match, the teenager brought his arm over again – yet this time snapped his fingers at the top of their arc, causing the ball to turn a yard across the wicket and fool the batsman.

'Did you do that purposely?' exclaimed a watching Hempelman.

'Yes, Mr Hempelman,' responded young Grimmett.

'That leg-break?'

'Yes.'

'You've never done it before. Not when I've been here.'

'I can bowl them whenever I like.'

'I've never seen you bowl them in a match.'

'Oh, Mr Hempelman, I wouldn't think of bowling them in a match.'

'Look here, from now on you're going to bowl leg-breaks. I forbid you ever to bowl fast again.'

Shortly afterwards, Hempelman was called away and a school match got underway. The little boy still fancied himself as a quick bowler. Despite his earlier tiredness, he came in off a long run-up, and in half an hour the opposition were all out for twenty. Little Clarence had taken 7-3.

In his next match, a fortnight later, Clarence was playing for Wellington Schools against Wairarappa Schools. By a terrible stroke of luck, Hempelman was umpiring on that day, forcing the boy to bowl his less-favoured leg-spin when called on to open the bowling. Clarence had been trying to avoid the captain's eye, thinking that if he had to bowl leg-spin in public he would forever shame himself, and so hoped not to be asked to bowl at all. Having considered making an excuse, he confronted the reality of trying to bowl leg-spin in a proper match. He ambled in off four paces and brought his arm over, giving it a rip as best he could at the top of the delivery arc. Before very long, Wairarappa had been bowled out twice, and Wellington won by an innings. Young Clarence's figures were 6-5 and 8-1. The course of his life had changed for ever.

This tale of fortitude overcoming adversity, with its sense of the joyfully improbable, captures something essential about Grimmett. If all the best features and eccentricities of Twirlymen through the ages could be distilled into just one bowler, the result might resemble little Grimmett. He was short of stature, with a curious action, and his exceptional Test record came despite – or perhaps because of – seemingly interminable obstacles to his development: his lack of growth as a child, the outbreak of war, the lack of organised sport at technical school (which caused him to give up cricket from the ages of fifteen to seventeen), the stiffness of competition in New Zealand, and, finally, the fact that his native country didn't play Test cricket until 1929. This last impediment he overcame by doing something that then, as now, is considered close to heresy in Wellington – he relinquished his Kiwi roots and became an Aussie. Born on Christmas Day, he was the greatest present the Kiwis ever gave their neighbours.

From the age of five Grimmett's little fingers would be wrapped round spherical objects – apples, oranges, tomatoes, rubber balls, leather balls, early modern Antipodean kitchenware. And, as he grew up, he took ever more obsessively to discovering the new frontiers of spin bowling. Few players in the history of the game have treated spin bowling more scientifically than Grimmett. His round-arm action, reintroduction of the flipper (along with other associated thumb-generated back-spinners) and brilliantly erudite books make it almost surprising to learn that he didn't take his 216 Test wickets wearing a white lab coat. 'The Fox' – also known as 'Gnome' or 'the Pimpernel' (references to his diminutive stature and elusiveness respectively) – is unique in having struck up two great spin partnerships, with Mailey and O'Reilly, despite having only made his Test debut at the age of thirty-three.

His longevity therefore acts as a bridge between eras, and it was his associated stamina that marked him out as being so special. His move from New Zealand to Australia was far from his last in search of success. He started in Sydney, supporting himself financially with a job as a signwriter. Unable to make a breakthrough there, he moved four years later to Melbourne. But fate seemed to conspire against him: selected to play against an MCC touring side at twenty-nine, and with time ostensibly against him, he was hit on the leg while batting, and left with severe bruising. His bowling was consequently poor, with 1-104 in the first innings, and, by the time he came on to bowl in the MCC's second knock, Jack Hobbs was well set. The master batsman thundered a drive back at Grimmett, badly splitting his third (and spinning) finger. He would hear nothing more from the Victoria selectors for three years.

But still he persevered. Another migration was in order. So, now well into his thirties, he moved to the Prahran district, five miles from Melbourne. In the backyard of his small home he put down a turf mat and started spinning balls, spinning and spinning and spinning, hour after hour after hour. First a short distance under-arm, then graduating to over-the-shoulder deliveries at progressively greater distances. It was now that he trained his fox terrier, Joe, to sit still until he had bowled an over – then to run and retrieve the balls one by one. It was a mutually beneficial arrangement. Among the deliveries he would experiment with here were several thumb-generated spinners, where revolutions were imparted using a clicking action between thumb and middle finger. Some were released with the back of the hand facing the batsman, imparting over-spin; others had the back of the hand facing either his right cheek or skyward, imparting back-spin. These latter deliveries would become his legendary flippers, each one a mini resurrection of a tradition almost a century old but by now dormant.

The practice paid off: Grimmett's record for Prahran was phenomenal – but still the Victoria selectors ignored him. He resolved to move again – this time to Adelaide and South Australia, and secured a new job there, only for the Victoria selectors finally to call on him after their three-year silence. In a comeback match for Victoria (ironically, against South Australia) he took 8-86 in the second innings, but so disgusted was he at his treatment that he went through with the move to Adelaide anyway.

This brief chronology gives some indication of what the poor man endured. There were further nuisances, too – when he finally made his Test debut *The Times* of London referred to 'the South Australian left-handed bowler' – and the impression he gave of being a man who had suffered unjustly for too long seemed apparent in his disposition, which was somewhere between reticent and laconic. He always bowled in his baggy green cap, ashamed of his baldness. He seemed to have prematurely aged: his wiry little physique, and slowness around the field, made him look like a frail old man. And yet when, after long years in the wilderness, he finally made his Test debut, justice would begin to be done.

Against England in Sydney for his first Test, Grimmett took 5-45 and 6-37 as England lost heavily. Frank Woolley was his first wicket, bowled through the gate. His accuracy was exceptional, the result of years of relentless practice, and he would bowl upwind, slow for a wrist-spinner (probably rarely over 50mph, just like 'Tich' Freeman), probing at the batsman with a modulating flight and awkward length. The ball should stay above the level of the batsman's eye for as long as possible: that was his dictum too. He only bowled one no-ball in his entire career, and came in off a short run-up at about 45 degrees, after a pronounced skip in his first stride, while caressing the ball paternally with his fingers on his way in. Like Sonny Ramadhin in the post-war years, he got through his overs very quickly; so quickly, in fact, that he was once told to slow down so as to give the bowler at the other end a chance to catch his breath.

The position of his back foot at delivery, directly behind his front foot despite a chest-on action, was unorthodox, and must have put immense strain on his lower back. His low arm would certainly be considered round-arm today, and his action made him look as if it was a discus rather than a leather ball in his hand. But Grimmett was moved to write to Ralph Barker, the man who first told the story of his awakening under Hempelman's tutelage, saying: 'Everyone refers to me as a round-arm bowler. This is wrong. The whole of my bowling technique was based on deception of flight and speed off the pitch. To acquire this, the arm has to move fast.'

If this last point seems a conflation of categories (Grimmett seems to imply that round-arm bowlers could only bowl with a slow arm, a claim for which there is scant evidence, while Sri Lanka's Lasith Malinga seems to disprove him), it is worth noting O'Reilly's analysis, which offers some defence:

Unlike Arthur Mailey, the first of the Australian spin trilogy of the inter-wars era, Grimmett never insisted on spin as his chief means of destruction. To him it was no more than an important adjunct to unerring length and tantalising direction. Grimmett seldom beat a batsman by spin alone. Mailey often did. I cannot remember Grimmett bowling a long-hop, whereas Mailey averaged one an over. So much, in fact, did inaccuracy become a feature of Mailey's success that he himself came to believe that it was an essential ingredient. Such wantonness was anathema to Grimmett, who believed that a bowler should bowl as well as he possibly could every time he turned his arm over.

Sharp turn didn't seem Grimmett's primary motive, which, if anything, recommends him to us even more forcefully. One of his favourite methods was to push the batsman further and further into the crease, before trapping him with the skidding back-spinner which cut in from the off – in other words, the flipper. And the comparison with Mailey in terms of economy rate was significant: whereas Mailey said he didn't bowl maidens, because that's what medium-pacers did, Grimmett said he did, because maidens led to wickets. This made him the miser to Mailey's millionaire.

Our debt to Grimmett is largely constituted of his popularisation of this skidding, back-spinning ball, and, further, to his willingness to write about it. Uniquely for bowlers of his generation, Grimmett set down his technique in hundreds of thousands of words, producing three books – *Grimmett on Getting Wickets* (1930), *Tricking the Batsman* (1932) and *Grimmett on Cricket* (1948) – that are among the most remarkable publications in bowling history. They expound at length on the techniques, grips, stratagems and concerns he had as a master Twirlyman. They are, in every sense, gripping reads. In *Grimmett on Getting Wickets*, the author devoted several pages of amateur physics to explaining why cricket balls behave the way they do, and even distinguished between 'spin bowling' and 'swerve bowling' in a manner that would have pleased the Swift Pioneers of the late nineteenth century.

In his years of practice, Grimmett made three observations that seemed pleasantly congruous with each other. First, the googly put such strain on the shoulder, and had destroyed the careers of so many bowlers, that it seemed an intolerable burden. Second, even if one did bowl the googly, the over-spin on it would often cause it to bounce so high that the potential leg-before hoped for by spinning the ball back into the right-hander was discounted. This was a special problem for Grimmett (and Freeman and Gupte, two other short men): his low arm meant the ball had to go sharply up before it came down, giving it a loopy trajectory that umpires disliked when considering lbw decisions. O'Reilly, writing his former spin twin's obituary, said: 'He seldom bowled the wrong'un because he preferred not to toss the ball high.' And third, in the transition from under-arm to over-arm bowling, a brilliant tool had been needlessly discarded. The thumb, with its soft padding and considerable span from the rest of the hand, was an invaluable lever. Why abandon it? Grimmett explains with reference to the extraordinary lobster George Simpson-Hayward, a man who looked as if he had benefited from future-directed time travel:

In most of my experiments I bowled under-arm with a tennis ball and afterward adapted the principle to over-arm.

I was impressed about this time by a very fine under-arm bowler named Simpson-Hayward, who toured New Zealand with an English team. He could spin a ball more than any bowler I had seen at the time. How could such vicious spin be applied under-arm, I wondered. Surely some different principle of spinning must be involved.

If I had asked Mr Hayward [sic], perhaps I should have evolved my Mystery Ball sooner. But as it was, I went on experimenting and eventually realised that much more spin could be applied by holding the ball between the thumb and second finger. The problem was, however, to adapt this to over-arm bowling.

I put in hours of practice at this [as did his fox terrier], and it was only after much hard work that I was satisfied and decided to use it in matches. The reason I waited so long was that pride in my bowling wouldn't let me bowl a ball that didn't fit into the main scheme of my methods. This conception of bowling, too, caused me to use the pruning knife from time to time; so that when I had perfected this new kind of spin, I practically discarded the old googly. I used it only on very rare occasions, usually when I was opposed by a left-handed batsman. I realised that the new delivery had great possibilities. And it was sound in principle to concentrate on my leg-break and straight ball, since the fewer other balls I bowled the less risk I ran of losing control.

It is false to suggest that Grimmett 'invented the flipper' (as Simon Hughes does, and so, too, Bruce Dooland, in *Cricket: The Australian Way*, adding for good measure that he did so in his fortieth year), that it was 'originated' by him (as O'Reilly does in his obituary), or that he was 'the first man to bowl [it]' (Trueman). Even Frith suggests that the flipper 'came several decades later' as compared with Bosanquet. We know from descriptions of Mead and Grace in earlier chapters that thumb-generated back-spinners which skidded into the batsman from a low trajectory –

that is, flippers – had long been employed in England. But Grimmett certainly did most to bring it back into fashion. His low arm accentuated the characteristic skidding trajectory, and, unlike later flipper-bowlers such as Bruce Dooland and Shane Warne, Grimmett often kept the seam close to vertical, causing his flipper to skid in occasionally. This was in stark contrast to the 'Mystery Ball' he extols in his later book, which seems really to be a conventional off-break bowled with the thumb.

A crucial point on which there simply isn't enough evidence either way is whether Grimmett occasionally released the flipper with the back of his hand pointing towards his face – in other words, with the wrist in the same position as for the leg-break.

One of the wonderful points about the physics of spin bowling concerns how the ball's behaviour changes according to top-spin and back-spin. We have already seen that top-spin makes the ball dip, and so bounce steeply. And back-spin makes the ball float on to a fuller length, and so skid on. What about how this affects turn off the wicket?

With deliveries such as the leg-break, googly and top-spinner, the top-spin on the ball makes it turn in the direction of the seam. So for the leg-break, the seam points towards third man, which makes the ball turn from leg to off. But what if the ball has back-spin? In that case, instead of spinning in the direction of the seam, the ball skids in the *opposite* direction. This is usually referred to as 'check-spin'.

In other words, if the ball is released so that the seam is pointing towards third man, and it has top-spin on it (as with the conventional leg-break), it will dip and turn from leg to off. But if the ball is released so that the seam is pointing towards third man, and it has back-spin on it, it will float on to a fuller length and then – by 'check-spin' – skid from off to leg.

In the case of the flipper family of deliveries, this creates a delicious opening. By bowling a flipper with the back of the hand pointing towards the face, and the seam pointing towards third man, the wrist-spinner has an amazing new weapon. This is a delivery which looks as if it should be the conventional leg-break (because of the wrist position and angle of the seam); but, in fact, instead of dipping and turning away from the right-hander, it will float and then skid into him. Against the right-handed batsman comfortably leaving the ball outside off-stump, this could prove invaluable. If Grimmett did bowl it regularly he didn't expound on the matter at length – perhaps because he wanted to keep it secret. But in the absence of firm evidence – and conscious of the fact that all patents are frauds in spin bowling – I shall shamelessly lay claim to this delivery myself. For the avoidance of all doubt, I hereby name it Rajan's Mystery Ball.

The deployment of various flippers, including possibly this one, allowed Grimmett to prolong his career, because he bowled very few googlies. Herb Collins, the Australian batsman, had told him not to bowl any more googlies on the 1926 tour of England, though Grimmett reckoned this was more because Collins feared that it would cause him to lose his leg-break altogether.

In the fifteen Tests in which he and O'Reilly bowled in tandem they shared 169 wickets, with Grimmett taking eighty-eight of them. And yet, despite his late flourishing in cricket, and despite the extraordinary success of his partnership with O'Reilly, Grimmett was dropped from the Test side, as if the misfortune that had dogged him in his younger days was destined never to leave his side. It is curious that one can say he left prematurely, given that he played his last Test at forty-five, but O'Reilly wasn't the only one who felt 'he was shoved aside like a worn-out boot'. Bradman, who, remember, said he thought Grimmett was the greatest spinner ever (counting O'Reilly as a medium-pacer), was nevertheless taken with another spinner named Frank Ward. And the Don's word was final. This rejection seemed a fittingly unwarranted climax for Grimmett. He was a man who, through remarkable perseverance, sacrifice and scholarly devotion, had mastered his art, and confounded his many doubters, despite seemingly insuperable obstacles. And yet, perhaps because of the manifold obstacles placed before him, he seemed always to be a sad man, as O'Reilly understood.

Social life meant little to Grum [Grimmett]. Not until late in his career did he discover that it was not a bad idea to relax between matches … later he told me, with obvious regret, that on previous tours he had been keeping the wrong company and had never really enjoyed a touring trip. That I thought was sad, but not half as sad as I felt when, at the very zenith of his glorious career, he was dumped out of business altogether.

In so many ways, Grimmett's career is a perfect microcosm of the trials, both public and private, a committed spinner must endure. He was rare in having the determination to reach the top, despite constant setbacks. The extent to which this is attributable to his Roman Catholic faith (which O'Reilly shared) cannot be known. Were it not that he had eventually achieved some success (indeed, he held the record for Test wickets until Alec Bedser overtook him in 1953), the depressive bouts described by O'Reilly would be utterly intolerable. But that he wrote so well about his art, shared in two great spin partnerships and patronised schools of bowling in which back-spin and the thumb play an essential role, gives his legacy both charm and joy, even if, as was so often the case, O'Reilly did the celebrating and smiling for both of them.

The contrast between them was plain to the eye, as were the contrasts within O'Reilly himself. Among the most wonderful things about him was the fact that the very *joie de vivre* that Bradman found so grating existed concurrently with his ferocious disposition once the ball was in his hand. Never in cricket was a nickname more deserved than the 'Tiger' that attached itself to O'Reilly. He was the most feared bowler in the world during a decade (the 1930s) dominated by batsmen and flat wickets. When rough outfields would cause the ball to deteriorate rapidly, his scowl and incandescence illuminated any pitch on which he was playing.

O'Reilly spelt out the need for this aggression in some of the vast journalism he produced (not least as correspondent for the *Sydney Morning Herald*):

You can never become a good attacking bowler if you do not develop a bowling 'temperament'. A happy-go-lucky, good-natured and carefree outlook is of no use whatever to an ambitious and competent bowler. He must be prepared to boil up inwardly on the slightest provocation, and opportunities are so common that there is no need even to cite one.

Conceal that desirable temperament from the public, but reveal it in all its force and fury to your opponent, the batsman.

His run-up and delivery were unorthodox and unsmooth: 'plunging and rolling like a ship in stormy seas, O'Reilly bucketed up to the wicket, wrist cocked, arms flailing, face contorted with pain and emotion', according to Ralph Barker in *Ten Great Bowlers*. A pronounced stoop over his collapsed front knee meant he never took full advantage, in the eyes of contemporaries, of his six-foot-three-inch frame, though he was still able to extract sharp bounce. His tight grip differed from most leg-spinners in closing the gap between first and second fingers completely, almost like a seam bowler's grip but with his first two fingers going across the seam rather than along it. Even though he was quick for a spinner, he had a much faster ball – probably around 75mph – that was known as his 'Irish special'. For the leg-break, his wrist did most of the work, with the fingers being more involved in the variations. Indeed, his fingers were long and unusually powerful. Time and again, O'Reilly was told to change his grip. Time and again, he listened to the advice – then ignored it. Even, indeed, when it came from a legend of leg-spin:

Arthur Mailey, then approaching the end of his career, was watching my first appearance at the SCG [Sydney Cricket Ground] nets in 1926–7, where I bowled for the first time under the gaze of the New South Wales selectors. Himself a selector, Mailey drew me aside, to show me the grip he used, fundamentally different from mine, with the ball held in the fingertips of his right hand. He suggested that I should imitate it if I ever hoped to be able to spin a leg-break noticeably. He went so far as to describe my own grip and to draw lines of similarity with the manner in which he held a golf club.

This advice appalled me. Here was a man trying to get me to dump all the lessons I had taught myself for nearly ten years: personal lessons which I had learned well enough to find myself in attendance at the nets that afternoon.

Not likely. I thanked Mr Mailey for the great interest he had taken in me but went on to say that I thought it was much too late to be fiddling about with an action which even by that time had become second nature to me.

What is this, if not the spirit of rebellion, the two-fingers-to-authority, that animated such early pioneers and brave originals as the four

Williams, Lamborn and Tom 'Old Everlasting' Walker? It gives some indication at least of the assurance O'Reilly had in his own method. So complete and unflinching was his self-belief that once, when asked what he thought of bowlers who ran out batsmen at the non-striker's end who backed up too early, he replied that in his experience no batsman had been that keen to get down to the other end to face his bowling.

Wisden of 1936 describes him as negative because he bowled straight at and just outside leg-stump, but this doesn't seem to have been his favoured approach for long; rather, he aimed at middle and leg to make the batsman play at every ball, inviting him to play against the spin, but never allowing him to let the ball go through to the wicketkeeper. His stock ball was a fast leg-break and his main variation was a slower and more flighty googly. He would send the googly along the same path – which is why he took so many wickets at short leg with deliveries that popped off the wicket.

O'Reilly claimed to have learned the googly in a couple of days after his brother Jack discovered the technique from spying on Mailey in practice nets at North Sydney. 'The bosie became my most prized possession,' Tiger would write. 'I practised it day in, day out.' As a result his arm came over at great speed and with hardly any discernible change of action for different deliveries, making him very difficult to pick.

Writing in old age, O'Reilly gave a fuller account of his method. It is worth restating for at least three reasons. First, it happens to be the core of the advice he gave Richie Benaud; second, it shows the importance to young leg-spinners of focusing on the spot on the wicket they intend to hit, if they want to bowl accurately; and, third, it conveys the need for spinners to resist the 'expensive' label, which too often allows them to forgive the occasional four-ball:

With my bowling, my cardinal rule was that I always had my eyes glued on the spot where I was going to pitch the ball. I wasn't a slow leg-spinner, I bowled medium pace. The leg-spinner was my stock ball, but I bowled the wrong'un more frequently than any other leg-spinner I've seen. It was nothing for me to bowl it three times in an eight ball over: I had complete confidence in my ability to bowl a wrong'un to length and direction, and I could really get it to bounce, so I used it as a variation of flight and bounce as well as spin.

When I started I used to bowl the orthodox off-break, but I gave that up because it interfered with my rhythm, but my straight faster ball got me lots of wickets – I even had a bouncer of sorts.

It was with his three brothers that he had learned the basic skills, 'playing with a gum-wood bat and a piece of banskia [Australian wildflower] root chiselled down to make a ball', according to Jack Fingleton in *Cricket Crisis*. When he was thirteen he watched Victoria play an up-country match in the mountain city of Goulborn. There his eyes were 'riveted on a wiry little leg-spinner whose name on the local scoreboard was Grummett'. It was from this that Tiger extracted 'Grum', his lifelong nickname for the man named Clarence who went from being his boyhood hero to his junior partner in spin bowling's greatest duo.

Learning the basics came easily to a boy of O'Reilly's athleticism – he held a state record for the hop, skip and jump, and was a champion triple jumper just like Craig McDermott, the Australian seam bowler, six decades later. The heaving action for which he became notorious is thought to owe something to his imitation of the windmill his forefathers had built in the town of Wingello, a monument he was curiously fixated with.

When training to be a teacher at the age of twenty (to follow in the footsteps of his schoolmaster father), he was passing through Bowral station and heard his name across the platform. He stuck his head out of the window of his carriage to be told he was needed for a game Wingello were playing against Bowral, a match to be played over two days but separated by a week. So he played. On the first day, a seventeen-year-old called Bradman scored 234 not out. Seven days later, O'Reilly bowled him first ball with one that pitched outside leg and hit off, doubtless not all that different from Warne's accounting for Gatting sixty-eight years later, though not captured on film, and therefore absent from YouTube. 'Suddenly', he later wrote of that moment, 'cricket was the best game in the whole wide world.'

Of the 144 wickets he took in twenty-seven Tests, 102 were Englishmen including, tellingly, ten dismissals of Wally Hammond in just nineteen Tests. Hammond was reckoned to be second only to Bradman in the world at that stage. O'Reilly might have taken more but for the war and his determination to be a schoolmaster. He announced his retirement in 1934 to concentrate on teaching and raising a family, but a teaching colleague convinced him to return to Test cricket. This he did, taking forty-seven more wickets in the series against England in 1936–7 and 1938. These included that of Len Hutton, out for a then record 364, as England scored 903-7.

After that match, O'Reilly asked for a gun with which to shoot the Oval groundsman, who had 'doped' the pitch specifically to nullify the predatory Tiger. O'Reilly was probably at least half joking, but over the course of the next five decades he owed much of his reputation to a remorseless disgust for those who, in his opinion, had undermined the game by making it too easy for batsmen. A terrible consequence of this, he said, was the fading of leg-spin into apparent obsolescence.

It is very sad that he didn't live to see Warne flourish, let alone the many other outstanding spin bowlers of today. He said he would never forgive English cricket for trying to kill off its leg-spinners. He regularly suggested, again not altogether in jest, that left-handers be barred from playing at the top level, because of their unfair advantage in facing leg-spin. It's just possible the strength of his feeling on this matter was related to the fact that two of the few batsmen to play him with relative ease were England's Eddie Paynter and Maurice Leyland, left-handers both.

Martin-Jenkins reports the Tiger's incandescence in the commentary box when Pakistani captains failed to set appropriate fields for Abdul Qadir. He would never fail to stick up for his fellow leg-spinners, seeing in their travails the efforts of a hunted species facing extinction. This was partly why, like so many other great spinners, he did his utmost to pass on his knowledge.

In the early stages of Australia's 1953 Ashes tour, Richie Benaud, then a promising young all-rounder, had heard via Tom Goodman, a correspondent for the *Sydney Morning Herald*, that Tiger was getting dismayed at Benaud's bowling, and wanted to talk to him about it. So Benaud and O'Reilly had a meal in the Scarborough hotel, and retired to the latter's room. There, in axiomatic terms, O'Reilly imparted what he thought were the fundamentals of spin bowling. These had been the key to his own success, and Benaud later averred that they were the main reason he completed the bowling half of becoming the first player to take 200 wickets and score 2,000 runs at Test level. They can be summarised as follows.

First, 'give the batsman absolutely nothing'. Second, 'develop one ball as your stock ball and perfect it'. Third, 'that ball should be your leg-break, and from your point of view it should be both an attacking and defensive weapon'. Fourth, 'don't try to take a wicket every ball'. Fifth, 'never forget, even for one moment, that the batsman is an enemy on the field'. Sixth, 'bear in mind that almost every captain under whom you play will be a batsman ... with very few exceptions they [batsmen] know nothing about the technique of spin bowling'.

As Benaud says in his autobiography, like all the best advice this was brief, clear and simple. It is a penetrating summary of the attitude that spurred two of cricket's finest spinners, and is a serviceable manifesto for aspiring leg-spinners the world over. It also seems, in its forthright, assertive and generous manner, to encompass the best qualities of a great of the game. With his pace, limited variations and whirligig action, the Tiger was unconventional, but it was precisely the spirit and aggression of the hunter within him that ranks him among the very greatest of all bowlers.

ARM BALL

Grip   *Batsman's Point of View*

The grip for this is different, and puts the spinner in the mind of the seam bowler. The first two fingers are splayed again, but this time the index finger runs along the seam. As the arm comes round, the wrist position doesn't change. The ball is released with the wrist in the same position as when the off-spinner is released. But with the shiny side of the ball facing towards leg, the index finger pushes the ball out with the seam pointing towards second slip.

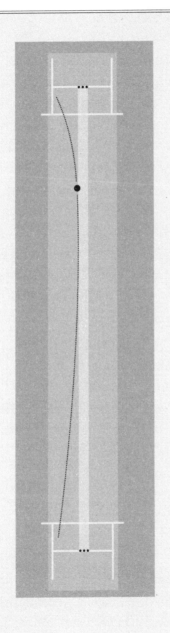

The ball should swing from leg to off as it would with a conventional fast bowler, and then continue along its trajectory (leaving the right-hander on pitching).

Chapter Seven

SPIN GOES GLOBAL

At Lord's where I saw it,
Yardley tried his best,
Goddard won the Test,
They gave the crowd plenty fun,
The second Test and West Indies won,
With those little pals of mine,
Ramadhin and Valentine.

Lord Kitchener, 'Cricket, Lovely Cricket'

Walcott, Weekes and Worrell held up their name
With wonder shots throughout the game
But England was beaten clean out of time
With the spin bowling of Ramadhin and Valentine.

Lord Kitchener, untitled song

Given that John Goddard's touring West Indies team had never won a
Test match, let alone a series, in three tours of England, you can forgive
fans sympathetic to his cause for getting excited when, having gone

1–0 down after the first Test of the 1950 series, they stormed to victory at Lord's in the second. Watching that game, and getting progressively more ecstatic as his countrymen marched to victory, was Lord Kitchener (Aldwyn Roberts), a member of the Windrush generation and author of the lyrics that founded calypso cricket.

The Times reported his celebration thus: 'Right round the ground he went in an African war dance ... all in slow time. Kitch, with a khaki sash over bright blue shirt, carried a guitar which he strummed wildly.' This he also did while leading a victorious, dancing procession all the way to London's Piccadilly, ending close to that monument to another great spinner, the Lillywhite's store. That night, he sang 'Cricket, Lovely Cricket' for the first time at two nightclubs frequented by London's vivacious new Caribbean immigrants, the Paramount and the Caribbean, and thus was born a whole genre of music. The song was in fact written after the game, not (as is sometimes reported) during it, and later recorded by Lord Beginner (Egbert Moore). The verse above referring to the Three Ws was, by contrast, the closing section of a melody sung by Lord Kitchener in the post-match celebrations on the field.

That evening, the whole of London erupted into a carnival of Caribbean delight, with spontaneous outpourings of reggae and calypso uniting Brixton, the Edgware Road and queues of people waiting to get into the Paramount and the Caribbean. And it was two spinners who were the toast of the town, two bowlers of whom nobody in England had heard – though many would later claim otherwise. The same two spinners of contrasting technique, deportment and character, through their mastery of flight and turn, would make a splash on newspaper back pages for the whole of the next week.

One of them, the most gregarious member of the visiting party, quaffed champagne in the team hotel and led the city's celebrations.

The other, never keen to party, repeated his habit of turning inwards just as the crowds outside demanded more.

They personified so much that is dear to cricket fans the world over – and fundamental to the argument of these pages: first, the great Caribbean surge after the war; second, the capacity of cricket in general, and spin in particular, to unite people of seeming differences, creating a common language; and, third, the internationalisation of cricket as a whole, and spin specifically.

Indeed, the post-war years of cricket were marked by the globalisation of mystery. The arrival of Test-playing nations from India (1932) and the West Indies (1928) facilitated the emergence of a range of brilliant spinners, so that, aside from the present day, the 1950s was the period in which spectators had the privilege of seeing the finest Twirlymen there have ever been. And, in a marked difference to previous eras, they no longer had to rely on the English and Australians to provide them.

Long before they had all of England – never mind the Caribbean – pulsating with Lord Kitchener's classic lyrics, from a calypso tune written for and about them, 'Ram' and 'Val', as they were universally known, were pioneers for inter-island and inter-racial harmony. (In this way, they upheld the radical, history-making instincts of spinners before them.) And, not long after, they were branded among the finest spinning twins ever to bowl in tandem, arguably as menacing (albeit through very different methods) as O'Reilly and Grimmett, though in my view one rung down on the spin twin ladder.

It was precisely their contrasting appearance and style that gave the combination its enduring majesty and charming harmony. Sonny Ramadhin – short, brown-skinned, shuffling through the crease, bringing over a fast, high arm with deliveries that were often on to the batsman in a hurry – bowled off-breaks and leg-breaks with barely distinct actions.

Given that he was five foot four, it's possible to claim that, even with his arm at twelve o'clock, it wasn't particularly 'high'. Ramadhin was the first East Indian to play for the West Indies.

Alfred Louis Valentine – tall, bespectacled, black and flighty, with the lithe, feline manner of Barack Obama – was a classic left-arm orthodox bowler, spinning the ball vigorously with an arm at times so low it seemed to come at the right-hander from a straight(ish) mid-off position. In fact, it's a reasonable guess that the counter-effect of their relative arm positions caused them to deliver the ball from about the same height, albeit on a different trajectory. They were brilliant men in their own right, but such was the nature of their exploits on the 1950 tour to England, in which they dominated a series as no other spin partnership before or since (including O'Reilly and Grimmett), and such is the charming symmetry of their biographies, that to unyoke one from the other would be to take something ineradicable and irreducible away from both.

When, on 1 May 1929, a plump little boy was born in the small village of St Charles, Trinidad, with no name, the birth certificate simply referred to him as 'boy'. Orphaned, he was brought by his Uncle Soodhai to Esperance village, south of San Fernando, where he would go to school. The boys there, adopting him as their own, called him Sonny, and the name stuck. He was unusually reserved, sometimes to the point of seeming awkward or anxious. Eventually he moved to the Canadian Mission School in Trinidad's Duncan Village, by which time he had been introduced to cricket, using coconut branches for bats, and coconuts, stones and limes – especially limes – for a ball. It was with the last of these that his fascination with spin erupted: much as Peter Philpott, the Australian leg-spinner, recommends spinning oranges to learn the basics, Ramadhin would spin limes for hours to acquire the essentials of his method.

As he played for, and rose through the ranks of, the Palmiste Club in Trinidad, his exceptional talent soon acquired attention. A friend (and namesake) of his, Sonny Beekie, who was then playing for Trinidad's South team, brought him to the attention of one Mr C. I. Skinner of the Trinidad Leaseholds Oil Company. Skinner offered the short nineteen-year-old shifts as a storekeeper, to provide him with a small stipend that would save him from penury. But it was in Skinner's other capacity, as an all-rounder for Barbados and former member of the Inter-Colonial team, that he had really taken Ramadhin on. He wanted Ramadhin to have access to the higher standard of cricket, and better facilities, the company offered.

Buoyed by Skinner's encouragement, Ramadhin showed up at two trial games for Trinidad, on matting wickets against Jamaica. They would be his only first-class games before a Test debut, and in them he took 12 wickets at 19.25. Jeffrey Stollmeyer, Trinidad's captain, extolled his new protégé's virtues; John Goddard, the West Indies captain, had seen enough to demand Ramadhin's selection for the forthcoming tour of England. The year was 1950.

In the same two trial games, another spinner caught the selectors' eye, albeit one playing for Jamaica. He was taller, toothy, clearly had poor eyesight (at least clearly to his teammates), and yet unlike Ramadhin was seemingly at ease with the world. He took only two wickets in those games, but they were enough to get young Alf Valentine aboard the ship to England. As Tony Cozier put it in his elegant obituary of Valentine for the *Independent*, the presence of the Three Ws (Frank Worrell, Everton Weekes and Clyde Walcott), Stollmeyer and Alan Rae at the top of the order meant those two trial games were specifically about solving the selectors' bowling dilemmas. In 'Ram' and 'Val' they had an unconventional answer.

Here were two names the English had never heard of. Experienced leg-spinner Wilfred Ferguson, who had taken twenty-three wickets in four home Tests against England two years earlier, was inexplicably omitted (it was of only partial consolation to Ferguson that Subhash Gupte should be given the nickname 'Fergie' in his honour a few years later).

Born a year later than Ramadhin in the poor suburb of Spanish Town, about twenty miles outside Kingston, Jamaica, Valentine was an apprentice machinist who came under the tutelage of Jack Mercer, the Glamorgan and Northants player, who guided him to some impressive returns for St Catherine Cricket Club. After leaving school at sixteen he had played briefly for the police, but a year later a chance meeting with Mercer led to the Englishman recommending Valentine to the Jamaica cricketing authorities. Mercer had spotted a tall, affable teenager who landed the ball on an awkward length, and had told him he would be a handful if he learned to wrap his long fingers around the ball and tweak it fiercely. It was good advice, and not least because Valentine showed no interest in batting.

Still, their relative performances for Trinidad and Jamaica in those trial games made for different levels of expectation on the part of the selectors. Ramadhin had wickets to his name, and was a bold gambit; Valentine came with little more than a recommendation, albeit from the influential Mercer, and was a shot in the dark. It was whispered that he only sneaked into the squad because of the variation the angle of his left arm would provide, and to the extent that the jibe hurt Valentine it did so because there was truth in it.

Never in the history of cricket did two novices make such a sensational joint impact. And in what a context, too: Goddard, remember, led a side that had never won a Test match, let alone a series, in three tours of

England. Hopes were so low as to be offensive. And, in losing the first Test at Old Trafford by 202 runs, they were true to form. Goddard would later call this an 'aberration', his reason for so doing prompted by the fact that 'Ram' and 'Val' had begun to show a glimpse of their genius. Valentine had taken five wickets by lunch on his first day in Test cricket, and would end up with 8-104, still the best figures by a West Indian on debut. He was helped by the groundsman having been told to go easy on the heavy roller and avoid overwatering the track. A week of baking sun reduced the pitch to a dust heap. Valentine got the ball to spit off a length, often making it jump over Walcott, even though, at six foot four, he was an unusually tall wicketkeeper.

The West Indies would win the next three Tests respectively by 326 runs, 10 wickets and an innings and 56 runs. At Lord's for the second Test, Valentine's figures were 116-75-127-7; Ramadhin's were 115-70-152-11. It was this performance that prompted Lord Kitchener to lead celebrations on the pitch with what *The Times* called 'guitar-like instruments'.

At Trent Bridge for the third Test, by which stage they were famous across England, 'Ram' and 'Val' achieved combined figures of 173.2-74-275-8. At the Oval they took 14-261 between them. Over the four-match rubber their figures were: Valentine, 422.3-197-674-33 (still a record for a West Indian in a four-match series); Ramadhin, 377.5-170-604-26. The other eight West Indian bowlers took only 18 wickets between them; these two took 59 of the 80 wickets available to them in the Test series. Valentine took 123 in all first-class cricket that summer; Ramadhin took 135. They were both named Wisden Cricketers of the Year in 1951. It was utter, phenomenal domination by the spin twins. How did they do it?

'Ram' and 'Val' probably got through their overs faster than any other bowling pair in the history of the game, including any pair of which one half was 'Bomber' Wells, he of the one- or two-step run-up (it varied according to the weather). This wasn't a chance by-product of their having the short run-ups common to spinners; rather, it was part of a deeply intelligent strategy, which involved conducting a war of attrition on batsmen who would find themselves exhausted and emotionally drained by the lack of let-up in the pair's examination of their technique. They made a habit of bowling six or eight consecutive maidens. The fizzing attack was relentless.

Yet in style and method they were sharply distinct. With narrow eyes and a pencil-thin moustache that brought linear detail to a round face, Ramadhin was, as Richie Benaud put it, 'basically an off-spinner with a deceptive leg-break'. He bowled both of these out of the front rather than the side of his hand, so that his fingers (first and middle for the off-break; middle and third for the leg-break) did most of the work, ensuring he was redolent of Sydney Barnes. Unlike Barnes, who had his wrist cocked back, as if screwing or unscrewing a bulb above and slightly in front of his head at the point of delivery, Ramadhin seems to have minimised the involvement of the wrist altogether. And yet he must have adjusted its position at least slightly for the off- and leg-breaks, not least because Len Hutton said that he never saw anyone turn an off-break more (dying in September 1990, the great Yorkshireman probably didn't see the best of Muralitharan, who definitely did turn it more).

Nevertheless, much of the time he bowled in the manner of Ajantha Mendis today, firing the ball in at a brisk pace on or just outside off-stump, pushing it wider and bowling slower if the pitch was taking spin. He had a straight ball – something akin to Shane Warne's slider – which he often bowled twice an over, and a leg-break speared into the stumps that took countless wickets leg-before or caught in the infield. Fred Trueman wrote: 'It was generally thought that the delivery which left the right hander was like an ordinary bowler of that type, who bowled what was called a "floater" or arm ball.'

This description is intriguing for several reasons. It conflates Ramadhin's leg-break with his straight ball; he bowled a delivery that turned from leg to off as well as one that went straight through, often skidding into the pads, which is here described as the '"floater" or arm ball'. The other fascinating thing is that, confronted with a delivery from an off-break bowler which spun the other way, batsmen were unwilling to believe it really did turn in the opposite direction. This is precisely how batsmen on the English county circuit, including Michael Atherton, reacted when Saqlain Mushtaq's doosra, which really does turn from leg to off, first emerged. They convinced themselves that it was just a top-spinner which drifted away in the air. Whether these misunderstandings are wilful or not, and whether they were motivated by an attempt to minimise dressing-room anxiety, they show the confusion that mystery spinners are apt to spread. That confusion ultimately works to their advantage.

Ramadhin's different deliveries demanded disguise, and for this purpose he employed a rather curious habit, namely bowling with his sleeves buttoned up. Together with the fact that he wore his cap when he bowled, and that his shirts were too big, this gave the five-foot-four, nine-stone bowler more than a passing resemblance to those schoolboys whose parents, being less well off, buy their children oversized uniforms in the hope they will grow into them, and thereby save them money on future purchases. One of the darker accusations made about Ramadhin's apparel was that its purpose was to cover up the illegality of his action.

It is impossible, even with the benefit of (grainy) slow-motion replays, to decipher whether or not Ramadhin straightened his arm – especially since it came over at such speed. Certainly we can say, from the pictorial evidence we have, that his arm was often bent as it came over, and there not being any deformity that stopped it straightening (as Muralitharan argues is the case with him), the temptation to straighten it must have been immense. All this made him frightfully difficult to pick, especially in poor English light, or when, as with the old Nursery End at Lord's, there was no sightscreen. Yet seasoned observers swore they could pick his leg-break through its slower pace and higher arc (much as Mendis's googly can be picked today). Jim Sims, the Middlesex leg-break bowler, was one who tried to demystify Ramadhin in this way, claiming he could pick the higher arc of the leg-break from side on.

Valentine approached the crease in jerks and with ill-disciplined limbs, seemingly lacking rhythm. This seemed bizarrely out of character for a man so lithe off the field. But by the time the ball came out of his hand, all seemed in perfect order. Benaud said of him: 'He was a wonderful bowler, slightly ungainly in initial movement to the bowling crease, but he nevertheless finished up with a nice action and the ability to spin the ball even on the most perfect batting surface.' His low arm, and full use of the width of the crease, forced the right-hander to play at almost every ball, since even those pitched six inches outside off-stump could knock it over if they didn't turn, and especially if he was getting drift into the right-hander. Trevor Bailey reckoned 'his trajectory was fairly flat but, because he spun the ball so much, it did tend to dip'. He usually bowled an arm ball at least once an over, forcing the batsman into two minds about playing every delivery.

Valentine's fingers were so frequently lacerated that he carried surgical spirit to games, and dipped his spinning fingers in a healthy amount at the end of the day. Ramadhin's skin was even more prone to deep tears, and the problem got so severe that he abandoned the orthodox grip for his off-break, instead spinning the ball off its smoother part (with his middle finger running down rather than across the seam).

Both were undone, albeit to varying degrees, by events on the 1957 return tour to England, a series that was later compared to the Bodyline series of 1932–3 because it seemed to contravene the spirit of the game. In the Edgbaston Test, Colin Cowdrey and Peter May, England's premier batsmen, decided that the way to counteract the spin twins was by using their front pad to nullify the threat of balls outside the off-stump. Ramadhin had taken Peter Richardson's wicket to leave England 113-3, and still 175 runs behind. But then Cowdrey and May, and especially the former, planted their front pads down the wicket, blocking the path of any ball too short to drive. The England pair took the score to 524 before the loss of a further wicket, while Ramadhin lodged close to a hundred appeals with the umpire. They grew steadily more outraged, eventually being more like squeals than appeals, and rendering his voice hoarse. He would later call them 'blood footballers'. Cowdrey finished with 154, May was 285 not out, and their partnership did much to force a change in the lbw law. That was of little use to Ramadhin or Valentine: neither was ever as effective a bowler again.

The emotional pounding of that experience gave some insight into the contrasting characters of these two greats, as did their careers after retirement. Ramadhin, who, after playing for Lancashire, would run a pub in a village on the Lancashire/Yorkshire border called Delph, seemed at times a fragile character, prone to bouts of depression, comfortable in solitude. It was an impression reinforced by his schoolboy appearance on the turf, where he had been so terribly bullied by those two excellent English gentlemen. An early indication of it was the time, during the Melbourne Test of 1951–2, when an unlikely tenth wicket stand of thirty-eight stole victory for the Australians, that Ramadhin trudged off the field, apparently overcome by the pressure and demands of teammates.

Even after the extraordinary win at Lord's in 1950, when Lord Kitchener was dancing his way through London, and the Kingsley Hotel where the team were staying had been draped in Caribbean flags, he would later say: 'I used to wait outside in the street until everybody had finished, just biding my time ... All I ever drunk was ginger beer. When everybody went out celebrating in London, drinking champagne, I just had a quiet meal with some friends from Trinidad who were in England as students.'

This is eerily reminiscent of Clarrie Grimmett's lonely episodes, as recalled by Tiger O'Reilly. It is instructive to dwell for a moment on the similarities of temperament between the two men, because therein lies an insight into a type of Twirlyman who has shimmered through the ages.

Ramadhin and Grimmett were united in being small men whose vulnerability excited sympathy in those around them. They were both conservative in disposition, preferring, as Michael Oakeshott put it, known goods to unknown betters. They were reserved, uncomfortable with the demands for exuberance occasioned by their regular, match-winning performances. On tour they often prefered to linger in the team hotel than join the party. What's more, they spent much of their careers feeling overshadowed by their taller, more gregarious and more sociable spin twin. O'Reilly and Valentine positively pursued the limelight, indeed wanted it to be theirs to keep.

The avuncular and optimistic disposition that Valentine in particular brought to the game could hardly be more different from that of his spin twin. It can be said of Valentine that he was a man of deep and unflinching virtue, and probably among the most altruistic players ever to bless Test cricket. Except for the time when, having been shockingly dropped by the selectors during Australia's tour of the West Indies in 1955, he left his phone off the hook in disgust, knowing that the selectors would regret their decision and call him, begging him to play (which they did).

Unfailingly humble in his dealings with fans (if not umpires), he would stand in front of the team hotel for sometimes half an hour, signing autographs. He did this game after game, even after heavy defeats, lingering long after teammates had left the ground in low spirits. In spare moments, he would sign scraps of paper, which he would keep in his pockets and throw from the tour bus at crowds baying for his affections and seeking autographs. Possibly his only sin was indulging an addiction to jazz records and fancy shoes – but then his fame peaked during the 1950s, when those two things were the height of cool.

Once, when a particularly stubborn umpire turned down two lbw appeals and was then slow to assume his position ahead of one of Valentine's overs, he shouted to a teammate 'Hey, Gerry [Gomez, the West Indies all-rounder], tell that likka blind umpire to come stand 'ere'.

It was on a visit to a boys' home in Sydney in 1960–61 that he was moved to devote his later life (he would be a popular coach first) to helping poor children. This noble occupation he fulfilled when, after the death of his first wife (with whom he had four daughters), he married Jacquelyn, an American, and moved to Great Oaks near Orlando, Florida. There they both looked after neglected and abused children in a fostering capacity. Being surrogate parents of up to twelve children at a time (from five to eighteen), they steered several hundred young Americans to a better course in life.

In their later years, then, the path of these two Twirlymen would diverge (though they often met). The differences between their characters were brought to the fore – 'Ram', the boy with no name, living the quiet life, said to have kept his sleeves buttoned down even when he played golf; 'Val', the team joker, devoting himself to other people. But, in the annals of the game they would forever personify one of the more extraordinary Caribbean summers in post-war England. Uniquely complementary spin twins, they had a deserved place among the legends of the game, owing as much to their statistical records as to their bifurcated heritage.

It was that synthesis – of a black man and a brown man – that made 'Ram' and 'Val' seem like revolutionaries, and true Caribbean greats. No visitor to the West Indies can reasonably doubt that its irresistible charm derives largely from its heritage from Indian and African cultures. As an East Indian, Ramadhin's brand of mystery in many ways prefaced the outburst of spin that took place in the land of his forefathers during his own rise to the top.

Indians, as everybody knows, love to bowl spin. But the emergence of a spin-bowling culture in India was initially a jerky affair. First hinted at by Vinoo Mankad, an exceptional all-rounder who bowled slow left arm, it came in two major spurts thereafter – first, 'Fergie' Gupte; and later, notoriously, in the second great spin-bowling quartet of cricket history, composed of names which conjure up all the majesty of Hindu (and Sikh) civilisation: Chandrasekhar, Prasanna, Venkataraghavan and Bedi. Between them, these five bowlers fortified the impression that Indian teams in search of the twenty wickets needed for every victory would always prefer to turn to spin.

Always excitable and loyal to the land of his birth, but generally not prone to exaggeration, Mihir Bose contends that Subhashchandra Pandharinath 'Fergie' Gupte was the finest leg-spinner that ever played. Among Gupte's rivals who might not argue with that statement is his brother Baloo, who also bowled leg-spin for India, though with far less success. (Gupte was not, incidentally, named after Subhas Chandra Bose, a leader of the Indian nationalist movement in the years before partition, as is sometimes reported.)

The evidence for Bose's view is not borne out by statistics or superficial appearances, but it does exist. That no less an authority than Sir Garfield Sobers ranked him as the finest spinner he ever faced, never mind Everton Weekes (he of the celebrated Three Ws), and Hanif Mohammad (the brilliant Pakistani) shared his view, and Laker labelled him 'the best of the modern leg-spinners', puts Bose in estimable company. Martin-Jenkins told me that Tom Graveney, the former England captain and President of the MCC, a brilliant judge of talent, reckoned Gupte was 'exceptional'; indeed, he thought Gupte the best spinner he'd faced, after Bruce Dooland. Rohan Kanhai, the maverick West Indian batsman, said mastering Gupte was one of the biggest prizes of his career. Sobers, who faced Richie Benaud in his prime, was even moved to affirm in his 2003 autobiography that he thought Gupte a better bowler than Shane Warne, to answer those who presumed his original opinion, stated four decades earlier, was outdated by the emergence of the Australian. The 'Gupte-was-the-greatest' contention is one that Bose makes repeatedly over lunch (generally at minimal prompting) and is the conclusion of an argument found in his *A History of Indian Cricket*. A distillation of it will serve us well, but before we come to that it should be observed that the reason Gupte's record in Tests is not foremost among leg-spinners is inextricably linked to the manner of his departure from the Test scene. And thereby hangs a tale – one involving Gupte, a hotel lobby, a phone call and a priapic member of an early Indian cricketing dynasty by the name of Kripal Singh.

Between the third and fourth Tests of England's 1961–2 tour of India there was a twelve-day break over Christmas. It had been a dull series, but two days before the Calcutta Test, Singh and Gupte, known to have been fit, were dropped (Gupte was replaced by Prasanna). Harangued by journalists, India's delightfully named captain, Nari Contractor, admitted a disciplinary hearing had been called over their behaviour in Delhi after the third Test. Finally, the story came to light. A girl at the Imperial Hotel, where the team were staying, had alleged – shock horror! – that Singh and Gupte, who were sharing a room, had invited her upstairs for a drink.

This outraged the Indian public, whose sexual mores, it may be said with confidence, are more aligned with those of the Pope than Don Juan. 'She complained to the Indian manager, an Army man, saying she didn't expect Indian cricketers to behave in this way,' Gupte recalled many years later. He was married at the time, though Singh was not, adding another twist to the tale. Eventually Contractor told Gupte which way the wind was blowing. His star bowler rushed to the airport, where he found Singh. 'I cornered him at the newspaper stand. He said, "You had nothing to do with it". I saw Chidambaram [President of the Indian board] having breakfast at the airport and told him, "Your culprit is confessing". He said, "We will talk on the plane".'

Alas, that conversation never took place, and the subsequent investigation had all the integrity of a Stalinist show trial. With the press screeching, an official enquiry into the scandal, scheduled to take place in Calcutta when the team arrived, failed to materialise, and the pair, instructed not to board the plane, were dropped implicitly. Eventually a hearing was held in Madras, but so pathetic was it that neither player was given the chance to make his case properly. At one point Gupte was told by a member of the Indian board that he should have stopped Singh from picking up the phone. Disgusted at this absurd claim, he retorted: 'He is a big man. How can I stop him?' He never played Test cricket again.

Gupte emigrated to Trinidad – where he had married a girl a couple of years earlier – to contemplate his garden. The man who emerges from all this chicanery has something of Malvolio about him. There was his bitter and discomforting departure from the stage, though he stopped short (in public at least) of declaring he'll be revenged on the whole pack of them; and, further, there was the sense that he was undone by timing, by mere unfortunate circumstance. Indeed, in many senses timing was the undoing of this briefly great cricketer: his sin was not so much to be in the wrong place at the wrong time, but to be in the right place at the wrong time, or the wrong place at the right time. This is Bose's argument, and it has cogency.

The career of India's first world-class spinner was terminated at thirty-two because of a phone call by his room-mate, which may have been wholly innocent. But timing undid Gupte in another sense. He played in an India team whose fielders, with extraordinary consistency, performed a trick familiar to club cricketers the world over: they could turn an approaching mid-air ball into a bar of soap. Dozens of chances were dropped off Gupte in his short career. His captain, Datta Gaekwad, was tactically naive. He is the only bowler – pub quiz alert – to be denied a ten-wicket haul by a dropped catch, his 9-102 against the West Indies in Kanpur in 1958 being, in any case, in a losing cause (he opened the bowling in the second innings, taking 23-2-121-1 as Sobers smashed 198). And he also had the misfortune to play regularly not only on dry, placid wickets, but constantly to face an outstanding West Indies line-up, for whom the Three Ws, among others, would think nothing of bludgeoning their way to massive scores. He played in two series against Pakistan which failed, over ten Tests, to produce a positive result – utterly disheartening for any bowler. Abysmally supported, on the West Indies tour of 1958–9 he bowled three times as many overs as any other bowler over the five Tests. Seen in this context, his 149 wickets at 29.55, in only thirty-six Tests, are sterling work.

In method he was rare among the finest leg-spinners in relying very heavily on his extremely supple wrist, and rather less than most on his fingers. Rare, but similar to 'Tich' Freeman nevertheless. Two significant advantages accrued from this: his fingers tended to last longer, without lacerations in the skin; and his googly was very hard to pick. Benaud thought Gupte's googly one of the finest he ever saw, since its similarity in appearance to his leg-break made it very difficult to pick – both being looped deliveries which seemed to come down from a great height, causing awkward bounce. Neil Harvey, the Australian left-hander, once rocked back to Gupte's googly and slashed it through point for four in a manner that suggested he had picked it. This caused Gupte to think his googly a vulnerability with Harvey, so he never bowled it again, and perhaps a few other batsmen should have thought about doing the same, if only they'd known they could knock his confidence and make him keep it in the locker.

Of all Gupte's achievements before his disgraced and sad exit from the Test arena, perhaps the greatest was his fathering the culture of spin that blossomed in India thereafter. There can be no doubt that the inspiration he provided directly aided at least part of that great quartet. 'I was listening to radio commentary when Gupte took nine for a hundred and two against West Indies at Kanpur in 1958', said Bedi, reweaving that thread of continuity linking Twirlymen through the ages. 'I was so inspired by that performance that I took up spin bowling. Gupte's feats really spurred me on.'

And how: just as Dennis Lillee's searing, side-on action seems the very epitome of fast-bowling technique, so Bedi's hovercrafting approach to the crease, in anticipation of release at the highest possible point, while perfectly side-on, is as pure a spinner's action as there has been. Indeed, Tony Lewis, who captained England in 1972–3, said he was the Lillee of slow bowling, while Jim Laker reckoned his idea of paradise was being at Lord's on a sunny day with Ray Lindwall bowling from one end and Bedi from the other. 'He moved to the wicket to bowl,' Martin-Jenkins observed, 'with all the lightness of a cloud.' Among slow left arms, he rivals Verity and Rhodes as the greatest. His 1,560 wickets in first-class cricket are more than any other Indian bowler has achieved – 424 more than Anil Kumble.

His different angle provided a variety lacking in that earlier quartet of googly-obsessed South Africans. Bedi had purity. His method seemed very basic: he went round the wicket to the right-hander, gave the ball a huge amount of air, landed it on off-stump, and invited the batsman to drive, often by leaving the cover area vacant. He would do this again and again.

There is a charming story which rather sums up Bedi's approach to bowling. Playing against England at Lord's in 1974, Bedi kept tossing the ball up to England opener Dennis Amiss, who drove him through cover with aplomb. Ajit Wadekar, Bedi's unsympathetic captain, sought additional protection on the off-side, but Bedi resisted. He kept looping the ball up. Amiss kept driving him for four. Eventually Wadekar went over to his star man and, increasingly frustrated, asked him specifically to bowl flatter, shorter and faster. Too bad, Bedi said. I'm a spinner. This is how I bowl. So he kept giving the ball air. Amiss finished on 188, eventually dismissed leg before by Prasanna. Bedi finished with 64.2-8-226-6, and his name on the Honours Boards.

This tale also hints at other aspects of Bedi's character – obstinacy, and its subsidiary trait, a quarrelsome temper. As quick to laugh as to blow his fuse, Bedi is one of the more colourful, and by extension popular, characters the game has thrown up. Not least because his luminous patkas (most often pink or bright blue) made him a fans' favourite. He would make a song and dance about keeping his fingers and wrist supple while fielding, a habit he cultivated by, as we have seen, a combination of yoga and doing his own laundry to keep his digits strong. He skipped for hours, and climbed stairs, to develop fitness for long spells. He was never shy to let a captain know he was prepared to take on some batsmen.

Reticence was not part of Bedi's make-up. 'Bishen is very much in the Sikh mould,' Bose says, 'a warrior who is stout of heart. He could be very difficult to control, and sometimes just go off on one.' Captain of India for twenty-two Tests, Bedi courted controversy because, in his own words, 'I couldn't stand foul play.' At Sabina Park in 1976, he sparked fury when declaring India's innings closed, in protest against the West Indies' intimidating approach to bowling, after two Indian batsmen had been injured. Also in 1976, he publicly accused England's John Lever of using Vaseline to keep the ball surface shiny. The England physio had indeed recommended the team use strips of Vaseline-soaked gauze on their brow, and Lever's ten wickets in the match were achieved with prodigious but suspect swing. Ultimately, Lever was cleared of any wrongdoing. In 1990, as Indian coach, Bedi's suggestion that he would throw the Indian team into the sea if they kept up their abysmal form was met with howls of disdain from a despairing public. He later said of that job that he was glad it was a short-term contract, and 'I didn't enjoy the role much.'

This is the same man whose self-censorship was so inactive that he could say of a fellow spinner, in apparent breach of the fraternity that binds most Twirlymen, 'That man [Muttiah Muralitharan] is the best shot-putter in the history of cricket. People like him are just killing the game and nobody is doing anything about it.' Not content to stop at that, Bedi added that Muralitharan was a 'chucker', a 'monster' who is 'going berserk with his action' and, just for good measure, 'Murali will complete one thousand Test wickets but they would count as mere run-outs in my eyes.' The Sri Lankan threatened legal action, but a defamation case never materialised. And in the autumn of 2010, Bedi issued a widely-publicised dig at Harbhajan Singh by declaring: '[Virender] Sehwag is the best off-spinner in the Indian team'.

Despite all this, his popularity is huge. Although he was forthright in his opinions, he would often demand better remuneration for the players, who he felt were getting ripped off by the Indian board. His protests were decisive in altering the balance of power in India, and in opening the way for national and international megastars such as Sachin Tendulkar and Mahendra Singh Dhoni. When a newspaper appealed for blood donors, Bedi, who belongs to a rare blood group, gave blood in Karachi, away from the cameras. The late politician, Benazir Bhutto heard about it, and sent him two carpets and a tea set; and once word was out, it was said that he could enter any shop in that city and name his price for anything that took his fancy. As he was a Sikh Indian in Pakistan, while partition was still such a recent memory, that speaks of a man with exceptional popular appeal.

Even on the pitch, there was a palpable sense of virtue about him: he would say aloud 'Well played' if some batsman of whom he thought highly had driven him through the covers. When, in the Gillette Cup final, David Hughes of Lancashire hit him for three consecutive sixes, he applauded each one, an act of humble recognition that didn't altogether endear Bedi to his teammates, who had a match to win while he was serving up maximums. Still, he believed in playing the game the right way – respectfully – and so, while quick with anger, he was quicker still with gratitude. When Mike Brearley greeted the bowler at Lord's with a namaste – the Indian clasped-hand greeting – his appreciation was clear.

The main reason for his enduring influence and authority is that, with ball in hand, he was an athlete of beauty and a joy to behold. The gods of cricket would take special satisfaction from each of Bedi's wickets, so completely did they answer to the aesthetic possibilities thrown up by the game. Only ever intimidated by Ken Barrington among batsmen, he seemed abnormally endowed with the patience and bravery required to overcome opponents of the highest calibre. He was slow through the air, but had the subtlest of pace changes, and bullied fielders into the most marginally adjusted positions, so considered was his plan of attack for each individual batsman.

This turbaned aggressor, who had never even seen a Test match before his debut, could call on a crop of outstanding close fielders – India's board having demanded improvement after all the costly chances dropped off Gupte and others in the previous decade. Farokh Engineer was an excellent wicketkeeper to spin, as good as Ian Healy keeping to Warne; and the mercurial Eknath Solkar, one of the first truly great short-leg fielders, was complemented by excellent close catching from Sunil Gavaskar, Gundappa Viswanath, Wadekar and Abid Ali. In Mansur Ali Khan, the ninth and last Nawab of Pataudi, Bedi had an astute captain for part of his India career.

Speaking outlandishly about his national team's fortunes in recent times, Bedi has insisted that India is at its best when producing top-class spinners, and he has chided the authorities for not doing even more to promote spin. He might be forgiven for that when one recalls that many of Bedi's own wickets were taken while Chandrasekhar (cart-)wheeled away from the other end.

Bhagwat Subramanya Chandrasekhar was one of the most flamboyant of all bowlers, as much of an extrovert and showman with the ball in hand as he was an introvert and everyman without it. Nobody who saw his dazzling 6-38 against England at the Oval in 1971, in which he led India to their first Test and series win in England, could fail to put him in the top class of leg-spinners. In method he was most similar to Tiger O'Reilly, bounding in off a long run-up which started with him ostentatiously holding the ball in front of his face, sometimes squinting with one eye, like a rifleman. Bowling at anywhere between slow and brisk medium pace, he relied heavily on top-spinners and a slider bowled out of the front of his hand with a scrambled seam. His stock ball basically behaved like an off-cutter. He also bowled a googly and, just like Anil Kumble two decades later, responded to the suggestion that he had no leg-break by mastering that delivery, so that at the peak of his career he could land it on a sixpence five times out of six, and turn it twelve inches.

The remarkable thing about all this was that the arm he brought over to achieve such fizz and bite off the wicket had been withered by poliomyelitis when he was just five years old. Invalided for three months, he returned from hospital to two loving parents who tried to return his life to normality. They were as thrilled as he was when their defiant boy turned his withered elbow into an instrument of great success, practising for hours at little prompting. As *Wisden* observed, when making him Cricketer of the Year in 1972, 'The belief is that the thinness of his arm gives it the flexibility of a whipcord, enabling him to produce the extra bite in his top-spinner.' We can revise the second half of that sentence, to say that it gave *all* his deliveries extra bite, not just the top-spinner. He threw with his left arm because of the deformity, and was ambidextrous, even bowling left-arm in the nets to help batsmen in need of a different angle. A bone missing in his right wrist meant that sometimes when he brought his arm over the wrist would be cocked more inward than he intended, turning a leg-break into a googly. This made him wild and unpredictable, qualities which suited his extravagant appearance and action. At times he could actually be the fastest bowler in his side, and with the scraggly beard he adopted early on, and the flourish of his flailing arms in a dramatic follow-through, the sight of him, especially as captured in still photographs, suggested all the speedy prowess of a great fast bowler. He even bowled a bouncer once, ironically at Charlie Griffith, the West Indian paceman, hitting him plum on the chest, and causing a delay of an hour that allowed the West Indies to draw the match. Some had it that this was revenge for Griffith hitting Contractor on the head in 1962, leaving the Indian captain with a fractured skull, unconscious for six days, needing two emergency operations, a metal plate in his head, and unable to play for India again. Several of the players in that game gave blood; Chandra, as he was universally known, made his debut two years later, and hit Griffith with that bumper in Madras in 1967.

Although he provided more four-balls than his captain liked, it was at times impossible to judge the length of his deliveries, so quickly did they come off the wicket or rip through the air. Eventually batsmen tried to get forward to him – Cowdrey, Sobers and Barrington had some success doing this, and he felt the last of these was the best he'd bowled against – but that only brought into play the close fielders, primed especially for catches off the shoulder of the bat prompted by the higher bouncing googly.

Chandra opted never to use his arm as an excuse for his other exalted status, as a rabbit without equal. At least he was back then: now he is merely one of only two players in Test history (the other is New Zealand bowler Chris Martin) who scored fewer runs off his bat (167) than he took wickets (242). He completed his fifty-eight Tests with the grand average of four, and with twenty-three ducks, the highest percentage of ducks to innings in Test history. During the 1977–8 tour of Australia, the

Australians gave him a Gray-Nicholls bat with a hole in the middle, in recognition of his unswerving commitment to troubling the scorers as little as possible. Once, when he nicked the ball to 'keeper while playing the West Indies, the umpire called no-ball but Chandra walked. The umpire called him back but he kept going, all the way to the pavilion. His teammates knew it was a no-ball, but didn't bother sending him back because they knew it would make no difference.

Entirely free of airs and graces, he took up a job in a bank, to which he would eventually retire, but a serious scooter accident curtailed hopes of a longer career at Test level. His wife eventually left him, moving to the United States. Controversy attached itself to him once in particular – though not because of any wrongdoing on his part – when there were (unproven) allegations that Pataudi sent him home from a tour of Australia not because Chandra was injured, but, rather, to engineer the call-up of a friend as his replacement. This was bizarre because the friend was an all-rounder who didn't bowl spin, and was therefore not a like-for-like swap.

At his best, Chandra was certainly the most feared of India's great spinners, more so even than Anil Kumble in recent times, and the most likely to make a decisive breakthrough. Precious insight into the terror of facing him was provided by Viv Richards.

It took me a long, long time to come to terms with Chandra. He was the most teasing bowler I ever had to face, and I never quite knew whether I was in charge or not. That was his greatness. His ability to lure opponents into a false sense of security was deadly. How is a batsman supposed to dominate such a man? How can he build his own confidence when he does not know whether the bowler is faking or not? ... To this day he probably remains the one bowler for whom I have most respect. He could do things with the ball that seemed supernatural.

The contrast of both pace and angle between him and Bedi seemed to make an ideal and complete combination of its own accord, but when allied to the off-spin of Erapalli Prasanna and Srinivasan Venkataraghavan, or Venkat – the nickname he has acquired as an umpire (where his trademark raised finger sits on an arm of perfect perpendicularity), and which Brian Johnston opted for after it was suggested that 'Rent-a-caravan' was, as mispronunciations go, a bit impolite – they were even more unplayable.

Perhaps I may be forgiven for remarking that, of the quartet, Prasanna had the closest resemblance to a Bollywood villain with his upturned collar, sleek black hair and arched eyebrows. This helped him very little in his career-long rivalry with Venkat, who emerged as marginally the lesser bowler but went on to play more Tests, and to captain India in the 1975 and 1979 World Cups. In fifty-seven Tests Venkat took 156 wickets at 30; whereas Prasanna, in only forty-nine Tests, took 189 at 30.

More austere in appearance than Bedi or Chandra, Prasanna was originally the bowler with whom that pair were most associated. Years before Warne and Muralitharan arrived on the scene, Trevor Bailey asked Tony Greig who he considered the finest slow left arm, off-spinner and wrist-spinner he had seen; Greig instantly replied Bedi, Prasanna and Chandrasekhar, respectively.

However, Prasanna took time out to complete his degree at the National Institute of Engineering in Mysore, the city from which Chandra emerged. Both were sons of Karnataka. Prasanna's departure from the sport meant there was a five-year gap in which he didn't play Test cricket, and it was during this period that Venkat emerged. As a result,

Prasanna felt to some extent wronged by history – less flamboyant and successful than Bedi and Chandra, and forever compared with his rival off-spinner rather than standing alone. His sense of injustice was compounded by the fact that when Wadekar took the captaincy from Pataudi, he seemed to favour Venkat, and dark mutterings from English and Australian players, suggesting the jerk in his action made it illegal, never quite left him.

It's a measure of just how good Prasanna was that Sobers thought him the best off-break bowler in the world at one point, even though Lance Gibbs was of roughly the same era. In India, they said that he was an even better bowler than Bedi. Like Bedi, he gave the ball plenty of air, inviting the right-hander to drive against the spin, and his functional, uncomplicated action meant he was capable of bowling very long spells. By contrast, Venkat, also an engineer by training, was a spinner much more in the mould of recent English bowlers like Peter Such or John Emburey, spearing the ball in at off-stump, and giving the batsman no width. He could spin it sharply, and had a beautifully side-on action, but was ultimately used as a stock rather than shock bowler.

By the time these Indians had established themselves on the world stage, and shown the Test arena that there was nothing wrong with a spin-dominated attack (indeed, at times it felt like Indian medium-pacers were only in the side to take the shine off the ball as Benaud put it to me), spin was flowering all around the world. Pace thrived, too, of course, but the international men of mystery were by now asserting themselves simultaneously on several continents. In England, the deadly combination of Jim Laker and Tony Lock broke records, while Wardle did something few others had done as well, only for Derek Underwood to come along and bowl even deadlier left-arm spin. In Australia, an axis of flipper merchants continuing the work of O'Reilly and Grimmett were supplemented by possibly the most enigmatic of all spinners, himself the subject of direct imitation a decade later. In the West Indies, lacerated fingers didn't stop Lance Gibbs becoming the first spinner to take three hundred Test wickets. And even South Africa, of all places, produced an off-break merchant of note. To get a full measure of the Second Flourish of spin bowling, and to fully appreciate the terror of what followed, it will serve our purpose to examine these in the order just mentioned.

Interlude Seven

ZOOTER
(OR SLIDER OR NOTHING BALL)

Grip ⠀⠀⠀⠀⠀⠀⠀⠀⠀⠀ *Batsman's Point of View*

 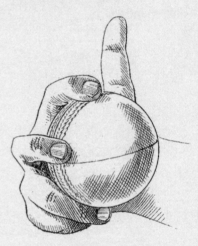

The grip for the zooter is the same as that for the leg-break, googly and top-spinner. The tops of the first two fingers are across the seam. The spin is imparted by the third finger, which straightens from a bent position. But this ball is best thought of as a back-spinner. As the arm comes round, the wrist unfurls, with the back of the hand initially facing the sky, but facing mid-wicket at the point of release. The seam is positioned towards extra cover, and is again spinning along its own axis.

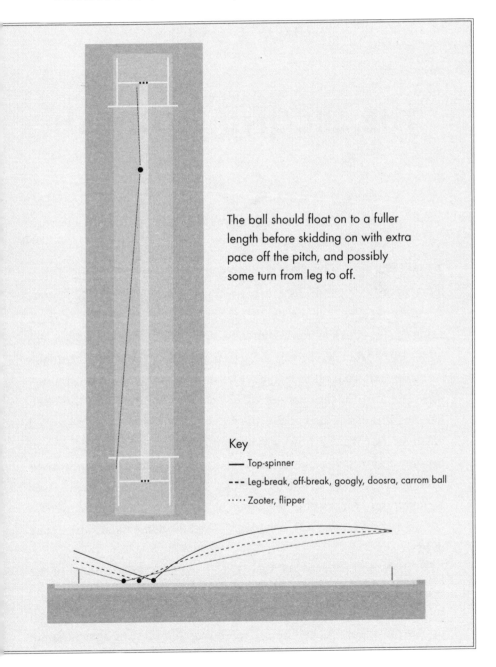

The ball should float on to a fuller length before skidding on with extra pace off the pitch, and possibly some turn from leg to off.

Key

—— Top-spinner

--- Leg-break, off-break, googly, doosra, carrom ball

····· Zooter, flipper

Chapter Eight

THE SECOND FLOURISH

Johnny Wardle, it can safely be said, was the greatest exponent of slow left-arm orthodox and Chinamen bowling that ever played. 'Chinamen', it will be recalled, are the deliveries produced by left-handed bowlers using the leg-break action. Whereas a right-arm bowler's orthodox leg-break turns from leg to off, the left-armer using the same technique turns the ball from off to leg. Most left-armers prefer to bowl orthodox slow left arm (in the manner of Rhodes, Verity, Bedi and the like), because it is easier, and allows the stock ball to leave the right-handed batsman. Not Wardle, however: he wanted to spin it both ways, and so mastered both techniques. Half a century later Muralitharan bowled beautiful leg-breaks at will, but then his stock ball – the off-break – was so much the product of a helicopter wrist that he and Wardle aren't a fair comparison, even if they had both used the same hand, which they didn't.

At the start of the 1950s, Wardle was the best wrist-spinner in the world; and at the same time, only two men, Valentine and Lock, could match him as an orthodox slow left arm. On his day he was better than both in this regard. Laker himself rated Wardle's bowling against South

Africa in 1956–7, when he bowled a left-handed googly (going away from the right-hander) to complement his Chinaman, as the best spin bowling he ever saw. Coming from the man who just months earlier had taken nineteen Australian wickets at Old Trafford in the greatest bowling performance cricket has known, that opinion has some clout. Especially, perhaps, when one considers that during the Durban Test of that series, Peter May specifically instructed Wardle not to deploy his unorthodox method of Chinamen and googlies, thinking it vulnerable. When Wardle bowled Roy McLean, the South African danger man, with an impeccable wrong'un, he let May know his preferred method was working. May, clearly a captain with limited grasp of the nuances of spin, instructed him, again, to revert to orthodox slow left arm. Truly, spinners have always been forced to negotiate their captain's ignorance tactfully.

There have been better pure slow left arms – Rhodes, Verity, Bedi, the former two also from Yorkshire – but never has a bowler used orthodox left-arm spin and Chinamen interchangeably with such efficacy. He learned much of his craft watching Dick Howorth, the brilliant Worcestershire all-rounder, on the MCC tour of the West Indies in 1948, and practised assiduously at every given moment, including on deck while sailing to Australia in 1954. Wardle tended to bowl orthodox slow left arm at Yorkshire because the pitches were slow; but overseas, on quick wickets with true bounce, his Chinamen were deadly. That his arm was bent behind his back until the last possible moment added to the efficacy of disguise, though a fielder standing at short mid-wicket would have a privilege not afforded to the batsman of seeing the grip he was planning to use. Given the substantial difference between his various grips, this made standing at short mid-wicket great fun. Willie Watson, his Yorkshire and England comrade, paid extra close attention to Wardle's grip. If he saw the splayed second and third fingers, he knew it was the Chinaman, so took a few steps back as Wardle approached the crease. Watson snaffled many a catch by doing so.

Just as Freeman didn't play more Tests because of Rhodes, or Venkat because of Prasanna, or MacGill because of Warne, Wardle would be better remembered if Tony Lock hadn't edged him for the slot alongside Jim Laker. And he might have been better, or at least more fondly, remembered if the manner of his departure from the game hadn't been so sour (Gupte presumably had some sympathy for him on hearing of his inglorious departure from professional sport). In 1958, Wardle ghosted a series of articles in the *Daily Mail*, savaging Ronnie Burnet, a forty-year-old appointed captain ahead of him despite his lack of first-class experience. Burnet actually managed to win the title with Yorkshire the following year, and Wardle's incendiary remarks cost him dear: Yorkshire sacked him, and the MCC withdrew the invitation to tour Australia that year. He only played one first-class game after that, in India a decade later, and instead had to take to the lower leagues. This added to the general impression, developed over several years, of a somewhat frustrated man – an impression confirmed by his fierce denunciations of younger players who dropped catches off his bowling. Wardle never forgave Lock for occupying the England slot he felt was his, and was happy to stir rumour – partly true, as it happened – that Lock chucked his quicker ball, if not all the others, too.

It was a bitter end for a bowler who had promised so much, and was clearly exceptionally talented (not least at bridge, which he practised assiduously given a spare hour). From a family of miners, Wardle became an apprentice fitter at the Hickelton Main Colliery at the age of fifteen. Two years later, Major Frank Buckley, that great professional footballer then manager, gave him a trial as inside-forward for Wolverhampton Wanderers. Wardle was good enough to make the next step, but cricket paid better – what a very, very different world that was. He joined Yorkshire, where the great line of spinners would continue in the supremely intelligent fingers and wrist of his left arm. With the stamina required of all great spinners, he survived the trauma of completely losing his rhythm, and his place in the Yorkshire side, when in 1948 an imbecilic coach tried to make him change his action, getting him to cross his legs in the delivery stride.

With ball in hand he was equally happy going over and around the wicket, and rare in his lack of discomfort when there was both a right- and left-hander in the middle. He was one of the most effective of all bowlers at the defensive ploy of bowling a leg-stump line, from over the wicket, at the right-hander in a groove. Incapable of the zip off the wicket Verity achieved, and armed with fewer variations of flight and line than Rhodes or Bedi, he was nevertheless capable of spells of unplayable bowling, especially on sticky wickets. As the cricket writer Rob Steen has argued, his record at Test level, where he took 102 wickets, bears out his dual capacity for attack and defence.

Of the 149 bowlers who have taken more than a hundred wickets at Test level, only six (S. F. Barnes, Colin Blythe, Johnny Briggs, George Lohmann, Bobby Peel and Charlie Turner) have averaged less than his 20.39. Only three among those 149 have a more miserly economy rate than Wardle's 1.89 runs per over: Trevor Goddard (1.64), Lohmann and Verity (both 1.88).

And yet, for all that, Wardle would be forever in the shadow of another bowler, Tony Lock, somewhat ironic when you recall that Lock himself seemed forever in the shadow of Jim Laker. Lock and Laker's association runs very deep, and goes far beyond the sharing of twenty wickets at Old Trafford in 1956; but perhaps the more illuminating parallel for our purposes is that between Lock and Derek Underwood. Both were left-handed spinners for England, yet the appellation 'slow 'when talking about their left arms could hardly be more insulting, so hastily did they come over in both cases.

Lock got fatter rather than flatter with age, but when in his prime during the mid-fifties, two things marked him out: one broadly good, the other broadly bad. The first was his speed. Bowling at slow-medium or medium pace, he was frightfully quick off the wicket, sometimes skidding in with the arm, sometimes fizzing sharply away in the direction of slip.

The second was his crooked arm. Everyone knew that Lock chucked his quicker ball, but there was an influential camp in cricket's fraternity that said he chucked every ball. This led Lock to prolonged bouts of anguish and self-enquiry. He excited little sympathy, despite the known provenance of his technical difficulty, which was the low roof beams at the indoor school in Croydon where this son of Surrey learned his trade. Lock had started out as a flighty slow left arm in the mould of Rhodes or Bedi, but his winter in this indoor school caused his arm to bend, and fundamentally altered his approach to bowling. He pounded his way through the crease with such effort that he needed a steel toecap in his left boot, to stop the sole tearing off. His bent arm was causing consternation, and was the subject of endless gossip. When, after India were beaten in three days in 1952 (including being bowled out twice in one day, both times for under a hundred), Fred Trueman raised the subject with Len Hutton: 'Isn't Tony's new action a bit strange?' Trueman asked his captain, during a drive over the Pennines. Hutton smiled wryly, and added: 'It is, but I think I will beat the Aussies next summer with him.' Sir Len was never one to be distracted from the chance to put one over on the Great Enemy.

In a sign of that perseverance which separates the spinners in these pages from the also-rans of cricket history, Lock remodelled his action not once but twice, having seen film footage of his shortcomings. Still, the remark made to an umpire by Doug Insole, who had just had his stumps rearranged by Lock's 'thunderbolt' delivery, never left him: Insole enquired if he'd been bowled out or run out. Perhaps it was that infamous comment that Bedi was drawing on in his later insults towards Muralitharan. Some claimed this faster ball was genuinely lock-up-your-daughters quick; more likely, it sometimes nudged 80mph.

An obsessive watcher of westerns, which he would frequently scurry off to catch in a local cinema if a new one came out on tour, Lock was an inspirational and successful captain of Surrey during their glory days of the 1950s. He later migrated to Australia where he continued to be an outstanding leader of men. He was one of the first great short-leg fielders, held exceptional catches off his own bowling (Trueman considered him the best catcher he'd ever seen) and appealed as vociferously as some modern-day Pakistanis (well, nearly). But even in his adopted homeland, a sense of controversy lingered around him. In 1964–5, he was sent from the field in a game to wash the Friar's Balsam from his hand. Again, he received little sympathy when pictures were released showing the appalling lacerations on his hand: Lock suffered more, and for longer, than most spinners from raw, bleeding, swollen fingers. Scars from the wounds proved useful weapons in countering the argument that he was a medium-pace bowler rather than a spinner, as did his appearance in the dressing room. As Bailey put it, he was a 'mystifying collection of bandages, elastic stocking supports and various plasters, while his spinning finger was treated by a magic formula which was intended to harden the skin and heal the cuts'.

Friar's Balsam was one thing, and forgivable in the eyes of those who know what spinners suffer for their shilling; but further controversy followed when he was twice accused of assaulting some young girls he was coaching in Australia. He was cleared of both charges, but his reputation never fully recovered.

It's hard to know what makes a man behave in ways that land him in such difficult situations; but it's a consistent thread of Lock's life, sympathetically conveyed in Alan Hill's fine biography, *Tony Lock: Aggressive Master of Spin*, that he seemed insecure at some deep level. He had vulnerabilities, and a sensitive character, and though his anxieties were sometimes the butt of team humour, as when they produced the sleepwalking or vivid nightmares Bailey introduced us to in an earlier chapter, at other times they were more sobering. When he was called for throwing against the West Indies by a square-leg umpire (the uncle of Clyde Walcott, in fact), Bailey reports:

I will never forget the look on Tony's face. He was shattered, as was the team because he was a vital link in our bowling attack. It took quite a time for him to get over that pride-wounding incident and he cut the fast ball out of his repertoire.

But, as Hill argues, it's inevitable that a major cause of Lock's anxiety must have been his association with Laker. It's not widely known that the two didn't speak for about a month after their twenty-wicket extravaganza in 1956, though they were slightly closer friends in later life; and it seems somehow unfair that Lock's fate is to be remembered, in some quarters at least, as simply an appendage to the greatest bowling achievement of all time. Lock said years later that he wished he hadn't denied Laker all twenty, and perhaps from his point of view that would have lessened the focus on his comparative failure in that July Test. It might then have been *all* about Laker, and not just 95 per cent about him, which naturally draws attention to the conspicuous 5 per cent remaining, Lock's solitary wicket (Jim Burke, caught Colin Cowdrey, bowled Lock for twenty-two, first innings). He bowled one more over than Laker in the game, but took eighteen fewer wickets. Peter Richardson, who scored a hundred on the opening day of that Test, recently wrote: 'Lockie would attack; Jim would chip away. It was no secret they didn't get on. They were always competing.'

It's not just what happened at Old Trafford that would have fuelled his inferiority complex: the two were conjoined at Surrey, the alliterative energy of their names forming a music heard down the ages, not least through the immortal lines

Ashes to ashes, Dust to dust
If Laker don't get you, Lock must

(These words were later bastardised and adopted by those fabulous but far simpler creatures, Dennis Lillee and Jeff Thomson, the terrifying Australian fast-bowling duo).

And who couldn't feel inadequate, when bowling at the other end to a man who was essentially unplayable, and in the business of acquiring match figures that, though they may hypothetically be passed, are likely to stand the test of time? As the ever useful Bailey pointed out years later, the tragic thing from Lock's point of view, the thing that must have given him sleepless nights, was that Laker took nineteen of the twenty wickets despite Lock bowling his heart out:

The most remarkable thing was not that Laker took nineteen wickets but that Lock took only one and the reason, of course, was temperament. The more wickets that Laker took, the more Lock tried and tried and the faster and faster he bowled. Meanwhile, Jim just carried on putting the ball on the spot and letting the pitch do the work.

There was no question that Lock felt terribly hard done by. Keith Stackpole, the Australian, asked Lock years later why there was only one wicket in his sixty-nine overs. Lock's answer was blunt – and bitter: 'Destiny was against me: catches fell short, batsmen played and missed, appeals were turned down, nothing went right for me.' This was remarkably similar to the popular account of Laker's ten-wicket haul for Surrey earlier in that season, when Lock again struggled in vain, only to be outshone by Laker. William Keegan, the legendary economics writer still penning his brilliant column for the *Observer*, was at the Oval when Laker took all ten. 'No one was in any doubt,' he told me, 'that Lock was absolutely going hell for leather in both innings. There was no suggestion of him trying to send down long-hops for Laker's benefit.' There is a lesson for young spinners in this, but it speaks of something rather sad and iniquitous, namely that Laker made it look easy while Lock toiled from the other end. The pitch *did* do the work, but only for one of them.

'The mere idea of [Laker] showing enthusiasm,' said Peter May, who captained them both at Surrey and at England level, 'is absurd.' The black-and-white footage we have of that magnificent spell testifies to Laker's method: he loped in with that lackadaisical approach of his, lobbed the ball up to the right-hander from around the wicket and watched the Australians tumble one by one. If the first great lesson of this spell, of letting the pitch do the work, is harder to translate into the modern game because we have covered pitches, the second important lesson – that off-spinners going around the wicket to the right-hander can be a devastating form of attack – is not so hard to translate into the modern game, and should be learned urgently.

Of course, Laker did have the advantage of a sticky wicket – rain dampened, but drying out because of the sun. But posterity should know that from the very start of the game the pitch had been the talking point. Treated with red marl (known as 'treacle') earlier in the season, it seemed certain not to hold together. Gubby Allen, chairman of England's selectors, had instructed Bert Flack, the groundsman, to shave the pitch. He duly did so – and covered the pitch to conceal it from the press. The Australians suspected a conspiracy, knowing what great form the English spinners were in (strange to think there was a day when that sentence didn't seem absurd). But England, batting first, amassed 459 at a speedy rate, dampening the disquiet of the Australians temporarily. As for Flack, his infamy was short-lived, but mainly because of events elsewhere. 'Thank God Nasser had taken over the Suez Canal,' he reflected years later. 'Otherwise, I'd have been plastered over every front page like Marilyn Monroe.'

Half an hour after he started bowling in tandem with Lock, Laker switched to the Stretford End, from where he would take all of his wickets. (This trick has worked well much more recently too: Graeme Swann took 5-76 against Bangladesh in June 2010 by switching to this end.) Less than an hour and a half after Laker and Lock began their partnership (including the tea interval), Australia were bowled out for eighty-four, with Laker having taken 9-37. In the Australian dressing room Ian Johnson, the visiting captain, lambasted his players for their shortcomings against spin, but then declared that they could still win the game if they batted their hearts out. As Benaud has subsequently confirmed, Keith Miller then piped up and said '6-4 we don't'. The Australians left the dressing room deflated.

Their spirits were raised, as so often when one team is being battered, by the arrival of rain. When most of play was washed out by rain through Saturday and Monday – all of it thirstily consumed by the wicket – the Australians thought Miller's prophecy, and cheek, might be trumped after all. But when opener Colin McDonald fell to the second ball after tea, Laker's calm annihilation unfolded. Five bowled, three leg-before, ten caught in the slips or leg-trap and one stumped: footage of the nineteen-wicket rampage is deceptive in how straightforward it makes his approach seem. Around the wicket Laker goes, arm coming over at one o'clock, sometimes lower, a big pivot of his braced front foot, plenty of air, the ball dipping violently on to a fullish length outside off-stump, and the Australians, terrified of coming forward, mostly playing, or failing to play, from the crease. When he took the tenth wicket, John Arlott's commentary came as close to Kenneth Wolstenholme's 'They think it's all over' as cricket can: 'Old Trafford has redeemed itself with a last hour of glorious sunshine. Laker comes in again, hair flopping, bowls to Maddocks, it turns and Laker appeals, and he's out leg-before and Laker's taken all ten!'

The great man responded with the kind of understated emotion you might expect of a chap whose career started in a bank. Throwing his jumper over his left shoulder, and uncrossing his legs from the position they acquired as he made his final appeal, that loping gait of his carried him from the pitch, with what must have felt like a thousand handshakes causing his giant, and now swollen, spinning finger to ache further. That afternoon, a round of interviews finally having been completed, Laker drove away from the ground, heading to London. He stopped off at a pub in Lichfield, Staffordshire, for a pint. Sitting there sipping his beer, not long after producing the greatest of all bowling performances, he wasn't recognised by a single person. And yet all around him the pub was abuzz with chatter about the Test result. When he got home that evening, his wife – who, being Austrian, didn't have a strong cultural affinity with the philosophy of off-spin – said she was perturbed by the dozens of congratulatory phone calls. 'Jim,' she said, 'did you do something good today?' She had her answer when the next morning's *Daily Express* splashed with 'Ten Little Aussie Boys Lakered In A Row'.

That 'something good' would have been more than enough to mark Laker out as a sporting great, but his imprint on the game was strengthened by events after his retirement. He became a dry, witty and perspicacious commentator for the BBC, his voice loved by millions, and his partnership with Benaud made one wonder what they might have done if they could have bowled in tandem as well.

Here, too, was a spinner who, despite the everyman, classless aspect of his character, was not as uncomplicated as that subdued celebration upon his tenth wicket in Old Trafford might have intimated. In the dressing room he was a loner and stubbornly introverted, his favourite companion often the fag in his mouth. Indeed, there seemed an incongruity between his status as a living legend and his boy-next-door lack of glamour. He wrote an angry autobiography which led to his being stripped of honorary membership of Surrey, the club he had served so well as a player. They felt that he had misrepresented them, and were irate at the perceived discourtesy. The MCC felt obliged to show solidarity, stripping Laker of honorary membership with them, too. Both Surrey and the MCC eventually recanted and restored membership, but it left a sour taste. Nor were the game's administrators united in support when he honourably declined the offer to work on Kerry Packer's World Series Cricket in 1970, a decision interpreted as stubborn and old-fashioned.

Born illegitimately in Shipley, near Bradford, in 1922, Jim Laker was the only boy of five children. His father left when he was two, and he was spoilt by a doting mother who was dead by the time he returned from war aged twenty-three. His aunt, a teacher named Ms Ellen Kane, was a cricket nut and introduced him to the game. He had initially wanted to be a batsman or fast bowler, but took up off-spin in time to practise it while serving in the Middle East, partly because even as a child the enormous knuckle on his index finger – that is, his spinning finger – had inspired comment. Some said he was deformed; Laker said he was lucky. It would eventually be the source of his greatest successes in life, though finally it developed arthritis and led to a premature end of his playing days. Before the war he had worked for two years at Barclays in Bradford; later, when billeted at Catford while posted to the War Office, he joined the local club, and soon made it to Surrey, but not before he had enquired as to whether or not he might get into the Yorkshire side. Failure to do so, and the rejection he felt, led to his briefly returning to a career in the bank. In the interim he also missed a trial for Essex because of the lacerations on his spinning finger, and took ten wickets in an innings in a club match, something he would make a habit of.

Laker made his breakthrough relatively late by modern standards – though having seen the case of Grimmett, we can forgive him for so doing. In 1956, aged thirty-four, he had played in only twenty-four Tests, roughly half of those for which he was available. He made that statistic look silly when he took those nineteen wickets, but it wasn't simply that performance that suggested he'd been underused by England. Laker had taken the phenomenal figures of 8-2 in the Test trial at Bradford, his home town, in 1950, a performance he rated as his finest ever. The Australians knew about this reputation before they arrived in 1956, but if there had been any lingering doubts about his skill, they would have been dispelled by that 10-88 he took when they played against Surrey early that very season. He later said he thought this a better performance than his Test 10-fer, given the quality of the pitch (as against the deteriorating track in Manchester). By painful irony, Laker only got the ten Australian wickets narrowly: Miller was dropped at extra cover when the Australians were nine down. The bowler? Step forward, Tony Lock. He seems wronged many, many times over.

Sometimes known by the same epithet as that other great spinner – Tiger – because of his energy in the gully, there should be no doubt that Laker's best attribute as a bowler was ferocious, devilish, air-munching spin. It was said that even in Test matches, with packed crowds, you could hear from the boundary the rip he gave the ball. This spin he allied to unfailing accuracy, and on rain-affected pitches he would go around the wicket to right-handers with sometimes five close fielders on the leg-side. 'A craftsman in a great tradition,' wrote Cardus, 'a classic exponent of off-spin, the most classic of all kinds of bowling.'

Such competence made him probably the finest orthodox off-spinner to play the game, though it's hard to account for the exact benefit he derived from uncovered wickets. He was the best spinner to play for England and on his day the finest bowler, too. Certainly, if Barnes could claim to be the most complete bowler, Laker could claim to have been intermittently the most unplayable. And yet, for all that, the wonderful thing is that he had, at least in the years before that Old Trafford Test, genuine rivals for the status not only of best bowler in the world, but best spinner, too – and the two men who came closest to rivalling him were both bowlers whose stock ball came in from the off.

One of them was a South African. There are many things worth knowing about Hugh 'Toey' Tayfield, but two stand out: first, he is the finest spin bowler South Africa has produced, notwithstanding the googly quartet of the early twentieth century; second, he derived his nickname from neuroses even more fundamental to his character than those that afflicted many other spinners in these pages. As ever, the sharpest explanation for its provenance is to be found in *Wisden*, which, when naming him a Cricketer of the Year for 1956, provided the following:

He belongs to the breed of cricketers who compel the interest of spectators. His habit of kissing his cap for luck at the start of each over has been criticised as ostentation, but it is characteristic of Tayfield that he should remain quite unmoved in his determination to continue the ritual. It began during the triumphant Melbourne Test of 1952–53. Australia were 84 for no wicket when Tayfield kissed his cap in desperation. Immediately A. R. Morris gave a return catch and the habit was born.

Tayfield has no explanation, however, for the other mannerism that led the Australians to christen him Toey at the outset of his Test career. Whether preparing to wheel into his brief, lopsided run or waiting for the next ball to be bowled to him while batting, he taps the toe of each boot firmly on the ground two or three times. Yet such is his intense concentration that he is hardly aware of doing so.

He really did challenge Laker for the best bowler of their kind. In the same entry, from Laker's year, *Wisden* said: 'Tayfield came to England again last year, not this time as a late reserve but with the reputation of being the best bowler of his type in the world.' (Laker himself wasn't a candidate for the honour of Cricketer of the Year having won it in 1952 – players may only receive the award once, though Jack Hobbs – 1909 and 1926 – and "Plum" Warner – 1904 and 1921 – are exceptions to that rule.)

Tayfield was like Underwood in being rare for a spinner because he flourished early. Born into a cricketing family – S. H. Martin, his uncle, played for Worcestershire, and his brothers Arthur and Cyril played for Transvaal, along with two cousins – Tayfield broke into the Natal side at the age of seventeen. And when the promising spinner Athol Rowan was struck down by knee trouble, Tayfield was called up for Test cricket at just twenty years old. He quickly developed a reputation as a man whose bowling had two foundations: parsimony and shrewd tactics. Turning the ball less than Laker, he bowled from very close to the stumps, often along a line of middle to middle stump, but such was the drift away from the right-hander that edges to first and second slip were always a possibility, and batsmen had to play every ball. He flighted the ball much more than Ramadhin, who bowled a similar line around the same time. Tayfield's great innovation was to bowl with two silly mid-ons, often nearly shoulder to shoulder, while leaving extra cover open for the batsman to drive through. Quite apart from snaffling many of his 170 Test wickets with catches in this way, it cut off one of the few risk-free scoring possibilities for batsmen getting bogged down by his relentless accuracy.

His economy rate is some indication of their reluctance to take up this invitation. Over the course of his career, he conceded just 2.06 runs per over in first-class cricket, and even fewer – 1.94 – in Tests. And that was in eight-ball overs.

He bowled 137 balls – that's twenty-two six-ball overs and five balls – without conceding a run against England at Durban in 1956–7. At the

Oval in 1955, he came on at 12.30 on the third day, bowled unchanged until close of play and acquired figures for his spell of 52-29-52-4.

This meant he was regularly more stock than shock bowler, though the fact that he still ran through so many sides, and took so many wickets against very strong England and Australia batting line-ups, counts in his favour. He was one of those spinners who suffered as a result of the rule change, circa 1960, that meant the leg-side field could only have five men, with two behind square, though as an off-break bowler who relied more on subtle variations of flight than turn, he got off more lightly than some spinners. Again, the deleterious impact of law changes on spinners seems to have passed with limited contemporary comment.

Tayfield nearly retired before his career had really got going: a rugby accident while playing for Durban High School Old Boys in 1950 damaged his bowling shoulder severely. A Durban osteopath put it right, but required of him that he give up tennis and squash, two favourite pastimes, for ever. Tall, strong and good looking – features he shared with Laker – he was married and divorced five times. In later life his business ventures were unsuccessful.

He must be seen, in the final analysis, as falling short of Laker's exceptional standard, and not just because Gentleman Jim took twenty-three more wickets (albeit in nine more Tests). In essence, Laker spun it more, meaning that in an age of uncovered pitches he was better able to exploit the full range of conditions. He could also use the angle from around the wicket more effectively; Tayfield, not being a big turner, couldn't bring it back into the right-hander as sharply. And the same elegant run-up and action that caused Tayfield to bowl from so close to the stumps while over the wicket, took him to the edge of the crease when bowling around it, so that his drift away from the right-hander, and lack of spin back into him, restricted his variety.

In such ways could Laker plausibly maintain, were he so immodest to do so, that he was a better bowler. The statistics and prevailing opinion of the time bear this out. But there was another bowler, one harder to classify, who for a few short years, perhaps just before Laker's prime, could claim to be fleetingly the most terrifying bowler in cricket. The irresistible charm of his contribution to the game not only comes from the fact that he was a spinner – so complex a character would never take up pace bowling – but also from his being a riddle, wrapped in a mystery, inside an enigma.

All serious students of cricket must surely be in debt to the brilliant writer Gideon Haigh, not least for his exemplary biography of Jack Iverson, *Mystery Spinner*. In it, we learn that the Iversons were estate agents in the part of Melbourne, St Kilda's, made famous by Shane Warne. 'Big Jack' was utterly uninterested in batting, one of the most comically inept fielders ever to play cricket and, it seems, one of the more insecure human beings produced by the Antipodes. At the age of fifty-eight, he succumbed to the mental fragility that had plagued him for nearly six decades and took his own life, by a gunshot to the chest. He had developed atherosclerosis of the brain in his fifties, and the depressive bouts proved too much. Yet for a few years at the start of the 1950s he employed a bizarre (though not unseen) grip to become one of the greatest bowlers of all time.

How can that be claimed of a man who played just one Test series – a mere five Tests, against England in 1950–51? Well, it can, and the testimony of those who saw him in action demands it. In that solitary series, he took twenty-one wickets at 15.73 runs apiece, including 6-27 in the second innings of the third Test at Sydney. Indeed, he played in only one game for the next two seasons, before giving cricket up for good, to return to the real estate business in Australia's suburban heartland whence he sprang. Benaud and Miller have always maintained that had Australia taken Iverson to England for the Ashes tour of 1952–3, they would have come home with the urn, rather than losing 1-0. But Iverson was something of a tortured soul, who would break easily under pressure, either if opposition batsmen got after him or if his captain for Australia, Lindsay Hassett, didn't place his field for him. It stemmed, many felt, from the same curiously quiet and anxious character who used to flick a table-tennis ball out of nervousness, almost as if to give him an excuse not to have to talk to those around him.

He had been a fast bowler at Geelong College, but started to contemplate the possibilities offered by spin when going 'on the land'. This Australian phrase, roughly today's equivalent of taking a gap year, means time spent away from home when rural isolation is meant to offer a young man the chance to think himself into adulthood. Iverson thought a lot about spin bowling as he worked as a 'jackaroo' – an Australian term for a young trainee stockman – in the Mallee, a district in the state of Victoria.

It was several years later, when posted to Papua New Guinea having trained as an ack-ack (anti-aircraft) gunner in the artillery, that his nervous tick with a table-tennis ball evolved, as he whiled away hours in the jungle, away from the front line. Sergeant Iverson found that with a bigger ball – a cricket ball – he was still capable of imparting ferocious spin. It is worth noting, before coming to Iverson's own account of his grip, that Peter Philpott, who played at Test level, experimented with the grip but tore a ligament in his middle finger and was out of action for a month. Iverson suffered for his art, teaching other spinners a particular lesson along the way: avoid the Iverson grip unless it comes naturally to you. As 'Big Jake' put it in a piece by R. S. Whitington for *Sporting Life*, in one of the most precious fragments of wisdom laid down by any spinner:

The idea was to try and spin the ping pong ball to beat the bat – the 12" ruler – and hit the pole. I found that by flicking the ball (as one does with a marble) with the thumb across the index and second finger, I could send it up straight, but could not impart any spin.

Then I got the idea of doubling the second finger of my hand back into the palm, placing the ping pong ball on the back of that finger and holding the ball in position with my thumb. With this grip I did not have to use my index, third, or fourth fingers. My second finger became a lever or spring and by releasing that finger I could get an abnormal amount of spin.

I also found that if I held my thumb horizontally to the left I could flick the ball far to the leg side of the tent pole and make it break terrifically towards the pole.

Under the rules of our French cricket we weren't allowed to lift our elbow and bowl over-arm, so I could not reverse the process and point the thumb to the right or leg side and deliver an 'off-break' or 'wrong'un' as it is called. So I started flicking the leg spinner. I found that I could flick the ping pong ball about six feet in the air with this one. It would drop quickly and bounce two feet in front of where the batsman played for it. I got a lot of catches at silly mid on or silly point with this ball. Also, with this action, the ball would come in as an in-swinger and, when it pitched, turn sharply to leg.

Here is the familiar drift into the right-hander for the leg-break, as demonstrated best by Warne's infamous delivery to Gatting. Returning to Australia, Iverson was interested chiefly in indulging his fondness for golf and tennis rather than cricket, but then, while out for a walk with his wife on Jolimont Park (just next to the Melbourne Cricket Ground), he saw something that would change his life, and cricket, forever. A game of cricket was underway, involving players from the Melbourne School for the Blind. Iverson found the sight of it utterly inspirational. As Whitington explained:

The courage and persevering determination of those blind players began a train of thought and resolve working in Iverson's mind. 'If those chaps with all their handicap can do as well as that, I'm going to give my bowling discovery a go', muttered Jack, more to the nearest oak tree and the summer air than to his wife.

'And Johnny [another nickname], if you take it up, I know you well enough to be certain you'll finish in there', said Jean Iverson, pointing to the adjoining MCG.

He did have a go, and he did finish in there. With the benefit of hindsight, and knowing how Iverson struggled with his inner demons for so long, there is something very moving about the image of him watching blind cricketers and resolving to make more of his own ability. He had only one life, he probably surmised – but that would be cut short.

His career at the top level was very brief, but while it was ongoing he struck fear into opponents as few others have done. Hassett, who also played for Victoria, stopped Iverson from bowling at New South Wales batsmen in nets sessions for Australia, so as to make him more effective in Sheffield Shield games against them. This certainly helped to preserve a bit of mystery about him, but the main source of his enigmatic presence at the crease – quite apart from the fact that many of his teammates felt they barely knew him – was the curious nature of his delivery.

With an audible flick, it looked for all the world as if he was bringing his arm over merely to dispose of a cigarette end. At six foot three, he was a huge and strong presence at the crease, giving his unconventional release an authority it might otherwise have lacked. Few players, as Johnny Gleeson remarked years later, could decipher how his digits were strong enough to flick the ball fifteen yards, let alone twenty-two, and the fact that his stock ball was a high-bouncing googly, with plenty of over-spin, simply added to the riddle. Each ball was spun with tremendous zest, and though there was a lingering impression that he didn't turn his leg-break much, it needed only to hold its line to be a deadly variant, so quickly did his stock ball come in from the off. Dozens of batsmen complained that, despite convincing themselves the next ball was a googly, they saw it come out of the back of his hand in such a fashion that it forced them to interpret the delivery as a leg-break. At times, Iverson would home in on the right-hander's leg-stump, making him play everything and using a phalanx of close fielders on the leg-side, to smother any opportunity that came their way.

He was possibly the first man to whom the label 'mystery spinner' was formally attached, and Iverson's aura was only strengthened by the brevity of his time in the Test arena. The strength of his digits ran contrary to the weakness of his spirit, and his overreliance on Hassett led batsmen to believe (correctly) that if they attacked him, his brittle confidence would snap.

It was in the fourth Test of his one and only series that Iverson suffered the ankle injury that would force him to limp out of the game altogether. The sense of anti-climax was both palpable and, in retrospect, fitting for such a profoundly complicated man. 'The overriding feeling,' Benaud says, 'is that was a sad ending for an extraordinary cricketer.'

That it may have been, and it is typically courteous of Benaud to say so, but one of the men who benefited from the demise of Iverson was Benaud himself. Had it not been for the brevity of Iverson's career at the top level, Benaud might not have broken into the Australian side. And given the quality of other bowlers in Australia at the time, including Bruce Dooland, the leg-spinner, there's no guarantee at all that Benaud would be known to us as the man he is today. But there is a further instance of amazing luck that made Benaud's career possible, and it stems from a story seldom told.

It is one of the less well-known facets of Richard Benaud's life that he owes his extraordinary career – in which he never lost a series as captain of Australia, became in 1963 the first man to take 200 wickets and score 2,000 runs in Tests, and over four decades became both the voice and the face of the sport through his trademark diction, extreme fairness and unflinching optimism – in considerable measure to his contracting dengue fever in India.

As he recounts in his autobiography, throughout Benaud's early career the webbing and calluses on his fingers were constantly being ripped because of the effort involved in spinning the ball. Even when struggling to bear the pain, its severity was a huge distraction as he came in to bowl. Colin McCool, a feisty character and another Australian leg-spinner, told him at the end of a day's play at the Gabba: 'Son, find some bloody way to fix those or you'll have an extremely short career.' Benaud had used methylated spirits to harden his skin, and Friar's Balsam to soften it. In the winter of 1956, a few months after Laker's heroics against them, Australia were playing three unofficial Tests in New Zealand. During a two-day warm-up game against Combined Minor Associations in a town called Timaru, Benaud decided to walk to a local chemist's he'd spotted earlier, to pick up a prescription for dengue fever, which he had contracted two months earlier while touring India and was causing him to black out. It was a pleasant, sunny afternoon on the quiet east coast of the South Island.

As he picked up the sulphanilamide with his right hand, Ivan James, the chemist, asked him why he had so many lacerations inside the top knuckles of his fingers. Benaud, then little known, explained he was a spin bowler and devoted to his craft. James replied that he had a lot of ex-servicemen who came in with similar symptoms, or with leg ulcers, because they were suffering the after-effects of being gassed. Free of charge, he passed him 'a small, wide-mouthed bottle about two inches high, and it said on it OILY CALAMINE LOTION BPC '54 [a reference to the year it was listed in pharmaceutical books]'. James also passed him a container of boracic acid powder. Within days, Benaud's fingers were fixed; he had worked out how to apply the lotion to the pressure points on his fingers, and so create thick, padded areas (entirely legal, of course), with which to impart sharp spin – but without Ivan James his career would have been unrecognisable as the one we know today. It is a debt that Benaud, typically, has repeatedly acknowledged in public, making special mention of James in many of his books and speeches (nearly as many as his wife Daphne, in fact). Though he might have prospered as a batsman, without James's intervention Benaud thinks he would have had to give up bowling, and his later captaincy of Australia would have been jeopardised. Amazing to think that if he'd reached over the counter with his left rather than right hand, most of us would probably never have heard of him.

His father Lou was a first-grade player and leg-spinner who once took twenty wickets in a match, and his brother John played three Tests for Australia as a batsman. Benaud grew up in Parramatta, western Sydney, where his father introduced him to cricket, and as a child he once saw Clarrie Grimmett at a game. Lou had regretted being posted to the country as a school teacher, where he spent twelve years. In *On Reflection*, Benaud recalls his father saying, 'If ... there were any sons in his family he would make sure they had a chance [to make a cricket career] and there would be no more school teachers in the Benaud family.' A philosophy of due diligence and industry, and a liberal attitude towards players getting rich, would be hallmarks of Benaud's career, not least when he was pivotal in pushing through Kerry Packer's limited-overs revolution in the 1970s.

Among the many maxims now widely accepted in the game that owe their provenance to this man of Huguenot descent – he still owns a house in the French village, about a hundred miles west of Lyons, bearing his name – is the claim that, for the best spinners, spin comes first, accuracy comes after. Which is not to say accuracy doesn't matter: the idea that spinners automatically go for plenty of runs has, as Peter Philpott argues, been hugely damaging. Rather, Benaud rightly says you cannot teach an accurate medium-pacer to be an on-the-spot spinner; but you can teach a bowler who gives it a rip, but lacks control, to land the ball in the right areas consistently. This Benaud did, with fabulous success, and it is a useful way of understanding his acquired rather than instinctive brilliance. The best sportsmen – as Matthew Syed, *The Times* columnist and former England table tennis number one, puts it in his book *Bounce* – owe their success above all not to genetic inheritance but to relentless practice. Benaud personifies that dictum.

He had a very high, classically side-on action, with a full sweep of the arm ending a sprightly jog on an angle of around 30 degrees. At the crease a pronounced retreat of his left arm would leave him looking over his shoulder at the batsman, before a considerable pivot involved his body wholly in the imposition of spin. He was reliant on over-spin (too reliant, on his first tour of England, according to Bailey), getting the ball to turn but not always sharply, and in the classical mould concerned to make it dip steeply at the end of its trajectory, and so beat the batsman in the air. And because the other side of the over-spin coin is steepling bounce, he would frequently have batsmen caught at silly mid-off while driving, or caught behind off a top edge as they went back to cut a ball short of a length, only to find it get up to nearly chest height. Accusations that he didn't turn the ball as sharply as other leg-spinners of the time hurt him, however. He once heard that Peter May, on seeing a nets bowler send down a leg-break that didn't turn sharply, remarked 'he's bowled me a Benaud'. This, Benaud says, 'had the effect of spurring me on to a considerable degree'. Not least when bowling to May, at whom he once sent down twenty-four consecutive googlies.

Yet it is true that Benaud's trademark as a bowler was his accuracy, the product of that relentless practice and discipline. He very rarely bowled a ball too short, and few batsmen took him on successfully. He had a googly that was often confused for his top-spinner, but inflamed tendons and bursitis were a powerful antidote to its overuse. That, and Fred Trueman. Having a drink with Benaud and Neil Harvey during the first Test at Brisbane on the 1958–9 tour, the Yorkshire great told Benaud that, for a top-rate spinner, his googly was too easy to pick. Benaud was surprised at this, and duly bowled a googly to Trueman in the game two days later. Trueman picked it, and hit it into the stand at long on. Benaud hardly bowled a googly at Trueman again that series.

Trueman also reckoned he could pick Benaud's flipper (learned from Dooland – see below), noting that his right elbow seemed to come out, 'pointing towards a position between mid wicket and mid on' during the delivery stride. Benaud went away to work on disguising his flipper, but the constant threat of googly disease put him off overemploying the wrong'un. Indeed, it was bowling a googly to Tom Graveney on 30 April 1961 that signalled the demise of his career. He had torn the fibres of the (aptly named, given the joy and misery it has given to Twirlymen through the ages) super spinatus tendon which runs along the top of the shoulder and is connected to the third finger, the spinning finger.

In all, Benaud captained Australia in seven series over five years, winning five and drawing two. He was one of the outstanding all-rounders in cricket history, a swashbuckling batsman and one of the first truly brilliant fielders. He was a late developer, too, flourishing as a batsman long before his bowling was renowned, and only being considered a world-class player after his exploits on the tour of South Africa in 1957–8. Indeed, on his first tour of England he took just two Test wickets, having been one of three bright young all-rounders (the others were Ron Archer and Alan Davidson) trying to be the next Keith Miller. And, on his second, he and Ian Johnson took sixteen Test wickets between them, while England's Jim Laker and Tony Lock grabbed sixty-one for their efforts.

The bowling high point of his career came when, at Old Trafford for the fourth Test of the 1961 series, England were 150-1 chasing 256. Despite having acute pain in his shoulder, Benaud came on, but unconventionally went around the wicket, using footmarks at the other end and bowling several pure top-spinners to bring his newly inserted leg-slip and leg-gully into play. He took 5-12 in twenty-five balls (not 5-13, as is often misreported), and Australia won comfortably. Later, at a press conference, Benaud said that, far from winning the match himself, it was Trueman's footmarks that the Australians had to thank for victory. Trueman was dropped for the fifth and final Test at the Oval, despite having match figures of 11-88 at Headingley in the third Test. He searched Benaud out to tell him that he had bowled from the Stretford End, not the Warwick Road End, so Benaud's thesis must be false. 'I know,' said Benaud, 'but we didn't want you to play in the last Test and it worked.'

Never short of cunning, he has always been distinguished by his thoughtfulness and intelligence. It is intriguing that, for a man known to millions for his talking, he was an exceptionally good listener, too – and especially when it was his fellow spinners doing the talking. There was, of course, his session with Tiger O'Reilly in a Scarborough hotel on the 1953 tour, where he learned, and took on, the Tiger's six leading principles of spin bowling. But it was from another of his countrymen that, on the next tour of England, in 1956, Benaud learned the delivery that really promoted him from top-class spinner to one of the greatest.

It's a good thing Australians like to talk. During that Ashes tour, Benaud found himself having a few beers in the dressing room at Trent Bridge. Play had closed on the Saturday of a tour match, and, with no play on Sundays in those days, Benaud was preparing to head back to his hotel. He was intercepted by Dooland, an avuncular Australian well established at Nottinghamshire CC, who congratulated Benaud on his 160 not out against Worcestershire ten days earlier in the tour opener. Asking how Benaud was getting on, Dooland received a reply to the effect that Benaud was a much better bowler now, because he'd calmed down and stopped trying to bowl six variations in a single over (having heeded O'Reilly's advice). Dooland expressed his pleasure at hearing this, but asked Benaud if he'd tried to master the flipper. Benaud said he hadn't. Dooland, who had shortened his run-up and changed his action to incorporate the delivery within his armoury, invited him to turn up an hour early at the ground on the Monday, where he would have a net set up especially at the Radcliffe Road End. Benaud duly did this, and, though his first few attempts at the under-the-wrist delivery went through as full tosses, he went on to practice it for a year. When he first tried it in a match, in a one-day game against Rhodesia at Kitwe in 1957, he took 9-16, six of them with flippers. Dooland's wisdom had been passed down a generation, and Benaud's deployment of the flipper would save this excellent delivery from obscurity for ever.

It was another Australian leg-spinner, meanwhile, who showed him the slider, the ball out of the front of the hand that skids on, usually with a scrambled seam, and looks deceptively like the leg-break. Doug Ring, who played thirteen Tests for Australia, picked up an apple on a railway journey after the Lord's Test of 1953, and showed Benaud how to bowl it. The ball, which Terry Jenner, ever one for clarity, also refers to as the back-spinner, became an essential part of Benaud's armoury – and that of his successors, right through to Warne. Jenner, who together with Allan Border would be Warne's most important mentor, was one of a countless number who profited from Benaud's generosity and had reason to thank Ring for passing the knowledge on. 'Richie never has been a guy who'd seek you out, but I used to seek him out, and he was always fantastic,' Jenner said. 'He showed me a ball called the slider, back-spinner, not to be confused with the flipper. It's one that keeps low, a good lbw ball, and in the end I bowled it pretty well.'

Unlike modern flipper merchants such as Warne, who release the ball with their wrist on top of it, and so set the seam spinning on the line followed by the equator around earth, Benaud, with his high action, sometimes released his flipper with the back of his hand facing gully. This meant the seam was, just occasionally, closer to vertical than horizontal, and by keeping the shiny side of the ball on the left – that is, the off-side – Benaud discovered his flipper would occasionally drift into the right-hander, before skidding on. Quite what it did off the pitch depended on how scrambled the seam was. This was a marvellous addition to his repertoire, not least because, since the ordinary leg-break drifts into the right-hander, too, the disguise was convincing.

But, variation being the key to disguise, the in-swerving, vertical-seam flipper was only an occasional ploy. As Benaud himself told me: 'The flipper I bowled, which was taught to me by Bruce Dooland at Trent Bridge in 1956, [generally] had the seam horizontal. It is true that my flipper often moved in the air into the right-hand batsmen, but it would have been unwise to hold the seam in the same position all the time because the batsman would straight away pick it as the flipper. Common sense dictated that I often varied the angle of the seam.'

Not just common sense, but wisdom; and it follows from this that if Benaud did bowl the occasional flipper with the seam pointing towards third man – Rajan's Mystery Ball, as I coined it in the context of Grimmett's flippers, which skids into the right-hander – it wasn't a regular, concerted ploy.

For years, Benaud's 248 wickets at Test level was a record for a leg-spinner. If that seems mere nostalgia now, his enduring influence in the game has ensured his legacy goes far beyond those statistics. Few players have influenced a modern, international sport to the extent that he has, whether in an informal, mentoring role to other greats, such as Warne, or in an administrative role, as when Kerry Packer turned to him to give World Series Cricket respectability. Most of all, those clipped Australian syllables, interspersed with vast, open vowels, have made cricket's artistic and moral merits accessible to millions. Together with Michael Holding, he must still be the finest of sporting commentators (though Warne is now pushing him close), owing an entire career to the basic philosophy that if you can't add to what the viewer can already see, shut up. When the novelist and satirist Anthony Powell edited a literary magazine, he told critics to write reviews concisely: 'say what it's about, what you think of it', and perhaps make a joke. Adopting this formula made Benaud, with his inimitable vocabulary (South African Lance Klusener hits his first ball for six: 'He's given that something. He's given it some humpty') no less than the voice of the game. 'Morning everyone', this Yoda would say, and you knew he didn't need the prefix 'Good'.

As captain, he had two maxims: first, captaincy is 90 per cent luck; second, eleven heads are better than one. Few professionals challenge either of these assertions confidently today. As a bowler, he was the first to go for really outlandish celebrations, albeit they were still rather mild compared to Monty Panesar, who would generally run for the hills (in the direction of third man) if he knocked a bail over. Benaud has the humility to say that, having watched Warne, he wishes he'd been more of a side-spinner, and thrown in more big-turning leg-breaks to discomfit the batsman. He says that despite the fact that he was constantly having injections in his shoulder to ease the pain. And, in writing his genuinely excellent autobiography, he lacked the self-regard of modern sportsmen in thinking the cricket more interesting than the character, and therefore calling it *Anything but ... an Autobiography.*

'If one player, more than any other, has deserved well of cricket for lifting the game out of the doldrums, that man is Richard Benaud.' So began *Wisden*'s paean to him in naming him Cricketer of the Year for 1962. Jack Fingleton compared him to Jean Borotra, the 'Bounding Basque of Biarritz' who captivated tennis fans in the 1920s. Wisden later settled for the description: 'the most popular captain of any overseas team to come to Great Britain'.

His contribution to the game is especially remarkable since on so many occasions it was nearly cut off before he'd really got going. Quite apart from his debt to Ivan James, there was a fractured skull after missing a hook while playing for New South Wales Second XI early in his career, and his nearly becoming a journalist after his training on the

Sydney Sun (a pastime to which he later returned with a vengeance). And he might have been an accountant, too: early on in his career, Benaud lost his job with a firm of accountants because they 'couldn't afford to pay the six pounds a week which would have been my due'. Had they been able to, he might not have suffered for long the minimal salary cricketers then received.

Never so conservative as to resist the march of the game, he always welcomed change, whether through the Packer revolution or, more recently, the emergence of decisive video technology and Twenty20. Marcus Berkmann summarises excellently: 'he sees the modern game as an enhancement on former glories, not as a disappointing echo of them'. Indeed, for all that Benaud hates the defeatism of nostalgia, we shall never see the like of him again.

The same was said of the Australian he had replaced as the best leggie from Down Under – Iverson. But with complete disregard for the natural rhythm of mystery spinners, a few years later along came another Australian leg-spinner who seemed to employ the Iverson grip to briefly bamboozle his way into the hearts of his countrymen, and the nightmares of his opponents. Johnny Gleeson is usually and best understood as a kind of Iverson 2.0. He used the same middle-finger grip as Iverson – though, as we have seen, it should really be called the 'Armstrong–Iverson grip' rather than the 'Iverson grip' – and, like his more immediate and illustrious predecessor, his career at the top level was short. Indeed, Gleeson spent only six years playing the game professionally.

He started as a batsman and wicketkeeper, touring the world with a collection of bush cricketers called the Emus, as reserve 'keeper in 1961, long before making his first-class debut at twenty-eight. The Emus were a collection of amateurs from across New South Wales, brought together by a Mr J. S. White for an annual competition and tour. Before then, Gleeson had studied at engineering college (just like Venkat and Prasanna) and been a postal technician, a career suited to a man who was among the most reserved individuals ever to play the game. In this respect, then, Gleeson shared attributes with those other quiet men of spin who played in the middle decades of the twentieth century, Grimmett, Ramadhin and Laker. Ironically, though he never played alongside Iverson, Gleeson was just like those others in living forever in the shadow of a more celebrated fellow countryman, in this case 'Big Jake'.

He watched Iverson obsessively, first coming across his grip in a photograph in a 1951 copy of *Sporting Life*, and, as David Frith observes, of the very many who were fascinated by that mercurial cricketer, Gleeson was one of the very few who could ape his method effectively. He met the object of his unrequited fascination while playing for New South Wales Second XI in Victoria. Iverson was at the ground and asked to meet his putative successor in the canon of mystery men. But their meeting was awkward; Iverson asked Gleeson how he bowled his leg-spinner, and the conversation foundered on Iverson's failure to grasp Gleeson's explanation – bizarre given their mutual expertise on the subject.

It was in Vancouver, Canada, of all places, on the Emus' world tour that Gleeson's years of practice with this unorthodox method finally paid off, and prompted him to abandon his pads and box in favour of spinning. Years later, in an essay for that delightful book *Cricket: The Australian Way* (1972), he documented the early development of these idiosyncrasies:

I had my delivery – bowled with two fingers, the thumb and middle finger, behind the ball – for about ten years before I used it in a match. I bowled it only in practice and had no idea of its value. The first time I let it go was against a group of school kids on a paspalum wicket with a jacaranda tree for stumps.

Later he would practise with a tennis ball, before graduating to a cricket ball, just as Saqlain Mushtaq did on the rooftops of Lahore. And the strength of his digits, he said, was down to the hours he spent as a child milking cows on his parents' farm in the outback. This, and the admission that 'My thumb has always been a bit "dicky" and bent, and seemed to just naturally go in behind the ball to support the middle finger for this grip', made him almost uniquely qualified to employ the Armstrong–Iverson method. This he did during a modest Test career, between 1967–8 and 1972, during which he bowled an orthodox off-break and a leg-break, googly and top-spinner delivered from the back of the hand using the Armstrong–Iverson technique. He used various labels to try to convey the difficulty and painfulness of this– 'knuckle-breaks', 'flickers', 'finger-crushers' – but decided 'none of these terms seem adequate'.

He bowled the leg-break as his stock ball to the right-hander (unlike Iverson), and the off-break as his stock ball to the left-hander, 'because the best way to get someone out is to take the ball away from the bat'. He was much shorter than Iverson – albeit with longer fingers – and a collapsed front knee meant he coursed a consistently flat trajectory, never really trying to deceive the batsman in the air, and bowling 'with the breeze', he said, rather than against it. He didn't turn the ball sharply, but got it to skid through and deviate at least the width of the bat consistently. Even in 1972, he was trying to learn the more orthodox method of delivering the leg-break and googly, and so intent was he on maintaining an air of mystery throughout that he boasted of not daring to bowl 'the Iverson stuff' at 'club, State, or even Australian practice'.

When Benaud saw him for the first time at Gunnedah in New South Wales in 1965, he watched him from his car and then, concerned at the ease with which he was bamboozling batsmen, watched him through binoculars from behind the bowler's arm. Benaud told Gideon Haigh that he thought he'd worked Gleeson out as 'simply a leg-break bowler who looked like an off-spinner'. Yet facing his first ball in the middle, Benaud, by now a venerated former captain of Australia, was looking to play a ball pitching on middle stump, and heading into his pads, behind square leg, only to see the 'keeper take the ball a yard outside off. Later, in the nets at the Sydney Cricket Ground, Benaud sought to play his first ball from Gleeson, which was outside off-stump, through point, only to see it turn into him and take the off-stump. Benaud shook his head and told Gleeson he was still in Gunnedah.

Those two deliveries seem to prove the virtue of a method employed, among other bowlers such as Ramadhin and Mendis, of targeting off-stump while moving the ball both ways, albeit not sharply. Geoffrey Boycott's 'corridor of uncertainty', usually reserved for medium or fast swing bowling, is a phrase most appropriate for bowlers doing this. It is a technique that caused some discomfort to the Don, too. When Gleeson was playing for New South Wales Second XI in Adelaide, Bradman asked to see him in a net. Wearing his suit rather than whites, Bradman stood close to the stumps, intending to get out of the way but keen to get a measure of Gleeson from the batsman's perspective. Gleeson threw the ball up more slowly, and Bradman, jumping to leg to avoid getting hit, misread the turn and soon found himself with a growing bruise on his hip. The Don, then chairman of the selectors, made sure Gleeson was fast-tracked.

In that same essay, Gleeson also wrote:

The enormous advantage the bent finger Iverson-type grip gives a bowler is that if the batsman starts to detect it, he can revert to orthodox spin. His entire range of deliveries is doubled, and this gives him more chance of staying one step ahead of the batsman.

And he added:

For me, the Iverson-type balls have to be delivered at a slow medium pace, which is probably faster theoretically than spinners should operate. I tried to bowl them slower and rely more on flight, but I found that the batsman could play back and wait for whatever turn was on the ball. Bowling at this pace you minimise the time the batsmen have in which to change their minds. With the bent finger grip, the ball does not cut down sharply onto the pitch as the orthodox leg-breaks do, and so the advantages of flighting the ball well up are partly lost. Maybe someday a bowler will learn variations of flight with the Iverson grip. But I can get an occasional ball to hang, as I bowl with the breeze, looking for a caught and bowled if the batsman fails to get to the pitch of the ball.

From this passage and those preceeding it we get a comprehensive picture of Gleeson's attacking mentality which, incidentally, included a desire to bowl with as new a ball as possible – even a completely fresh cherry – and on green, zippy wickets. The batsman shouldn't be given any time, to maximise the benefit of being able to turn it both ways; a flat trajectory will suffice because it is deviation off the pitch that will get you most wickets; the more variations the better; mix between orthodox and unorthodox methods according to the batsman's perspicacity; generally make the ball leave the batsman; and to hell with the textbook if it recommends the opposite for any of the above. As per usual with unusual bowlers, Gleeson had a self-assurance about his method that was disarming. (At other times, it was expensive: he once insured his right hand for A$10,000 before embarking on a tour of South Africa.)

But, to a greater extent than with Iverson or even Ramadhin, batsmen worked him out. The great South African Barry Richards reckoned he had Gleeson completely figured. He told his teammates that if you see one finger and the thumb, it was the off-break; but if you can see more than one finger over the top, it was the leg-break. This simple process is believable, and fits with the position of the hand after release, but doesn't account for Gleeson's googly. Presumably, though, Richards didn't have too much trouble picking that either, because not once in seven innings could Gleeson dismiss him.

It was partly as a result of the public dressing down Richards had given him that Gleeson's Test career ended. This prompted him to take up lawn bowls, to which by all accounts he devoted the same industry and dedication. He was always regarded as one of the most experimental of cricket's bowlers, obsessing over the mechanics of each delivery, a habit teammates suggested owed plenty to his days as a trainee engineer. He earned respect for being admirably straight-talking, even dismissing the idea of his being a 'mystery spinner'. 'I was not a mystery spinner. I did things a bit different to someone else,' he said in an interview in 2008. 'The papers started the mystery business. I was told I had six different balls. That was bullshit. You've only got three as far as I'm concerned: one goes straight, one spins from the leg and the other one spins from the off. You can't do anything else.' That, as any top-class spinner, and especially this Iverson 2.0, ought to know, is partly true, but far from the full story. A cynic might call it spin, and not in a flattering sense either.

The era in which Gleeson briefly shone was soon to come to a close. He played in his last Test in July 1972, and only two other bowlers who played during the seventies could be considered in the first rank of spinners. It's true that England had some highly competent off-spinners who had played through the previous decade and remained in or around the team in this one. David Allen, John Mortimore, Ray Illingworth and Fred Titmus were foremost among them, but none of these bowlers, in my humble estimation, was what you would call great. Illingworth, who made a huge contribution to cricket more widely, took many of his wickets with his arm ball; Titmus was relentlessly accurate and is one of few cricketers to have played in five decades, having made his debut in 1949. His 153 wickets in fifty-three Tests speak more of his longevity and reliability than true prowess, though he, like Illingworth, served the game exceptionally well after retiring.

Only two other spinners really stood out in this twilight period, before spin bowling plunged into the long winter of the eighties. Both these bowlers, one an off-spinner, the other a left-armer, were the finest spinners over the course of a Test match career, that their country has produced.

You could hardly call Derek Underwood a slow left arm. The more fitting appurtenance for him was the one that came to be his nickname: 'Deadly'. Though Laker is the greatest spinner to have bowled for England, Underwood is the finest spin bowler England have ever had if a whole career is considered. Revered now as one of the most effective administrators of the game, he would have taken many more than his 297 wickets in Tests – quite probably he would have been the first man to cross four-hundred – were it not for the lucre of Kerry Packer's World Series Cricket. That escapade, and his being banned from Tests for three years because of his membership of an unauthorised English touring team to South Africa, meant he never quite achieved what was his due, which was being regarded as the most successful of all post-war left-arm spinners, at Test level at least, and until the brilliant Kiwi Daniel Vettori came along.

Underwood's pace would have been regarded as medium by the club cricketers at Farnborough, where his father, Leslie, played, and his main attributes were exceptional command of length and the ability to make his arm ball swing sharply, and late, into the right-hander. This gave the batsman facing him a feeling of unrelenting interrogation: not many bowlers in the history of cricket contributed so few bad balls, though I suppose 'Toey' Tayfield would have had something to say about that.

Compared with most of the other bowlers in these pages, Underwood was unusual in being prolific when young. His father had constructed a net in their back garden, with matting over a concrete pitch, for Derek and his older brother Keith (who is now the Managing Director of Club Turf Ltd, the cricket company they run together). Although his plodding run-up betrayed the fact that he was no natural athlete, bowling came easily to him. As a result, he became the youngest ever bowler to take a hundred wickets in his debut season, in 1963, when aged just eighteen.

His making it to Test level owed a huge debt to Lock. Much as Mailey and Hordern might never have taken up spin had they not seen Bosanquet send over his mystifying googlies in the Sydney Test of 1903, so, too, is it possible that Underwood would never have devoted himself to left-arm spin if he hadn't seen Lock bowl in the Ashes Test at the Oval in 1953. It is no coincidence that the style of spin Underwood adopted, which owes so much to Lock's method, was taken up after his being inspired on that day, when he was just eight years old. And yet Underwood's debt to Lock is greater even than that, and still more practical: it was Lock himself who had recommended Underwood to Kent – as a batsman –

after a coaching session in a department store. Had it not been for that session, and for the influence Lock wielded in the game, Kent might never have got their young batsman, and England their 'Deadly'. Just as with the tale of Benaud's oily calamine lotion discovery in Timaru, and Iverson's captivation by those blind cricketers of Melbourne, the real wonder about these sensational spinning careers is that they so nearly didn't happen.

With a classical side-on action, including a high leading arm, Underwood had the self-assurance to resist countless attempts to remake him in the style of a Bedi or Rhodes. On a Cricketers Club tour of Cyprus and Malta, for example, his lack of success on matting wickets resistant to his unorthodox spin led to pressure for him to slow down, give the ball more air and try to spin it more. It didn't work, and he soon reverted to his more familiar method. This was focused on making the batsman play every ball, and exploiting uneven wickets with the subtlest of variations in spin, line and flight. As *Wisden* put it: 'He always bowls at the stumps; he has natural orthodox leg spin, not too much, and after rain he can make the ball stand up.'

In his autobiography he was emphatic that he considered himself 'not a cutter' – so much so that he might have found Trevor Bailey's assertion that 'he relied more on cut than break to achieve his spin' somewhat offensive.

Though he was much weaker against left-handers later in his career, by which time his captains had also come to rely on him as a stubborn nightwatchman, he never lost sight of the first of Tiger O'Reilly's dictums for spinners: 'Give the batsman absolutely nothing'. It was the aggression behind his commitment to this view that facilitated his most memorable triumph, the 7-50 with which he bowled England to victory against Australia at the Oval in 1968. Many things conspired to make that event a cause of national celebration, but more than most it was the fabulous photograph of him going up to appeal for leg-before to take the final Australian wicket, that of John Inverarity, with every single one of his teammates in the frame, so close were they to the bat in that desperate and fateful hour. Underwood wanted to salvage the ball for his souvenir cabinet, but it was snaffled by a fan as the crowds rushed on to the pitch, swallowing the players in the process.

It must have been sour enough for Underwood that he finished three short of three hundred wickets in Test cricket, which would have made him the first spinner to that landmark; but it was made worse by the fact that Fred Trueman's 307 wickets was at that time a record for all bowlers, and tantalisingly within reach. Where Underwood was lured by other temptations, Lance Gibbs, that marvellously calm son of Guyana, never veered from his ambition to trump Trueman's record. This he did when, in the very last of his Test matches, played a full eighteen years after his debut in 1958, he took his 308th, and then 309th wicket, to gigantic appreciation from the Melbourne crowd. There was a strain of thought, predominant in English circles (and especially in Yorkshire), that speculated as to whether he really merited selection for that game, given he was by then forty-one. The conspiracy theorists were emboldened by his immediate departure from the Test scene thereafter.

But by the time that came, few begrudged him his fleeting glory (Dennis Lillee would anyway break the record himself not long after). Much like Valentine, the lanky Gibbs had an effortless affability and instant charm, which recommended him to even the fieriest of opponents, just as it did his cousin, Clive Lloyd. He was part of possibly the greatest West Indian side of all – and by extension, perhaps the greatest of all cricket XIs – when partnering Wes Hall, Charlie Griffith and Gary Sobers in an amazing bowling attack. Sobers bowled both medium pace and spin, of course, but it's no exaggeration to say that Gibbs, far from being the fourth man, was the reliable stock bowler who glued that attack together. This is one reason among many why no West Indian has come close to matching his quality. Having played for the United States, to which he retired from the Test arena, Gibbs probably merits the distinction of being the only bowler in these pages to be the best spinner for not one, but two countries.

'Stock bowler' can sound like a euphemism, even an insult, and, given the generally optimistic tenor of my argument, and the broad emphasis on spin as a means of attack, perhaps it is partly both. But, just as with Tayfield, it's hard to avoid the phrase when considering the bowlers at the other end to him, the length of his spells, his dependability and, indeed, some of the extraordinary figures he produced. To give just one example, in the Bridgetown Test of the home series against India in 1961–2, the opposition were cruising at 149-2. Then, in the final session of the match, he took eight wickets in fifteen overs – fourteen of them maidens – in one of the greatest spells of bowling ever seen, dismissing the Indians for 187. His figures were 53.3-37-38-8. I suppose this is 'stock' and 'shock' bowling moulded into one. Not until the kangaroo-like Sulieman Benn did it in Jamaica in February 2009 has another West Indian spinner taken eight wickets in a Test match – let alone a single innings.

How did Gibbs compare with Laker – or, for that matter, Tayfield? The best answer to that is to say he is more similar to India's current turbaned aggressor, Harbhajan Singh, than either of those two. But if one had to choose between those nearer contemporaries, Gibbs's addiction to over- rather than side-spin would take him nearer Tayfield. Within the sub-category that is off-spin, there are essentially two types, as we have seen – those that bowl at off-stump, wicket-to-wicket, and those that bowl outside the off-stump and invite the batsman to drive against the spin.

Gibbs was of that breed of off-spinner, much like Harbhajan and the afore-mentioned Englishman Bob Appleyard too, whose chest-on action, and delivery from wide of the crease, angled the ball into the right-hander. These bowlers tend to generate a lot of over-spin, rather than big side-spin, and though Gibbs, too, lost out from the rule changes that limited the number of fielders behind square on the leg-side, he took many of his wickets in the classic leg-trap. Many of these were snaffled by his favourite short-leg fielder, Sobers (there really is very little this most accomplished of cricketers didn't do). With a bounding, springy and short run-up on a 40-degree angle, Gibbs was an affront to all coaching manuals, his back foot perpendicular rather than parallel to the bowling crease, and his left arm mostly uninterested in the delivery of the ball. These habits made it difficult for him to bowl effectively from around the wicket until towards the end of his career, where, under the guidance of M. J. K. Smith at Warwickshire he toiled for seemingly countless overs.

A short delivery stride produced the fabulous sight of his back foot, his right, hooking upwards towards his right buttock. All this gave the changes to pace and flight that he generated an air of imperceptibility, and led to a natural curve in the air away from the right-hander and into the earth, so that the ball that seemed to drop short would in fact need to be negotiated just below chest height. His very quick arm action and short run-up gave him the impression of constantly hustling, and woe to the man who tried to distinguish between the end of his run-up and the beginning of his delivery stride. That was a thankless task.

These features combined to make Gibbs a figure of beauty, one whose contours were sharpened by his incongruity with the blood-inducing pace of those around him. He was a very different off-spinner from his predecessor, Ramadhin, though it's widely reported that, like that curious little man, he too possessed a genuine leg-break by way of variation, a relic of the fact that he started his career as a leg-break bowler with the occasional off-break. There is a charming symmetry to the fact that the globalisation of spin bowling opened with a Caribbean spinning surge, while what I have called the Second Flourish of spin bowling closed with a Caribbean spinner becoming the leading wicket-taker in all Tests. That was despite his team's fame owing an ever-increasing amount to the fear engendered by its pace bowlers, a tendency that got much worse in the eighties.

To some, it was a welcome sight. Those tearaways Hall and Griffith gave way to bowlers who were magisterial and magnificent: Holding, Garner, Marshall. Their speed would come to define, and decide, cricket through the following decade. But from the point of view of spin – that is, from the point of view of those who care deeply for the game – it was a Dark Age. A few lights flickered in the background, but really the only man to keep the flame alive with any energy worth reporting was one whose contribution to cricket in general, and spin in particular, cannot be overstated. He was a Pakistani Samson.

Interlude Eight

DOOSRA

Grip 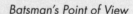 *Batsman's Point of View*

The grip is the same as for the off-break, with the first two fingers splayed across the seam. The thumb can rest on the seam, but for this delivery it is unlikely to be involved in imparting spin. The spin is imparted between the inside top knuckles of the first two fingers, with the index finger in particular straightening by the moment of release.

Imagine holding the ball in the release position for the off-break, with the seam pointing towards fine leg. Now cock your wrist inwards (that is, bring the ball closer to the inside of your arm). The seam position will move so that it is facing straight down the pitch, towards the batsman.

Now cock the wrist still further inwards, until the seam is now pointing towards third man. This is the release position for the doosra. You'll find that if you want to cock your wrist still further inwards, your arm has to bend at the elbow.

It's very difficult to release the ball from this position without bending your arm, but much easier to get the necessary propulsion in your wrist and fingers by straightening it from a bent position.

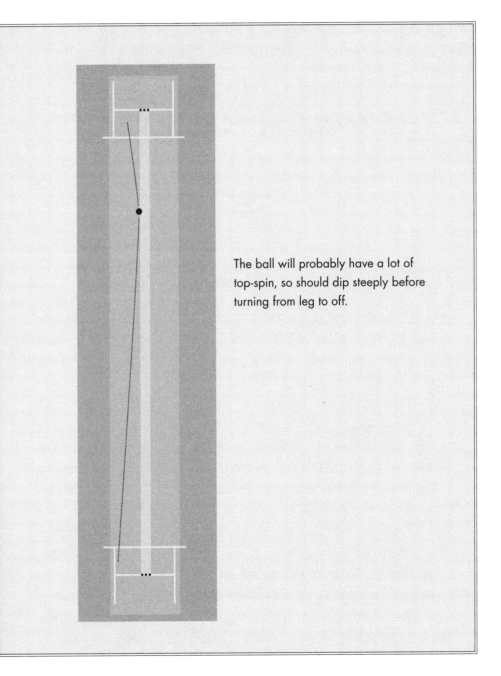

The ball will probably have a lot of top-spin, so should dip steeply before turning from leg to off.

Chapter Nine

THE WILDERNESS YEARS

It's a general rule of cricket literature that books surveying the Test arena of the 1980s will salivate over the power and aggression of the pace bowlers who dominated it without pausing to contemplate the flip side of their ascendance, and the horror of a sport thus emptied of its most cerebral and aesthetically pleasing pastime. I can understand why the sight of bowlers like Holding, Marshall, Ambrose, Lillee, Thomson and Hadlee is enough to whet the appetite of fans and connoisseurs alike; but the consequent neglect of attention to spin bowlers has been unforgivably myopic, and means lovers of the game owe more to those few keepers of the flame as existed in this dark period than is customarily thought.

Cricket has therefore yet fully to service its debt to Abdul Qadir, the Eric Cantona of the sport, in part because of that myopia, and no doubt also because, like the mercurial Frenchman years later, behind his upturned collar lurked a volatile and therefore divisive figure. More than any other bowler through this period, Qadir upheld the idea of using attacking spin bowling as a route to winning matches. With his sharp nose and goatee, flowing hair and tongue thrust out to be lodged between pursed lips at the moment of delivery, so great was his commitment to optimally ripping every ball, this Pakistani Samson was a dazzler, a showman, a man who exhilarated crowds with bowling they longed to see more of.

That he was so attacking a cricketer was particularly welcome because the few bowlers who did twirl away in the Test arena were becoming ever more defensive, such were the ostensible demands of the limited-overs revolution that marked the end of the previous era. It's true that these wilderness years for spinners were basically caused by Kerry Packer's colourful upheaval of the game: batsmen were becoming more aggressive, boundaries were becoming shorter, the premium was on scoring fast and the spendthrift label had become even more unwanted. When bowlers as successful as Underwood were tempted away from the five-day game, there seemed little to recommend it to other spinners. Young bowlers were being taught that the old virtues of flight, guile, calculation and deception were now inferior to the demands of economy and immediate impact.

I hope that real fans of the game have observed that the latest revolution, Twenty20, which seemed certain to accelerate the descent into brutality promised by a limited-overs game, has in fact proved that the wrong lessons were learned by spinners during the Packer revolution. As Benaud said to me, spin *is* compatible with a shortened form of the game – it just needs to be good enough.

Of course, when the Test arena has fast bowlers as good as those produced by the Caribbean during this era, for example, that makes spin a much less fashionable enterprise, regardless of the lessons being learned from the one-day game. But it does put a premium on those brave souls who continued twirling away through these years, and it's a curiosity of this period that, Qadir and the Australian Bruce Yardley aside, many of them were English. They include Pat Pocock, the Welsh-born off-spinner who returned to play nine consecutive Tests for England from 1984, a full eight years after his previous Test, and sixteen after his debut. His 67 wickets at 44.41 indicate the crisis in spinning quality teams were facing at Test level. Eddie Hemmings floated on the edge of the England team for the best part of a decade, and took advantage of Emburey's ban for three years for touring South Africa; but he managed only forty-three wickets, the last of them coming when he played his final game a few weeks before his forty-first birthday. Geoff Miller, now an England selector, managed thirty-four Tests, but more because he was a better batsman than Emburey or Hemmings than because his off-breaks made him a worthy successor to Laker.

Only three spinners from these years deserve our full attention, as having made decisive contributions to their respective traditions in this lowly period, and it's pleasant to note that they constitute a leg-spinner (Qadir), an off-spinner (Emburey) and a slow left-armer (Phil Edmonds).

Ah, Philippe. It's a pity that the man who ought to have succeeded Lock and Underwood as a great modern spinner for England has instead achieved notoriety for his intemperance. Raised by his Belgian mother after his birth in Lusaka, Northern Rhodesia, Philippe Henri Edmonds was briefly involved in the anti-apartheid struggles of the late 1960s, before heading to Cambridge, where he received a Blue. It was said that his recalcitrance as a character stemmed partly from his childhood, and certainly there was something deep and incorrigible about his fondness for conflict. This is the man who, having long aspired to be captain of Middlesex and England, is alleged to have once pinned Mike Brearley against a wall, after the latest in an endless list of spats, stared at him from an inch away and said 'lay off'. He's also alleged to have done something similar to his biographer, Simon Barnes.

This is the man who garnered little sympathy when he suffered from an attack of the yips. This is the man who read the *Financial Times* in the dressing room, who wore a Swatch watch as the only England player of his generation to have negotiated a watch-sponsorship deal, and who turned up to games in a Rolls-Royce, having once said, 'If someone in the United States sees a guy driving a Rolls-Royce, he'll say to himself, "Good on him". In Britain people just look on enviously and want to knock you.' This is the man of whom the normally reserved and gentle Bailey wrote: 'He has sometimes shown a remarkable lack of tact in his dealings with colleagues'; that 'he has the knack of saying, or doing, something instinctively without considering the consequences'; that 'he simply does not exude the necessary personal magnetism' to be a leader; and that he was, à la Laker, 'slightly remote and self-contained as he has never been "one of the boys".'

This is the man who was nicknamed Maggie because, like the then Prime Minister, he didn't suffer fools gladly. This is the man who was no-balled for bowling bouncers at Australian batsmen who had earned his ire. This is the man now reputed to be worth £50 million, with allegations – none of which have led to criminal charges – of shady links to Robert Mugabe and corrupt politicians in Sudan, places where his extensive mining interests are more lucrative than ever. This is the man whose wife, Frances, published a spiteful and bitchy account of the disastrous Caribbean venture of 1985–6, *Another Bloody Tour*, in which scores were settled on both her and her husband's behalf. This is the man who, after thirty years of marriage, was divorced in 2007, from a wife who once said of him: 'I want much more of a presence from Phil. Phil wants to be a tycoon like Jimmy Goldsmith. I am sure he will be one day, but I don't want it to be when I'm 97 and in the grave.'

But for all that, he was an electrifying and exciting spinner. With an action nearly as pure, high and rhythmic as Bedi's, Edmonds excited all those who saw him, and some who didn't, before his Test debut at the age of twenty-four in 1975, when he took 5-28, albeit mostly with bad balls. His first spell in Tests, indeed, yielded 5-17 from twelve overs, fuelling expectations he could never live up to. He then took only one more wicket in three innings over the remainder of the series. He had to wait until Underwood's departure for World Series Cricket before making a real breakthrough at Test level, and, though over the course of both his county and international career he profited from being paired with Emburey, there were times when England lacked the bravery to bowl two spinners, meaning that Edmonds lost out.

Slower through the air than Underwood and Lock, he was more in the style of Rhodes, looping the ball from wide of the crease, and on helpful tracks pitching the ball on leg-stump and trying to hit the off-bail with it. He imparted enough revolutions to achieve the necessary turn, but he, too, was undone by the new pressures of having to bowl in limited-overs games in between longer matches, and coursed the well-trodden path of becoming flatter and faster. This was one reason he didn't live up to the promise of his early days, and finished with 125 wickets at 34.18 from fifty-one Tests.

Like Emburey, he was a devoted servant of Middlesex. He served as chairman, and once, five years after he had retired, played in a match while stuffed with painkillers and on impossibly short notice, after an injury crisis had claimed Tufnell, his successor. Turning up at the ground in a Rolls-Royce, he pushed back the years, with 4-48 from beautifully flighted slow left arm – very slow, by then. As Peter Roebuck put it: 'He still broke bounds by fielding aggravatingly close, he still ostentatiously wore a watch, probably still pretended he was paid a fortune to do so, still disdained calisthenics, still clapped his hands, still rubbed them in the dust as he prepared to bowl ...' So stiff did Edmonds's back become that he took ever more painkillers, but, not realising his constitution was ill prepared for the onslaught, spent much of day two in a drug-induced haze. If it hadn't been for the washout on day three, Middlesex might well have taken to the field deprived of their star man.

That was an accolade they spent close to a decade bestowing on John Emburey, who was for much of this period the best off-spinner in the world. And it's instructive to examine how he could have achieved that status despite his being ostensibly without many of the key qualities of his England predecessor, Laker, who thirty years before had the same said of him. Emburey was in many ways a servant of the Packer revolution, a bowler who peaked just as the effect of that upheaval was rippling through the game. He excelled in both formats, but did so with a form of off-spin that was, in its essentials, defensive. When he came on he set out to bowl maidens, not to spin the ball vigorously, and he was never a huge turner of the ball. His action wasn't so much side-on as back-on. When he was bowling well, the batsman would glimpse the back of his left shoulder blade, so pronounced was the pivot over his braced front leg. He bowled a beautiful under-cutter that skidded through off the pitch, and also one of the great arm balls, a floater that just moved away from the right-hander in the air, and kept on going after pitching. It was a ball on which he'd received advice from Titmus, his mentor at Middlesex.

Standing at six foot two inches, getting very close to the stumps, and bowling with an arm at twelve o'clock – that is, as high from the ground as possible, Emburey bowled a similar wicket-to-wicket line to Tayfield, but with much less loop. Indeed, he was at times basically a flat off-spinner who utilised variations in pace to deceive the batsman; yet at other times he would bowl from twenty-four rather than twenty-two yards, and use the extra length to generate both dip and prodigious bounce, while stepping right up to the bowling crease for a much faster quick ball, one that owed its pace in part to his early days as a medium-pacer.

Made captain of England for two Tests in 1988, when he wasn't really ready, Emburey was the only England player to go on both the rebel tours to South Africa (1981–2 and 1989–90). He took up cricket after discovering that his maternal uncle had had trials for Surrey, and under the tutelage of Mike Gunton, his cricket master at Peckham Manor School, switched from medium pace to off-breaks. The presence of Titmus initially dissuaded him from trying to make a living out of it, so tight was that bowler's grip on the Middlesex side, but in time his chance came, and just as the influence of Titmus was decisive in the development of his game, so Emburey has as a coach been decisive in the development of many other spinners. Shaun Udal, the best recent England off-spinner aside from Graeme Swann, was persuaded out of retirement by Emburey's persistence.

Though there could be some debate as to whether Emburey was the best off-spinner in the world through this decade, there can hardly be any doubt who was the best leg-spinner. It was not until 1952 that Pakistan entered the Test arena, and in the first quarter of a century of their existence they produced some competent if unexceptional spinners, of whom Intikhab Alam and Mushtaq Mohammad were the best wrist-spinners. It was a shock to some, then, when Qadir rocked on to the Test scene and displayed, from the age of just twenty-two, a command not only of the leg-break, but the top-spinner, googly, and – even at this early stage – the flipper.

His philosophical approach to bowling could hardly be more different from Emburey's, though he, too, had started off as a seamer – one whose main interest was batting – only to discover in the nets that he could spin the ball a long way. The Englishman came on and looked to land his first dozen balls on an immaculate length, so as not to get taken off; Qadir wanted – and expected – a wicket from ball number one. His audible grunt at the crease conveyed the intensity of his application, and a beautiful chest-on action was the culmination of a bouncing, whirling, body-pumping approach to the crease, which was the antithesis of Warne's uninterested stroll. As he departed from his mark he licked the first three fingers of his bowling hand like a cat cleaning a paw. This was one-third practicality (it might improve grip, or it might not); one-third superstitious habit; and one-third gamesmanship. Qadir put it about in interviews that he conceived of his run-up as a way of causing maximum distraction to the batsman – a suggestion which, once it was ventilated in public, had the desired effect of diverting his opponent's attention from the ball to come.

Born into poverty in Lahore, he was the son of a preacher and as a devout Muslim took his prayer mat with him to each game. He didn't drink or smoke, and while stocky of build took extreme care of his body and fingers, knowing he owed his livelihood to them. It was because of his lack of height that, even though his arm came over nearly at the vertical, the ball spent plenty of time above the batsman's eye line: his loop was natural, and accentuated by the slight bend in his front leg. He bowled in an age light on high-class spin, and even lighter on high-class wrist-spin, and an air of mystery clung to him long after he was established at the highest level. Rumours abounded that he had two different googlies; then, that he had two different top-spinners (which he did: one bowled from wide on the crease, the other from very close to the stumps); and commentator after commentator was left embarrassed by his attempt to pick the delivery after it had been released.

India's batsmen, however, had slightly more success in picking his deliveries, which you'd expect given the diet of high-class spin they were served at home. The great Sunil Gavaskar and Mohinder Amarnath took especial delight in announcing to the world their detection of his googly. 'Every time he would bowl a googly,' Amarnath said, 'one of us would shout "googles" before hitting it away. Qadir felt quite bad about it and said to us, "It's bad enough you can read it, but can you please stop shouting it out aloud?"' This spurred commentators to attempt a version of the trick for themselves, though with limited success. Even Benaud was prone to venturing that such and such delivery was the leg-break, only for it to spin violently in from the off and disturb the stumps.

Violence, come to mention it, was something Qadir was associated with. In rare ventures from the peaceful strictures of his faith, he was known to threaten physical aggression, and sometimes to act on his threats. He certainly did so when, during the volatile 1987–8 tour of the Caribbean, umpire David Archer turned down two massive appeals against Jeff Dujon and Winston Benjamin. His sulky look as he returned to fine leg was irresistible to the West Indies fans, who jeered him relentlessly. Not long after that there was more excitement when the object of their taunts stepped over the boundary rope, climbed over a fence and threw a punch. It landed on a local twenty-one-year old named Albert August, and, though Qadir escaped unscathed from the ensuing kerfuffle, he was marched down to the local police station after the game. Charges against him were dropped after a few high-level phone calls, a contribution from the Pakistanis to local police funds and a US$1,000 out-of-court settlement.

His frustration was usually retained for obstinate umpires, but until his close friend Imran Khan came along and showed faith in him, he lacked the support of a top-class captain, and so made enemies who were sometimes closer to home. On the 1984–5 tour of New Zealand he was so annoyed when his captain, Zaheer Abbas, took him off that he ostentatiously sulked like a child on the field. The tour committee fined him for his actions but, unrepentant, he bluntly refused to pay. Not satisfied with causing this much anger among his teammates, he went on television and criticised his colleagues further. For this final outrage he was sent home 'for disciplinary reasons'. It wasn't the last time his on-air remarks got him in trouble either. In 2004, Pakistan Television (PTV) dropped him after he said that it was customary for Pakistani bowlers to tamper with the ball, and this was a long-nourished habit.

After taking 6-44 against England in only his second Test, he decided he would make a habit of relieving Englishmen of their wicket, so dumbfounded were they by anything that wasn't seam or swing bowling. Long before Warne tormented them, the English batsmen fell like lemmings under Qadir's spell. A full eighty-two of his 236 Test victims were English, while he only took a shade over three wickets per Test against other sides. That said, his first three tours of England were a disappointment, and it was only on his last visit, in 1987, that he really excelled (despite missing close to two months on paternity leave). And he reserved his best performance in any arena for the English batsmen who faced him at Lahore on the 1987–8 trip. There he took 9-56 with one of the greatest of all bowling spells. Graham Gooch, who played against Warne in his prime, said that spell rendered Qadir an even better bowler than the great Australian.

If that seems excessive praise, it's worth remembering that, unlike Warne, Qadir was bowling without the aid of a decent spinner at the other end (Warne had Tim May in his early days at least). And though few people would now claim that Warne was an inferior bowler, the impact these two had on cricket was about more than the number of wickets they took. It was about the manner in which they took them. Through a dark, painful period for spin bowling, Qadir kept the flame alive, inspiring a legion of followers, of whom the great Mushtaq Ahmed would be the most conspicuous, and attaching to wrist-spin bowling a razzmatazz and popular appeal it was desperately close to losing altogether. It's going too far, and stretching the laws of history, to suggest that, had it not been for Qadir, the Great Age of Spin bowling that followed him would not have happened. But it's reasonable to assume that in large swathes of the cricketing world, he alone ignited fascination in the wonders of the Twirlymen tradition. Had he not done so, the rest hardly bears thinking about.

Interlude Nine

CARROM BALL

Grip   *Batsman's Point of View*

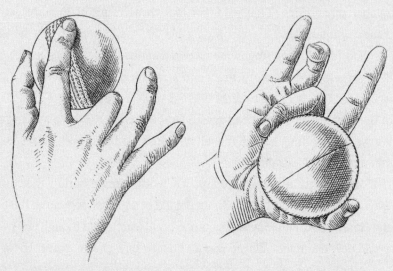

The grip is different from all the other deliveries. The ball is held between the fleshy pad of the thumb and a bent middle finger. The seam can either be positioned so that the index finger is running along it, or so that the index finger is perpendicular to it. As the arm comes over in the delivery stride, the wrist position remains unchanged, but the middle finger straightens – as if flicking a disc in carom – to propel the ball forward. In effect, this delivery can be thought of as a leg-break bowled between the thumb and middle finger, but out of the front of the hand and with no wrist involvement.

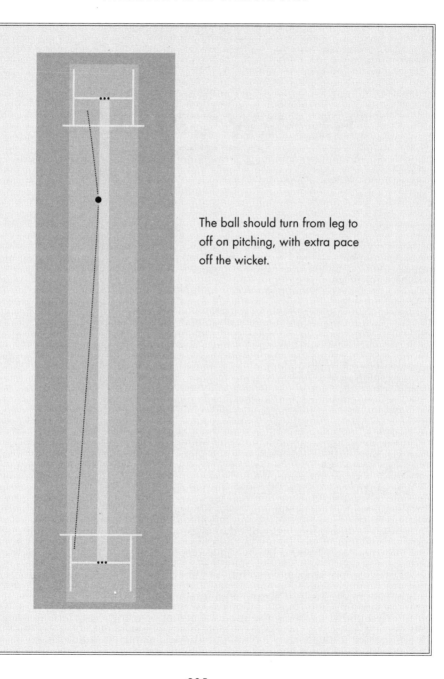

The ball should turn from leg to off on pitching, with extra pace off the wicket.

Chapter Ten

THE NEW GREAT AGE
OF SPIN

It's a typically otiose habit of sports correspondents struggling to convey the magnitude of this or that player's talent to take refuge in that old chestnut, the 'once-in-a-generation' bowler/batsman/striker/swimmer/skater/boxer/quarterback – delete as appropriate. This is, stating the obvious – which player, after all, *doesn't* appear only once in a generation? – but it's a phrase that pops up most either when some brilliant youngster emerges on to the scene or when a great career is being surveyed. It is, I suppose, a demotion from that other false note of praise, the 'once-in-a-lifetime' sportsman, and is designed to show that the writer has knowledge of previous eras of the particular sport they're covering. You'd have thought they'd know by now, having seen Mitchell Johnson described by Dennis Lillee as a 'once-in-a-generation' bowler, shortly before struggling to hit the cut strip in the Ashes series of 2009, that such phrases are hostages to fortune.

Two giants bestride the modern era of bowling. Both are spinners. Ironically, though they complement each other so wonderfully as to seem the object of some celestial decree, both were routinely described – often by the same correspondent – as a 'once-in-a-generation' bowler at the start of their careers, and now, having retired, suffer the fate of attachment to that even worse label: 'once-in-a-lifetime'.

What these writers are trying to get at is both the quality that makes each of them special, and their relation to previous bowlers. But such labels are restrictive, because by lumping Shane Warne and Muttiah Muralitharan together, they elide the essential contrariness of their methods, which make them a kind of yin and yang, or matter and anti-matter, of spin bowling. The Australian is a purist, the coaching manual's favourite exhibit, an example of orthodoxy achieving extremes of success. The Sri Lankan defies all convention and categorisation; he is unorthodox; he would never feature in a coaching manual, and ought not to. Instead, he, a wrist-spinning off-break bowler who mastered the doosra, is the lushest and most exotic growth in the garden of international spin. Warne, by contrast, is the proudest rose, the one to unite tourists and connoisseurs. Statistically it is not actually possible to say one is a better bowler than the other, though I may as well state my position on the two most feverish debating points that conjoin these two at the outset. Warne is a better bowler, and Muralitharan is a chucker. But he has been a wonderful bonus to the game.

They have both been exceptional servants of spin bowling and the game more broadly: Warne is an outstanding coach, and fast becoming the finest sports commentator in the world; Muralitharan is a wonderful mentor for many young players, and, as a Tamil in war-ravaged Sri Lanka, a precious ambassador for peace and goodwill. In terms of spin bowling, their careers offer one lesson above all others – the moral of these pages, to the extent that there is one: mystery is temporary, but mastery is permanent.

Technically, Warne rivals Barnes as the most accomplished bowler the world has seen. He spins his leg-break as much as any other bowler has done and unquestionably had a greater command of accuracy than any other spinner who has played. He owes this to a combination of natural talent, intense practice and brilliant coaching, mainly from one man – Terry Jenner, the Spin Doctor.

More than is generally recognised, Jenner has been one of the most influential of all coaches. He wasn't such a bad leg-break bowler himself either, playing nine Tests for Australia, including a 5-90 against the West Indies in 1973, when his victims included Rohan Kanhai, Alvin Kallicharran and Roy Fredericks. He didn't have Warne's command of length, but spun the ball vigorously and could achieve outlandish turn. Nor did he lack Warne's self-regard. Asked by Brian Viner of the *Independent* if Warne's ball to Gatting was the best he'd seen, he said it didn't match one that he had bowled himself. 'I got Gary Sobers stumped, playing for South Australia against the West Indies. It was a leg-break that curved away and spun back through the gate. I couldn't believe it was me.' His attitude to coaching is uncompromising. Within minutes of Viner showing up at a training session, he said to one boy, 'Remember Crocodile Dundee', then grabbed the ball from him, and said, 'When he says "That's not a knife … this is a knife". Well, that's not spin … this is spin.' Moments later he was chastising another one: 'You're six foot two but you've got the delivery stride of a bloke of four foot nine.' This intensity owes much to a sense that opportunities are precious, and failure to take them can lead people into dark places – a fact that his own life bears out. Addicted to gambling even in his playing days, he took badly to a rotation policy which saw the likes of Gleeson, Kerry O'Keefe, Ashley Mallett and Ray Bright chosen ahead of him. 'In 1976 I was dropped again and became very bitter,' he told

Viner. 'Within five minutes I wasn't even playing club cricket.'

Jenner's gambling continued to haunt him, and eventually he embezzled A$30,000 (£10,000) from car dealerships he worked for, to finance his habit. Jailed for six and a half years, he served two, and was released in 1990. A friend of his fixed up a job coaching at the Australian Institute for Sport (AIS: cynics said it stood for Arseholes in Sandshoes) in Adelaide, to speed up his social rehabilitation, and someone said there was a nineteen-year-old turning up the next week who he should have a look at. He had peroxide blond hair, a diamond earring and his name was Shane. Jenner, along with Jack Potter, would coach him. Jack Potter was the man whose main claim to fame was that he holds the record for being twelfth man for Australia the most times without winning a cap (three, for the record), but whose claim on these pages is that he bowled a doosra thirty years before Saqlain. Potter's first impression of Warne captured him perfectly: 'Chubby, bright blond. Great personality, adman's dream.'

The bond between Jenner and Warne has been intense, the former counselling the latter through various scandals and a painful divorce. Jenner knows Warne's action better than anyone – 'if he talks to one person about his action I think it might be me' – and had a curious ability to get the best out of Warne when others couldn't: wicketkeeper Ian Healy, who had a better view of Warne's bowling than anyone, once said to Jenner, 'What is it, Doc? You say the same things we say to him, but with you it works.'

Jenner, then, is the man to listen to for an explanation of Warne's genius for technical proficiency. It starts with his run-up – or, rather, his walk-up, father of a thousand imitations (including, dare I say it, my own – though as I have said, the breadth of my paunch necessitated it). Asked why Warne doesn't have a run-up, Jenner retorts:

This is one question I find annoying because a run-up is only for rhythm. Coaches who encourage people to run in like medium-pacers are not allowing the leg-spinner to go up and over his front leg. It is important that you bowl over a braced front leg. Warne had eight steps in his approach but walked the last three and had lovely rhythm.

And when he got to the crease, he took every last drop of wisdom from the coaching manual, and seemingly every lesson gleaned from nearly two centuries of spin bowling, and distilled it into the perfect execution of leg-spinning possibility:

Warne had the five basics of spin: he was side-on; to get side-on, your back foot needs to be parallel to the crease and Warne's was; his front arm started weakly but by the time of release it grew very powerful; he drove his shoulders up and over when he released the ball; and completed his action by rotating 180 degrees. Those basics came naturally to him and were the key to him walking up to the crease and jumping to bowl.

Side-on, back foot parallel to the crease, powerful front arm, shoulders driving up and through the action, pivot over the front foot: Warne did those better than any other spinner before, or since. And though he clearly has natural ability, it was through the intensity of his practice and training that he made it to the top.

It is some consolation to those prone to deify him, like me, that his career was in a fundamental sense the product of failure. Raised in the bosom of a stable and loving family, he hadn't dreamt of playing cricket until in his twentieth year a 'heartbreaking letter of rejection landed on the doormat' from his beloved St Kilda's Aussie Rules football club. He deduced from it that 'I was just too short', and 'I wasn't fast enough to cover the ground'. This sense of rejection, and the consequent determination that comes from having a point to prove, would be essential drivers of his success both in playing days and now as a coach, not least at Hampshire, where he has been a brilliant and decisive influence.

His hero when growing up, the man he wanted to emulate, wasn't a great Australian spinner of old, a Benaud or a Grimmett perhaps; nor even such recent twirlers as Abdul Qadir. It was an Aussie Rules player. He wrote in his autobiography, 'One player I liked watching because of his aggressiveness was Dermott Brereton of nearby Hawthorn', who was 'a real flamboyant character with a great sense of fun who gave no quarter on the field. He was a rough diamond, but a diamond nonetheless. He wore an ear-ring, dyed his hair peroxide blond and drove a Ferrari. Sound familiar?'

A year after Warne made his first-class debut he was playing Test cricket, but even then it was a baptism of fire: Ravi Shastri and his Indian comrades smashed him to all corners of the ground, leaving him with match figures of 1-150 (Shastri, caught Dean Jones for 206). Selected to tour England for the 1993 series, he came over as something of an unknown quantity. Then he delivered that ball.

It is true that, in and of itself, that ball, which had it not turned would have missed leg stump by two and half feet, and which Gatting had every reason to believe was initially destined to pitch on off-stump rather than outside leg, was a self-contained moment of sporting glory. Warne has described what was going through his head as he stepped to his mark. 'First one … obviously, always a little bit nervous for the first ball, so …

now Mike Gatting, good player of spin, I thought that ... bit nervous first time bowling against England, what we'll have to do here is, just bowl a nice leg-break that hopefully lands somewhere on the mark and, er, can turn.' He didn't know that he'd bowled Gatting until the batsman began his trudge to the pavilion; and Warne's initial celebration was in fact just a response to that of Ian Healy, who jumped with delight and was the first to know what had transpired. The wicketkeeper ran down to Warne and said: 'That wasn't a bad delivery to start with.' In the commentary box, Benaud put into words what had just happened: 'He's done it, he's started off with the most *beautiful* delivery. Gatting has absolutely no idea what has happened to it. *Still* doesn't know. He asked Kenny Palmer on the way out. Kenny Palmer just gave him the raised eyebrow and a little nod. That's all it needed.' That 'still' is shorthand for one spinner's deep affection for another.

But, as ever, context improves that sporting moment further.

Warne had been smashed around by Graeme Hick at Worcester in a warm-up match earlier in the tour, during which, under instruction from Border, he withheld his googly lest it be detected. Atherton told me that, since Old Trafford had been pounded by rain, 'the pitch looked like a swamp – you could practically put your hand through it – and we were convinced they would play Tim May [the off-spinner] alone. David Lloyd even said a wrist-spinner would be useless in weather like that.' So far from being the terrifying opponent of later years, as Warne ambled in to bowl at Gatting, he was a surprise selection, a man who flunked his Test debut, and who'd made an inauspicious start to the tour, suggesting he was averse to English conditions. Allan Border, whose grasp of tactics is almost peerless, brought Warne on as soon as Atherton had been caught behind off Merv Hughes. He did so despite the common (and justified) view that Gatting was one of few Englishmen comfortable against spin.

That context amplified the wondrous impact of Warne's delivery. So too did the English response. Before the series was over, Mike Gatting, Hick and Robin Smith had been dropped. Gooch would be dismissed by Warne five times. Gatting was by then already a man of substantial build, and it was specifically his chubbiness that made the baffled expression on his face, once that ball had dislodged the off-bail, immortal.

Phil Tufnell captured something of the hilarity of the situation when he said, 'The last time I saw that look on Gatt's face, someone had nicked his lunch', to which Graham Gooch added the immortal rejoinder, 'If it had been a cheese roll, it would never have got past him.' Jenner had just spoken at a dinner in Melbourne. 'And when I'd finished someone turned on the TV and said 'hey, your boy's on'. When I saw him bowl Gatting I said, "that's the problem with young kids of today. It took me two years to teach him that ball and I said whatever you do, don't show it first up". They realised I was joking.'

Ever since that ball, Warne has had a grip on the cricketing imagination. He was the best bowler in the world throughout almost his entire playing career, despite major operations on his fingers and shoulder towards the end of the 1990s that caused him briefly to lose some of his spin. He was only ever dropped once by Australia when available (in Antigua, 1998–9).

For batsmen facing him, he posed problems they simply didn't see the like of elsewhere. Only Sachin Tendulkar and Brian Lara conquered him, the former scuffing up an area outside leg stump in net practice by way of preparation. (Daniel Vettori's New Zealanders prepared for Muralitharan by batting on recently used and dry pitches, so as to replicate his unpredictable bounce.) Whereas some spinners, such as Ramadhin and Valentine, bustled through their overs quickly, Warne's approach was languid, thoughtful, considered. He may have got through his overs slower than any other spinner in the history of the game. Five minutes per over was nothing for him. He'd stand on his mark, scheming, approach the crease slowly, make huge representations to umpires, spectators and gods alike if the batsman did anything but hit him to the boundary – and even then sometimes – and thought nothing of moving his fielders three or four times per over.

Warne championed a much looser grip than other leg-spinners. Whereas Benaud, for example, would hold the ball tightly, with it sitting close to his palm, Warne was much more relaxed. Hold the ball too tight and you tense up as you approach the crease, he surmised. Hold it more loosely and you'll relax. To this end, his first two fingers were much closer together than with most wrist-spinners. He labelled his grip 'Two up, two down'. A relaxed approach meant he could focus on the task in hand. And, crucially, the object of Warne's focus was different from what the coaching manuals teach. All young spinners, encouraged by the likes of Benaud and Peter Philpott, are usually told to focus on the spot on the pitch they intend to hit. This is the way to improve accuracy. But as he approached the crease with his loose grip, Warne wasn't focusing on the spot on the wicket he wanted to hit. He had something else in mind.

'I'm a little bit different,' he says. 'What a lot of people think about is a spot on the wicket . . . I actually think about what shot I want the batsman to play. Whether I want to push him back and defend, whether I want to draw [him] forward to drive, whether I want him to sweep, whether I'm trying to push him back on the back foot . . . that allows me to bowl exactly where I want. Rather than focusing in on a spot, or anything like that, I think about what I'm trying to get the batsman [to do].'

Quite apart from vicious, and usually quick, turn and bounce off the pitch, he made the ball drift a long way in the air. One of Jenner's favourite maxims was that it wasn't just where the ball ended up but how it got there that mattered. 'You couldn't really come down the track to him,' Atherton explained to me, 'because the drift would mean you were playing against the spin and across your front pad, making it very hard to control the shot.' So batsmen tended to stay in the crease. 'But he bowled a different line to most leg-spinners. He attacked the stumps much more than other spinners. Border and Bobby Simpson got him bowling at middle-and-leg on most wickets, and leg and just outside when it was turning.' Right-handed batsmen had almost no option but to play against the spin, through the leg-side, where a tempting hole would often be left in mid-wicket. Some tried to shift their bodies, taking guard outside leg-stump, as Pakistani Salim Malik did, though with limited success. Atherton himself, having been bowled around his legs by Warne during the Lord's Test of 2001, shifted to a leg-stump guard for Trent Bridge. '[Warne] noticed the difference within three balls, bowled at off-stump instead, and I had half a bat dangling in extra cover with which to play.' He was caught behind shortly after.

These technical challenges were compounded by sheer force of character. More than almost any other player in the modern age, Warne's was a winning personality. He had extraordinary charisma. Australia won ninety-two Tests of the 146 in which he played. Nobody has ever been on the winning side so often. His exuberance sometimes tipped into vulgarity, as when he loutishly did his imprecise version of the Viennese waltz, stump held aloft between two hands, on the balcony of Trent Bridge after 1997, a kind of ritualised two-fingered salute to the English fans, and his very public problems with weight, compounded by his smoking during games when Australia were batting, endeared him little to some traditionalists.

He was also readily involved in sledging, on and off the field, and was charged with bringing the game into disrepute when saying of Arjuna Ranatunga, Sri Lanka's captain and a long-term adversary, 'Sri Lanka and the game overall would be better off without him ... I don't like him and I'm not in a club of one.' On the pitch his banter usually had big consequences. South Africa's Daryll Cullinan and Warne were prolific in their verbal exchanges. Once, when Cullinan was on his way to the wicket, Warne told him he had been waiting two years for another chance to humiliate him. 'Looks like you spent it eating,' Cullinan retorted. Yet the Australian usually gave as good as he got. He loved to flirt with umpires – though his barbed comment to Aleem Dar during his last Test in Sydney, when he told him not to worry about where his feet landed, and 'just take care of what's happening at the other end, mate', was an indication that he was ready to retire. But with batsman he swung between magnanimity, applauding good shots in the manner of Bedi, and brutalising them. Nasser Hussain and Mark Ramprakash were two of his favourite prey.

On England's Ashes tour of 1998–9, England needed around fifty off ten overs, with six wickets in hand, during a one-day international. Warne started to tease Hussain, who promptly hit him back over his head for four. Warne applauded sarcastically, and goaded him with a few choice words. 'This is where it's crucial not to get out,' he said. 'Don't let your team down now.' Hussain promptly charged down the track, only for Warne to see him coming, drop the ball short, turn it a mile and have him stumped by yards. Australia won.

In the Trent Bridge game of 2001, Warne detected that Ramprakash, never sure of his place in the team, was torn between a desire to bat out the day in what had been a low-scoring game, or come after him. So Warne started goading him, indicating with his hand that he wanted

Ramprakash to come down the wicket to him and take him on. 'Come on, Ramps you know you want to.' 'That's the way, Ramps, keep coming down the wicket.' Ramps did. Charging down the track, he was easily stumped. England finished the day six wickets down.

His favourite English target for banter has been Paul Collingwood. It was hardly Collingwood's fault that he came in only for the fifth Test of the 2005 Ashes triumph. But that prompted Warne, in the return series, to raise the small matter of his receiving an MBE. Warne had been batting, when Collingwood started sledging him. The retort we have on the record is 'You got an MBE, right? For scoring seven at the Oval? It's an embarrassment.' Warne later said of the exchange, 'It was making me concentrate. It was making me more determined. It was all a bit of fun. That's the way he wanted to play it and I was happy to play that game. It suits me fine.' But theirs has been an ongoing dispute. Warne said that Collingwood was 'too busy trying to drive his Aston Martin and fly around in helicopters [rather] than trying to work on his captaincy' (of England in the Twenty20 World Cup). And it's been reported that after Collingwood had attempted a few sweeps against Warne, and missed, the bowler muttered to wicketkeeper Adam Gilchrist, 'For Christ's sake, this guy can't hit anything' – to which Collingwood responded, 'Hey, Warnie, do you want to say that to my face or do you want to send me a text message like you did to those other hookers?' Allegedly.

'Hookers' indeed. Perhaps the word was a synonym for the shenanigans and sometimes shady dealings that have characterised what the public knows of Warne's life away from the pitch. As Simon Wilde put it in his excellent biography of the Australian, he may be a genius, but he is a hugely flawed one.

He had sex with a student, sex with a mother of three, sex with a TV assistant, sex – allegedly – with a woman on the bonnet of his BMW, sex in Kevin Pietersen's flat (not with KP himself, as far as we know). Nothing wrong with any of that, except he was married for much of it. His priapic tendencies, and the lewd text messages that came with each fling, made it into the national press. 'If you share something private with someone and it's consented by both, it should stay that way — not for the world to see in a paper. I think it's shit and unfortunately I've put myself in too many of those situations over the years,' he told Paul Kimmage of the *Sunday Times*. He endured a very public divorce through the summer of 2005, the summer of his greatest Ashes performance, forty wickets (sixteen more than the next bowler from either side) and 249 runs, albeit in a heroically losing cause. 'He'd only been alone for eight weeks,' Simone, now his ex-wife, said. 'Being faithful for eight weeks isn't too much to ask, is it?'

It wasn't just his dealings with women that struck some as un-Catholic behaviour. He foolishly took £3,000 from an Indian bookmaker in return for what he considered 'banal' information about pitch conditions. He had previously lost money in a casino (gambling being a habit he shared with the younger Jenner and his last Australian captain, Ricky Ponting, known with good reason as 'Punter'). He was sent home in disgrace from the World Cup in South Africa in 2003 for taking a banned diuretic, and garnered little sympathy when he claimed he thought it was a slimming pill. He blew (literally) a lucrative sponsorship deal with Nicorette by smoking in public, and was dropped from his A$300,000 deal with Australia's Channel 9, after Kerry Packer deemed his off-field antics made him a commercial liability.

All these salacious stories, eagerly reported and re-reported in both the upmarket and downmarket international press, created an aura, a degree of fame, that just made Warne more intimidating. It is true that he never fulfilled his great dream of being Australia's captain

(Steve Waugh and then Ponting were preferred); but it is a mark of his greatness that, despite endless distractions off the field, he remained focused and fiercely competitive on it. 'I have always had the ability to compartmentalise and get over things quickly,' he told Kimmage. 'You've got to get on with it. In a way that's been my downfall off the field but on the field it has made me very successful.'

It was inevitable, given all this, that he would confess 'Sometimes I feel as though I am playing a part in a soap opera' – but not as inevitable, perhaps, as the fact that his life would duly be put on stage, in the 2008 show *Shane Warne: the Musical*, a production which didn't flinch from exhibiting his personal vices. 'Muppets,' he said of the Australian comedian Eddie Perfect and playwright Toby Schmitz, 'there should be a law against it.' Then he turned up for the opening night. Perfect and Schmitz didn't have the scope to mention the fact that the advertising campaign for Advanced Hair Studio that Warne had endorsed, claiming the treatment could reverse hair loss, was dismissed as misleading (too much spin, said the critics). They were too early, alas, for the launch, in February 2010, of his new range of underwear – brand name: Spinners. Nor did they have time to mention his conversion to professional poker which, in a part-time capacity, he now takes nearly as seriously as his commitment to Twitter. @warne888 has more than 300,000 followers; his biography says 'father to my lovely 3 children, motto keep smiling, be true to yourself'.

More the quintessential Australian everyman than any player since the Don, Warne channelled this wider fame towards success on the pitch through a propaganda war, in which he was ably assisted by colleagues and a dumbfounded, ignorant press. Before every single one of his four tours of England, Warne put it about that he'd invented a new delivery. He never had. At one point, he said that he had sixteen in total. This is an absurd statement, given that anyone with a GCSE in maths ought to be able to tell you that there are, theoretically, an infinite number of deliveries. But the spin worked – literally. And Warne would talk it up.

One of the reasons he's such a brilliant and charming television commentator is that he can now be honest about this propaganda, and expose it for the pack of lies it really is. He has admitted, for example, to lying about his dismissal of Ian Bell at Lord's in the 2005 series. Warne bowled three leg-breaks to Bell, who shouldered arms to the first two, which spun sharply away to slip. But the third one skidded straight on and he was trapped leg-before. It looked like genius: even Benaud exclaimed that it was the slider, and an example of fabulously executed deception. In fact, it was a leg-break that simply didn't grip. Warne talked it up in the press, and had Bell completely flummoxed for much of that summer. It didn't help England's number three that the greatest bowler of the modern age had taken to calling him 'the Shermanator' – a magnificently cruel reference to a geeky virgin of that name in the film *American Pie*. It was almost as if a decree had gone out – the Australian players and coaching staff never failed to mention Bell's name without adding 'aka the Shermanator'. He averaged 17.1 over the five Tests.

In truth, Warne had only the standard range of deliveries available to the leg-spinner, though as a result of his shoulder trouble dropped the flipper altogether for a few years, and never relied on the googly (which he bowled with a discernibly much higher arm) as much as, for example, Qadir or Mushtaq Ahmed, two bowlers whose chest-on actions allowed them to cope better with the strain. He didn't invent any new delivery, or pioneer some new technique, and his challenge was to the record rather than rule book. If there is one sense, however, in which Warne moved the art of leg-spin forward, other than by doing it better than everybody else, it was in what came to be his reliance on the zooter, also known as the slider or the nothing ball (see Interlude Seven).

So skilfully did Warne rip his stock ball that it both drifted and dipped in the air more than almost any other leg-spinner's. Clearly that had intrinsic benefits, but it meant that his flight was usually parabolic, and, quite apart from the problem of bowling too many deliveries on the same curved path, this caused problems with his claims for lbw, because the top-spin component on the ball, responsible for its dip, made it bounce high. It was in response to this quandary, of course, that Grimmett, sixty years earlier, had resurrected the flipper from its dormant state. But Warne's shoulder trouble, and specifically an operation he had in 1998, made bowling the flipper difficult. So he turned to the zooter, the ball Doug Ring had taught Benaud on a train journey after the Lord's Test of 1953, using an apple.

Warne's leg-break dipped, drifted in, turned away from the right-hander and came out of the side and front of the hand. The zooter was the perfect foil: it came out of the front of the hand, with the wrist in a deceptively similar position at the point of release as for the leg-break, but instead of having a looped trajectory, it contained an element of back-spin, meaning that it floated on to a fuller length than the batsman expected. And instead of turning away, it would skid on with a scrambled seam. At times during the Ashes series of 2005, Warne was using this ball up to twice an over. He once bowled six of them, knowing it looked all but indistinguishable from his stock ball, so the risk of overexposure was minimal. This zooter, or slider, became the most effective variant weapon in Warne's armoury towards the end of his career. It achieved the effects of the flipper without putting as much strain on the shoulder.

He had initially learned this ball, and most of his variations, while at the Australian Academy in his younger days, where he displayed the strength of his forearm and fingers to onlookers by spinning small balls on a billiards table, in an echo of Bosanquet's twisti-twosti sessions which helped make the googly popular. That practice led to many of the most handsome deliveries cricket has seen, quite apart from the Gatting ball. The flipper that did for Alec Stewart at Brisbane in 1994 would have made Grimmett blush with pride; while it's possible that no bowler – not even Muralitharan – will make a ball turn as much as Warne did with his delivery to Shivnarine Chanderpaul at Sydney in 1996 and the ball that did for Andrew Strauss at Edgbaston in 2005 (Warne himself said he thought the former the biggest turn he'd ever achieved). The left-handed Chanderpaul, playing magnificently, went back to cut a ball that seemed only just to hit the cut strip, delivered from over the wicket, but was bowled – and not only that, but leg-stump, too. Strauss shouldered arms to a ball that went in front of his leading foot to hit middle and leg. Both were delivered with nearly pure side-spin.

Those sensational dismissals added to the aura of a man with apparently mysterious powers of sorcery in his fingertips. But, viewed with hindsight, and with the benefit of video analysis not available to other generations of players, the striking thing about Warne remains not that he was some great inventor, but rather that he took previous inventions and put them together to make a uniquely brilliant machine. He had the vigorous wrist and finger action of Mailey; the modulating flight and leg-stump line of Grimmett; the aggression and exuberance of O'Reilly, and the technical proficiency and work ethic of Benaud. He was a triumph of orthodoxy, not innovation.

On tour in Sri Lanka in 2004, he took 26 wickets at 20 runs apiece, while Muralitharan took 28 wickets at 23. Along the way, in one of Ponting's great achievements as captain of Australia (they won 3–0), Warne scored a victory for purists by beating Muralitharan to the magical figure of five hundred Test match wickets. Muralitharan's name, incidentally, is 'Muralidaran' everywhere but in England, in case you thought, while surveying scorecards in recent years, the Sri Lankans were lucky enough to possess another 'once-in-a-generation' bowler who just happened to have a very similar name. Muralitharan says he prefers it to be spelt with a 'd', not a 'th'.

It was during that 2004 series that comparisons between them were most readily made. Warne, the summation of the best that had gone before, stood in sharp contrast to Muralitharan, a kind of antidote to so many of the lessons taught by experienced players and coaches. 'You wouldn't really call him an off-spinner,' Atherton told me, 'because he was that different to face compared with conventional off-spinners.'

'Murali has been unique,' Warne himself says. 'Nothing about other bowlers prepares you for the challenge.' Wild-eyed and goateed, he is the television camera's dream. Transferring the ball from right to left hand as he leaves his mark – 'as if spinning it up a chute', as Martin-Jenkins says – and bobbing to the crease off thirteen yards, he then explodes in an orgy of flailing arms and roaring energy, expressed in a momentary skyward glance of his eyes and the cupping of his lips. His has been the most animated and electric of all the great bowlers' actions. So spirited is the sweep of his bowling arm that though he starts from a chest-on position at the point of delivery he finishes with a pronounced dip of the right shoulder towards the batsman, as if eager to catch a better glimpse of the sorcery he has just submitted for his enemy's attention. The revolutions are imparted by the clutching of an orthodox grip on the ball, but far from being the first and second fingers that do the work, as with conventional off-spinners, a wrist of almost superhuman suppleness – his fingertips can touch his forearm – suddenly unfurls, like a mini merry-go-round receiving an injection of kinetic energy. This technique has left more Test batsmen giddy with confusion than that of any other bowler the game has known.

It's not the wrist so much as the arm to which it is attached, however, that has made Muralitharan the most talked-about bowler in modern times, which, even in the Age of Warne, is testament to his impact on the game. Here are the facts of the matter. Muralitharan was born with a congenital deformity in his arm, which he cannot straighten fully. If you and I flop our arms down by our side, they will run broadly parallel to our legs, and the palms will be facing the side of our thighs. When Muralitharan puts his arms down by his side, something different happens. His left arm does what ours would do, but his right bends away from his body at the elbow, and his palm is twisted outwards to face in front of him, rather than inwards. This reveals not only the fact of his bent arm, which cannot be straightened, but also that he has an extraordinarily flexible shoulder. If you and I flexed our biceps to show off to our spouses, there would be a limit to how far back behind our bodies each arm could move while the elbow was bent. For Muralitharan, this external rotation, as physiotherapists call it, is significantly more pronounced.

His three brothers also suffer from this affliction. They bowl with a very similar action, albeit at amateur level. It defies the laws of probability, therefore, to suggest his bent arm is the product of anything other than biological inheritance. He could not have bowled like Laker, Gibbs, Swann or Tayfield even if he had wanted to.

His action raised eyebrows very early on. When Border faced him for the first time, he missed five balls out of six, simply unable to fathom that a wrist this active in delivery could be breaking it in the direction customary to an off-spinner.

Muralitharan's toughest examinations have come in Australia, a country where he was consistently unsuccessful on the pitch, and bullied by players and the public both on and off it. He was no-balled by Darrell Hair at the MCG on Boxing Day 1995, again in a one-day international that season, and by Ross Emerson at Adelaide on Australia Day 1999. After the first call, by Hair, the ICC used the latest biomechanical equipment to conduct extensive tests on his bowling arm, and as if to inflict further humiliation on him, carried the tests out at the University of Western Australia (guaranteeing spice and colour for the national media), and then at the University of Hong Kong. His action was filmed from twenty-seven different angles and put through computers capable of objective analysis far more subtle than any human brain could manage. They produced, however, a curiously human conclusion: Muralitharan's action created the 'optical illusion of throwing'.

This ordeal must have been trying for a man only three years into his Test career, but the reaction of the Australian crowd, who would thereafter make a habit of shouting 'no-ball!' as he released each delivery, was public torture. It came as a surprise to very few when, on his next tour, Emerson called him for throwing. Further tests were demanded by the baying public. Further tests were commissioned. These were conducted in Perth and England. They again cleared him. In 2004, Muralitharan declined to tour Australia, and nearly caused a minor diplomatic incident when the Australian Prime Minister, a genuine cricket nut, made his contribution to the debate. John Howard spoke for many of his countrymen (and voters) when he called Muralitharan a chucker. This may have been a genuinely held belief, but it was utterly predictable. As with most stories involving sport, it would have been more interesting if he'd said the opposite.

It was at the end of a three-match home series against – who else? – Australia in March 2004 that Muralitharan, who by now had learned Saqlain Mushtaq's doosra and improved it, was reported to the ICC by match referee Chris Broad (father of England's Stuart). Yet more biomechanical tests ensued; yet again, Muralitharan had to endure the ignominy of news stories saying that he'd been reported, and frenzied media coverage before, during and after each Test.

These tests finally convinced the ICC to examine the state of bowling more broadly, and whether or not all bowlers were in fact chuckers. They decided they were – to an extent. So the ICC changed the rules. They permitted a 15-degree bend in the arm, and the consequent straightening – anathema to traditionalists, but a compromise with reality in the eyes of the ICC. The international authorities were lambasted the world over. Australia were, naturally, lacking in reticence on the matter. I cannot surpass the words of Simon Barnes in stating the logical, necessary conclusion of the ICC investigations over a period of a decade. In naming Muralitharan the Wisden Leading Cricketer in the World for 2006, an exceptionally prolific year, he wrote:

There is no controversy about Muralitharan's bowling action. That has been examined by the ICC, and passed. There may be controversy about the ICC and its interpretation of Law 24, but that is a different matter entirely, and should be undertaken only by those seriously prepared to argue about 'the angle between the longitudinal axis of the upper arm and forearm, in the sagittal plane'. The regulations lay down a tolerance of up to 15 degrees of flexion in the bowling arm: Muralitharan fits within that. Most of his deliveries come with a flexion of two to five degrees: it is only the doosra that requires a full 15.

The change in the Law is a reflection of advancing technology, not politics. Almost every bowler examined under ultra-slomo has a kink in his action as great, if less superficially apparent, than

Muralitharan's. No: his action is legal, and if you dislike this truth, your quarrel is not with the bowler but the administrators.

Muralitharan caused a brief existential crisis in the highest echelons of the game, and a paradigm shift in the way bowlers and their actions are now seen, not in terms of binary bowler/thrower alternatives, but as being on a spectrum, where the differences between bowlers are differences of degree rather than kind – literally. That, perhaps more than the eight-hundred-plus Test wickets he has ended up with, will be his legacy. It is unlikely the law change will be reversed.

If you re-read the above passage by Barnes, you will note that he does not deny Muralitharan is a chucker (neither do I). He says his action is within the rules. The word 'chucker', which seems to evoke a spirit of foul play in the eyes of traditionalists, needs to be recalibrated in the cricketing imagination. It cannot be said enough times: the ICC thinks that all bowlers chuck – to an extent.

And why shouldn't Muralitharan extract an advantage from his deformity? Why, when bowlers have to bowl on flat, covered wickets, with shorter boundaries and bigger bats, with video replays interrogating their every trick – why shouldn't they be able to exploit this tiny benefit? At a time when batsmen in many forms of the game are not only reverse hitting, but using two-sided bats – two-sided bats! – effectively to double their striking range, what's a few degrees to an able-bodied bowler, let alone one who isn't?

To the extent that he has redressed the balance between batsmen and bowlers, and caused a wider examination to reveal the universality of bent arms in cricket, it's hard not to conclude that Muralitharan has obtained unfair advantage as compared with some bowlers, but he has been good for the game, too.

Those wishing to make the case for Muralitharan could be infinitely heartened by footage, recorded by Channel 4, of him bowling while his arm is in a cast. This restriction on his elbow doesn't prevent him from spinning the ball sharply, adding credence to the idea that a much higher than usual degree of kinetic energy carried in his spin originates in the wrist.

That said, his detractors will take heart from footage, readily available on YouTube, of him bowling leg-spinners to the South Africans in a Test match. Even I, as an instinctive supporter of Muralitharan and his contribution to the game, find it impossible to deny that these leg-breaks, delivered in the orthodox fashion off the third finger, and spinning sharply off a good length, seem to be bowled with arm rod-straight, and there is none of the 'optical illusion of throwing' reported by the ICC.

Such nuances and counterpoints make it inevitable that most people, including myself, land ultimately on the feeling that Warne was in his essentials a more wonderful bowler. There were similarities in their approach, Warne's leg-stump line to right-handers forcing them to play against the spin, while Muralitharan's prodigious turn meant he could bowl wide of off-stump and force batsmen to drive him, knowing that if they played no shot the ball could spin back in sharply and have them bowled or trapped before. Some batsmen refused to yield to these temptations, dragging him a long way from outside off through mid-wicket; and a sub-species of the same approach was the instinctive sweeping which batsmen from India, England, Australia and South Africa at different times adopted, not always with success. As England coach, Duncan Fletcher demanded England use the sweep more, thinking it obvious that the Sri Lankans themselves would use it to counter Muralitharan on spinning tracks. Fletcher reckoned his claim to enjoy being swept 'is just reverse psychology in my book. Muralitharan is one who often says that, but I have watched him closely when he has been swept early on in his spell. His walk back to his mark has always been a very timid one in that instance; the walk of a man who does not like what he is seeing.'

Just as Tendulkar and Lara mastered Warne above all with the speed of their footwork, sometimes charging at him, sometimes rocking back to good length balls, so those few batsmen who really had the measure of Muralitharan were adept at confusing his length with the nimbleness of their toes. In 2007, Michael Clarke did this better than anyone before or since.

Even this attempt to nullify his options was to a great degree undone by Muralitharan's adoption, and eventual advancement, of Saqlain's doosra. This ball eventually did for Saqlain, costing him his stock ball, the off-break, but Muralitharan could use it interchangeably with his off-break, and this made him literally twice the bowler. It added a huge range to his options. He started to go round the wicket to right-handers, bowling from very wide on the crease and spinning his stock ball in from just outside the off-stump, while sending the occasional doosra on to the very same spot, spinning it away and bringing his slip and gully into play. Using this approach, batsmen were forced to play every single ball. This begins to account for why 'bowled Muralitharan' is the most common dismissal of all in Tests. (Though it bears no relation to another test record – that of having registered the most ducks).

The reverse approach worked for left-handers. Before, and especially on helpful wickets, he would instinctively go round the wicket to left-handers, bowling from wide on the crease, attacking middle or leg-stump (just like Warne to the right-hander), and spinning the ball away so viciously that it would sometimes go directly to Mahela Jayawardena at slip. But cometh the doosra, cometh Muralitharan over the wicket to the left-handed batsman. Bowling, again, from wide on the crease, he would use the sharp angle to bowl several balls on off-stump, spinning away from the outside edge; then, having forgone it for several overs, a glorious doosra would follow the same trajectory, land in the same spot, but spin into the left-hander, quite often smacking him below the knee-roll as he shouldered arms. Few sights in cricket have been more glorious.

It is doing him a gross disservice to say, as Graham Thorpe did in 2005, that 'Warne was always varying the degree he spun the ball, while Murali generally just tried to spin the ball as much as he could'. Thorpe, a brilliant player of spin, was saying this before Muralitharan had really mastered the doosra, but the Sri Lankan had long varied his pace and degree of turn intelligently. Unlike Warne, there wasn't an optimum speed at which he achieved the most turn (Warne's was 50mph); and this meant he could bowl in very different styles, sometimes lobbing the ball along a parabola that would have made Gibbs smile, sometimes, as when I saw him in a day-night match against the Indians at Hambantota in 2004, bowling much, much quicker, and closer to 65mph.

Such is the fame these exploits have acquired that the ECB's ongoing reference to him as 'Sri Lanka's mystery spinner', as if he hasn't been around for the best part of two decades, now seems misplaced. He went from mystery to mastery long ago, and in so doing entered the national consciousness of his homeland in much the way Grace and Botham did in England, or Bradman and Armstrong did in Australia. To do so when his country has teetered on the brink of civil war, and to do so as a member of the Tamil minority, cannot be understated as a victory for the precious remnant of civil order in modern Sri Lanka. Nor can it be dismissed that, as the son of a biscuit maker, and the grandson of a tea plantation labourer, his ascent reflects the better hopes of many of his countrymen, just as Tendulkar's story is that of modern India. It was at St Anthony's College in Kandy that a coach, Sunil Fernando, thought his physique better qualified for spin than pace, and Muralitharan converted with initial reluctance at the age of thirteen.

His record in Tests, which will probably not be surpassed, despite the ever growing number of days each year when there seems to be more than one Test match being played, owes an incalculable amount to his positive outlook and fighting quality – a trait revered by the Sinhalese majority back home. He has endured tremendous interrogation and public humiliation, though, unlike with Warne, these have generally resulted from transgressions on the pitch. Just as Warne was in many ways the ideal overseas player at Hampshire, finally becoming so much more than that, so Muralitharan had a huge impact at Lancashire, not chiefly through his bowling, but rather his gregarious nature, work ethic and commitment to the spirit of the game – ironic, given how many people said he contravened it. Haigh picks out this illustrative paragraph in the veteran Lancashire player Ian Austin's autobiography, *Bully for You, Oscar*:

I've never known anyone who knew so much about cricket – or anyone who could talk about the game for so long. There's a hell of a lot of international cricket being played all year round these days, but Murali knew all about it. He knew more about Lancashire's record than Lancashire players themselves. We'd be sitting in the dressing room or in the bar in the evening at an away game and he'd suddenly start talking about one of our games from years back. He'd know all the facts and figures and couldn't believe that the rest of us didn't remember every last dot and comma of the game he was talking about.

This is a charming tale of immigration at its best, and chimes with Warne's assessment that 'on a personal level, I have always found Murali to be a really nice guy, with a great sense of fun, and he is very, very competitive'. These words contain more than a hint of affection, and the pair grew to be friends rather than simply rivals. Their association profited from the fact that neither of them was in the habit of bowling any of the other's deliveries: Warne couldn't send down a doosra even if he tried. But the close symmetry of their careers acts as a framing mechanism for an age in which spin bowling never dominated the game as pace bowling did in the 1980s, but broke new barriers, and became fundamental to the success of so many teams that we can now reasonably hope that spin bowling will never suffer the threat of extinction so recent in our memories.

Through the 1990s and the first decade of the twenty-first century, while Warne and Muralitharan tore the record books asunder, India and Pakistan both produced two outstanding Test match bowlers who spun their stock ball in opposite directions; New Zealand produced the best genuinely slow left arm since Bedi (assuming Underwood's pace puts him in a different category); Australia produced another erratic leg-spinner who turned the ball more than Warne, but had a different approach to his art; England produced both a bowler whose visual association with Bedi was explicit, and who briefly threatened to emulate his illustrious predecessor with ball in hand, while also producing the best off-spinner since Gibbs; and dotted all around were bowlers, some of whose careers have yet to finish, who, had they the privilege of bowling on uncovered wickets, would unquestionably be thought of even more highly than they already are.

Though Warne's extraordinary contribution to the game is emphasised by the bevy of mediocre spinners that followed him into the

Australian team, few of whom could hold down a place for long, there is some hope that Steve Smith, who bears an uncanny resemblance to Warne, can smooth out the rough edges of his action to add top-class leg-spin to his effective middle-order batting. (It will be galling for English fans to discover that, had his English mother had greater sway over his Australian father, he might have been playing for England now.) And in Sri Lanka, the world of cricket was quickly abuzz when the ex-army boy Ajantha Mendis bowled something called a carrom ball (see Interlude Nine) to make India's allegedly spin-savvy batsman look silly. His star has faded, though it may rise again; and, anyway, by far the most interesting thing about him is not his sainted new delivery, but the fact that it's neither 'his' nor 'new'.

In India, the only regret is that Anil Kumble and Harbhajan Singh weren't closer in age: by the time Singh was in his pomp, Kumble was waning, never having rediscovered the form that made him, against Pakistan in Delhi in 1999, the second man to take all ten wickets in a Test innings.

A comparison of the two 10-fers favours Laker's achievement. That's not just because the Englishman had overall match figures of 19-90, while the Indian's were 14-149. True, Old Trafford in 1956 was a rain-affected, uncovered wicket; but then by the time Kumble was weaving his magic in Delhi, you could fill a tablespoon with the debris thrown up from the pitch by each delivery. The key distinction is in what was going on at the other end. In Laker's triumph, Lock was bowling his heart out; by the time Kumble had taken his sixth, Harbhajan wasn't giving it his all. By the time Kumble was on his ninth, Javagal Srinath was bowling wide long hops at the other end, and the one time he bowled a straight one Waqar Younis skied it just beyond square leg, whereupon the attendant mid-wicket fielder made a less than wholehearted attempt to catch it. In the interests of authenticity, he could at least have dived. And the other point that detracts from Kumble's effort is that Shahid Afridi, the crucial first wicket, was wrongly given out caught behind when in fact his bat hit his pad. (We can't, of course, verify all Laker's dismissals.)

But watching and rewatching Kumble's nevertheless extraordinary performance, the highlight of one of the great Test match careers, is instructive, because, just like Underwood's spell to bowl England to victory at the Oval in 1968, it reveals a near perfect union of bowling style and conditions. Chasing 420 to win, Saeed Anwar and Afridi, Pakistan's openers, made India's bowling look impotent, to reach 101-0 at lunch. After the interval, Kumble, at this time still sporting a moustache and looking every inch a poster boy for the Hero Honda billboards plastered across his home town of Bangalore, roared into action. But not until he had Mushtaq Ahmed – ironically a fellow leg-spinner – caught in the gully off his glove, from a leg-break that bounced shoulder high off a fullish length, did Kumble appear to take a wicket with prodigious spin off the wicket. With other wickets lost leg-before or bowled to balls hurrying through, or caught by close fielders playing down the wrong line, you'd be forgiven, watching the ten balls in isolation, for thinking Pakistan had been overawed by a slow-medium, up-and-down club trundler, albeit one playing in front of 25,000 delirious fans at the Ferozeshah Kotla stadium. The pitch, which Kumble acknowledged to be decisive in his achievement, had had to be repaired after it was vandalised by thugs from the Shiv Sena Hindu nationalist movement a few weeks before the game. They went much further than the 'shave' given to that Old Trafford pitch in Laker's Test by groundsman Bert Flack, under instructions from England's chairman of selectors.

If you watch the whole of Kumble's spell, rather than those deliveries in isolation, however, you get closer to understanding his magic. Kumble was arguably the finest spinner of them all when it came to changing his bowling style to suit a particular pitch. Never a big turner of the ball, on a crumbling wicket he sent down top-spinners and back-spinners with exceptional command of length, while throwing in much more flighted googlies and leg-breaks for variation. On true, solid wickets he would often do the same, but the smallest adjustments in angle and pace would undo the world's finest batsmen. Most teams treated him not as a spinner but as a medium-pace bowler who swung the ball in. Ahead of the 1999 World Cup in England, Steve Waugh instructed his team to play him as an off-cutter bowler. 'Kumble is quicker than most spinners, and he doesn't turn the leg-break as much as many of us,' said Warne. 'He really comes into his own when the bounce is uneven. His height accentuates the difference, so he is very difficult to play confidently.' This was what Fletcher was getting at when he said Kumble was a bowler 'we always mentioned in team meetings as being someone not to sweep, especially early on in one's innings, because he can easily get under the bat with his skidding deliveries.' Martin-Jenkins left him out of his *The 100 Greatest Cricketers of All Time*, but, after reconsidering, is putting him in the next edition.

The pace at which he bowled was probably around 60mph on that afternoon in Delhi – a full 10mph quicker than the pace Warne considered to be natural for himself. The two became good friends, sharing net sessions with Terry Jenner, and exchanging their latest discoveries on points of technique. Kumble adapted his leg-break after Warne showed him his grip for the stock ball, so that Kumble involved his third finger in the delivery more. Warne's flipper benefited from a tutorial from Kumble on how he bowled his.

In style the bowler he has been compared most to is Chandrasekhar – and by extension, O'Reilly. Of the three, Kumble seems to have had the shortest run-up. He turned his leg-break more than Chandrasekhar when he really wanted to, and bowled slightly slower. Like Muralitharan, and for that matter Phil Tufnell, Kumble transferred the ball from his bowling hand to the other, spinning it as if up a chute, and seemed when he left his mark as if set for a 100 metres sprint, only to slow down and approach the crease with two big bounds and a long sweep of the bowling arm. This springy approach had the effect of denying the batsman a sight of the ball until the very last moment.

He was rare for a bowler classified as a leg-spinner in that he seemed to have no qualms with using completely different grips for different deliveries. For the leg-break his grip was standard, though that chat with Warne changed the emphasis between wrist and fingers; for the flipper, too, his grip was fairly orthodox; but he got many of his wickets with a zooter squeezed out of the front of the hand more by palm than by fingers. And, charmingly, his googly – of which, in a hugely successful spell at Northamptonshire, he would regularly bowl six to left-handers – was sent down from what can only be referred to as the Paul Adams grip, with the ball spun between middle finger and thumb, both of which would often run along the seam. This adjustment, a sign of the remarkable dexterity and muscle memory in his fingers and wrist, was done not with the intention of achieving accuracy; rather, he wanted to accentuate spin, and for that reason bowled the googly on a looped trajectory and much more slowly – rather as Gibbs would have sent his stock ball, for example. Speaking in 2008, he said:

Over the last six or seven years I have bowled more of it. I spin the googlies a lot more than the leg-breaks. I am more confident on a flatter deck. That's because it is a different grip totally. It's a natural action. I bowl [it] a lot slower and at that pace you get a lot more spin. With that grip, I do, but with my normal grip I can't bowl that slow. It's all about the pace. If you bowl at that pace, you spin it more.

Intriguingly, this suggests that Kumble felt the orthodox grip for the leg-break, with which Warne also spun his googly, necessitated a quick arm action and release. This doesn't appear to have been Warne's experience: he bowled the googly rarely, but when he did, it was usually a tad below his standard 50mph, and in any case he could easily have varied the pace had he wanted to – though bringing his arm over too quickly might finally have done for his shoulder.

None of this should detract, however, from the fact that Kumble is a leg-spinner at heart, who shares with those other Twirlymen who break the ball from leg an ineradicable fondness for beating the right-hander through spin. Asked what his favourite mode of dismissal is, he said:

A leg-break nicked to slip. People expect me to get people out on the back foot – lbw, or pushing one through. That gives me satisfaction, but at the same time this gives me satisfaction too. It gives me pleasure when I know that I beat him in the flight.

Spoken like a true spinner. And an exceptionally successful one, too: with 619 Test wickets, he is third in the all-time list, behind only Muralitharan and Warne. He acquired his first one hundred wickets in twenty-one Tests, two fewer than Warne took to reach that landmark, and when, in 1995, he took 105 wickets in first-class cricket for Northamptonshire (Mushtaq Ahmed, another leg-spinner, had the second highest tally on ninety-five), he was the first spinner since 1983 to pass one hundred wickets, and the first leg-spinner since 1971. He had been signed by Northants as their replacement for Curtly Ambrose. Mohammad Azharuddin, his captain for India, phoned Allan Lamb to recommend the youngster, who Lamb remembered rather well by virtue of being Kumble's first wicket in Tests, caught at silly point. When Northants phoned Kumble he was in a hotel in Madras (as it then was, Chennai as it now is). He accepted without talking money.

His father had been a management consultant, and, like so many of the other bowlers in these pages, young Anil started out with a tennis ball on the streets outside his house. He sought to exploit his height as a medium-pacer, but his brother Dinesh, aware of the paucity of spin bowlers in southern India, thought he had a better chance of getting on if he had a go at leg-spin. 'There was no one to guide me or coach me or show me how to grip the ball,' Kumble recalled. But he did okay by himself, finding that his height helped on the matting wickets that were rolled out over dry mud in Bangalore's club cricket. 'When I started my career we played on dustbowls in all these mofussil centres. But that was an education,' he says. He made his Test debut at nineteen, in heavily rimmed glasses that suggested a brooding intellectual. 'With his thick glasses and grim demeanour, he appeared a fellow who might be more comfortable in the first row of a classroom rather than spinning a ball on a cricket field,' said Rahul Dravid, the magnificent Indian batsman who became one of Kumble's closest friends. Indeed, the theme of education is one that has always attached itself to Kumble's character, whether through his own analysis or that of others. 'His greatness arrives from his ability to always see himself as a student. He is always learning, and through the years he has consistently made small improvements, extending his range and polishing his repertoire,' Dravid added.

Much as with Warne and Muralitharan, there was a sense that Kumble's champion class stemmed ultimately from a quality of character rather than technique. Dravid could speak with some authority on the subject. They played together in under-19 cricket, when Dravid was a terrified wicketkeeper trying to avoid getting a broken nose while standing up to Kumble on matting wickets. So Dravid had a better sense than most about the development of Kumble's career, one fortified by Kumble's replacing him as India's captain when Dravid couldn't bear the strain. Coming just after Kumble's thirty-seventh birthday, many said he'd acquired the responsibility too late. 'You felt that he was an intense, proud character,' Atherton told me, 'who wore his pride on his sleeve. A natural captain.'

After all, he'd shown he could be an inspirational leader for years, as when, in the Antigua Test of 2002, he was hit by a Merv Dillon bouncer, spat out blood, batted for a further twenty minutes, took to the field with a heavy bandage reattaching his mouth to the rest of his face, bowled fourteen respectable overs, took the wicket of Brian Lara and flew home to Bangalore the following day for surgery on what was, it transpired, a broken jaw. But it was in the tense series against Australia in 2007–8, when Harbhajan and Andrew Symonds got involved in a race row, that Kumble's leadership came into its own. Calm, dignified and diplomatic, he was told that Ponting had said in a press conference: 'There is absolutely no doubt this match has been played in the right spirit.' His instinctive response – 'Only one team was playing in the spirit of the game, that's all I can say' – was taken as a sharp and successful victory in the public relations war. Perhaps you'd expect no less from a man who, during his early playing days, had worked in PR for Triton Watches in Bangalore.

It helped that he had matinee-idol looks and was, at least in the days after the Delhi 10-fer, only one rung down from Tendulkar and Mahendra Dhoni in terms of the adulation he received from the Indian public. A teetotal, vegetarian and family man, he was every mother's wish even before the distinction he received for his Masters in Mechanical Engineering, a qualification that those other brilliant Indian spinners, Prasanna and Venkataraghavan, also acquired. Dravid, ever keen on the education theme, said of Kumble, 'He has a degree in engineering and a Ph.D. in leg-spin bowling.' With this observation, the master batsman revealed that very Indian form of humour that makes jokes out of favourable comparisons. This comic tradition, incidentally, explains why the cartoon in *The Times* the day after Kumble took all ten is my father's favourite from several decades of reading newspapers: a chap in the laundry is confused when he sees three options on the washing machine – Spin, Extra Spin, Kumble.

Some sages proffered the suggestion that Kumble's handling of the Harbhajan controversy marked the high point of his career, over and above the Delhi conquest nearly a decade previously. It's hard for many people outside India to understand the burden that he shouldered through a tortuous few weeks, not only because of the sheer scale of cricket's popular base in India, and the tribalism inherent within it, but because of the place of Harbhajan Singh in the modern Indian psyche.

Fans in England, South Africa, the Caribbean, or to a lesser extent Australia might be forgiven for thinking that Singh was merely a competent Test match spinner who, having had problems with the legality of his action (stemming, predictably, from his doosra), used to bowl off-spin with the chest-on action and looped parabola of Gibbs, but is these days so reliant on his lucrative income from shorter forms of the game that he is becoming a kind of exotic Shaun Udal.

That would be to ignore the bigger picture. Harbhajan, known to his countrymen as Bhajji, is dating Geeta Basra, beautiful Indian actress, Bollywood star and icon of modern India. Marriage is rumoured. As a celebrity pairing it makes David Beckham and Victoria Adams look like Eddie the Eagle and Sue Barker. Nor do his showbiz credentials end there. If you thought Darren Gough winning *Strictly Come Dancing* was hilarious enough, look up the victorious, and astonishingly accomplished, boogie with which Harbhajan won *Ek Khiladi Ek Hasina* (*One Player, One Beauty*), a show similar in style to *Strictly Come Dancing*, but distinguished by having a vastly bigger audience. Together with Dhoni, India's captain, he owns a sprawling 14,160 sq. ft office on the eighth floor of the Trade World Building at the Kamala Mills Compound in Lower Parel, Mumbai. Harbhajan might use the office for the TV production company he has started with friends; Dhoni might use it for the merchandise venture he has undertaken with the Bollywood superstar and model Dino Morea. That is to say, they are well connected.

He has a stake in a hair salon in Chandigarh called Sylvie's, owned and run by the eponymous Sylvie, who happens to be transgender. Once, in his school days, he found himself equipped with an air rifle. He fired it. At a beehive. 'There was complete chaos. When they found out I was the culprit, the teachers gave me a lot of stick.' It was this spinner, you recall, who in April 2008 was involved in an apparently farcical incident during a Twenty20 game that cost him £375,000. Harbhajan was captaining Mumbai, who had just lost their third game in a row, against a Punjab XI in Mohali. Going down a line of opposition players to shake their hands in the customary way, he alighted on Sri Sreesanth, his seam bowler colleague in the national side, and, instead of shaking his hand, slapped him across the face, completely without provocation. This led to his being banned for a whole season.

That last, and completely unforgivable, incident came a couple of months after the Harbhajan–Symonds saga. But in the context of his other extra-curricular activities it gives some indication of the combustibility of the man Kumble was sent on to the world stage to defend. Harbhajan was found guilty of a racial slur – calling Symonds, who was adopted but one of whose biological parents was Caribbean – a 'monkey', and banned for three Tests by Mike Procter, the match referee. He claimed Symonds, no stranger to controversy himself, had started the spat by telling him he had no friends on the Australian team, after Harbhajan patted Brett Lee on the backside with his bat, after having blocked out a Lee yorker. The Indian Cricket Board (BCCI) suspended India's tour of Australia pending the result of an appeal. The New Zealander Justice John Hansen eventually downgraded the charge from Level 3.3 to 2.8, finding Harbhajan guilty of using abusive language and fining him 50 per cent of his match fee, but, crucially, clearing him of racism.

I've long felt that, given no microphone picked up what he actually said, speculation on the precise content of his discussion with Symonds is reserved for the idle and the pedantic.

So let's speculate.

The indispensable Lawrence Booth has highlighted the key exchange during the Appeal hearing between Symonds, Justice Hansen, and Vasha Manohar, the Indian lawyer:

Manohar: 'I put it to you that apart from the other Indian abuses he said to you the words 'teri maki'?
Symonds: 'Possibly, I don't recall, I don't speak that language.'
Manohar: 'Thank you.'
Hansen: 'But you accept that as a possibility, Mr Symonds?'
Symonds: 'As a possibility I accept that, yes.'

'Teri maki' is Punjabi for 'Your mum'. Later in the hearing, Symonds said Harbhajan called him 'big monkey', but the fact that he admitted what he heard first might have been 'Teri maki', cast sufficient doubt on the incident to exonerate Harbhajan. Claims later emerged in India that, since Hanuman, the monkey god, is a revered symbol of Hindu tradition, Harbhajan would never deign to invoke a monkey as a form of insult. This seems a tenuous argument, not least because Harbhajan is a Sikh. Leading the anti-Harbhajan, pro-he-said-'monkey' charge was Matthew Hayden, a devout Christian, who later called Harbhajan an 'obnoxious weed'. On the field of play, Hayden said to Harbhajan: 'It's racial vilification, mate. It's a shit word and you know it.' He thought Harbhajan said monkey, though in the Appeal he, too, said it was open to doubt. Procter, when handing down the initial ban, said he was 'satisfied beyond reasonable doubt' that the word 'monkey' had been uttered.

The controversy lingered long after the result of the Appeal with the revelation that some Australian players had been leaned on by their anxious board to downplay their version of events. This came at a time when Ponting was not a popular man. The Indian Board was then shown to have chartered a flight out of Adelaide, as if that were a sin. An unnamed, contracted Australian player claimed in the *Sydney Morning Herald* 'this shows how much influence India has, because of the wealth they generate'.

Enmity between the two teams, three years on, has yet to be fully resolved. The taste lingers. And Harbhajan's fame, and status as a national hero, continues to grow, despite the setback of his Sreesanth provocation. But the above saga is an absolutely essential indicator of the raw material – the headlines, the rudeness, the adulation at home – that has turned a competent spinner into India's best in the post-Kumble age, and a pin-up of Twenty20 who is third only to Swann and Vettori in the ranks of spinner who excel at all forms of the game.

In Test cricket he will never again be as dangerous as he was in 2001, when in three Tests against Australia he collected thirty-two wickets, while the most any of his teammates could manage was three. He did this at the age of twenty-one. The wickets included the first hat-trick at Test level by an Indian, though the hat-trick ball victim, Warne, was wrongly given out when jamming the ball into the ground and to short leg. At this stage, Harbhajan was an exceptional young talent. He launched off his mark with a jump of declaration, and so wildly did he flail his arms that, had he not given the impression of swimming his way up to the wicket, the batsman could be forgiven for thinking Medusa herself had entered the attack, sporting a turban. His mostly one-armed, chest-on action produced a huge degree of over-spin, so that loop, and the consequent awkward bounce, were the chief destroyers in his armoury, much as with Gibbs a few decades earlier.

But a finger operation in 2003 diminished his spinning capacities, and he briefly lost form altogether. He remodelled himself as a bowler with more subtle variations, and started bowling the under-cutter regularly – an effective ball on slow, dusty tracks in India. He had always possessed a more than useful top-spinner, which, because of the speed of his arm action, hurried on to the batsmen, trapping many of them in front before they could get their bat down (including Ponting and Gilchrist in that hat-trick). Warne, who said of the Symonds affair, 'I thought he [Harbhajan] handled the situation ... pretty badly and should have been punished more than he was,' thought his top-spinner his best ball. 'On slow pitches in Australia, you have to try to push the ball through a bit quicker. In India, those balls can sit up to be cut or pulled,' Warne said. 'You need to try to slow things down, try to put over-spin on the ball and try to tempt batsmen to drive. Those conditions are perfect for Harbhajan's top-spinner.'

Even now, though still India's premier spinner, he lacks the fizz and bite of those early days. Most spinners get better with age, and Harbhajan, now into his thirties, should be reaching his pomp. (Muralitharan, asked who might surpass his record haul of Test wickets, said: 'I think only Harbhajan can do this.') Instead, he seems destined never to become what he might have been – the best orthodox off-spinner since Laker, a title that now sits more comfortably with an Englishman, Graeme Swann. I'd venture three reasons. First, his finger never fully recovered the strength and suppleness it had prior to 2003; second, his having allowed the experience of limited-overs cricket to change the way he bowls in the longer game, like Emburey; and third, his adoption and overuse of the doosra.

As Jenner, with customary insight, put it: 'I watched Harbhajan Singh help India win the 2007 World Cup in South Africa and he was bowling 100kph yorkers, wide of the crease. You wonder about the development of the spinner then. I don't think he has been the same bowler since.' He is right, and so, too, was Atherton when he was prompted, after the Chennai Test of 2008, to write:

Even though Harbhajan was in form, bowling at a ground he knows well and at batsmen short of match practice, he made little impression. I am not entirely sure that Harbhajan is the bowler he used to be, now that an overextended use of the doosra – the ball that spins to the off – has affected his ability to drift and spin his stock ball, the off spinner.

Harbhajan was once a young bowler with a sharp-turning stock ball, plenty of loop, a top-spinner that hurried on to the batsman, an arm ball that drifted away in the air and an under-cutter. But when first Saqlain and then Muralitharan started bowling doosras with extreme skill, he felt the soft tug of peer pressure and put into action a ball that is exceptionally difficult to bowl, and which cost him his stock ball. Harbhajan has accounted for his adoption of the doosra – which led to his being called for chucking – in a manner that suggests he would have started bowling it even if it hadn't been for that other pair; but we should be in no doubt that his challengers for the status of best off-spinner in the world hastened his demise by encouraging him to overuse it. It's no consolation either, to those who wish spinners well, that this account makes clear his awareness of the complications involved in bowling this variation:

It is very difficult to explain in words. All a youngster can do is lock his wrist and try to roll the ball over, making sure the seam position is towards the slips. The doosra came by chance to me – I was experimenting during my days at the Sports Authority of India Academy in Chandigarh, around 1996.

The thumb rule in bowling off-spin is to point the seam towards leg slip, but I wanted to send the ball straight. So I started to bowl with a straight seam, like a fast bowler. Once that started to happen I locked my wrist and tried to see if I could send the ball the other way. I practised really hard to perfect the delivery.

A lot of spinners lose their stock ball, the off-spinner, by bowling a lot of doosras, so I would suggest that they perfect one delivery as their stock delivery and use the doosra judiciously.

If only he had heeded his own advice, which was wiser than he gave it credit for. Or – a clearer illustration still – seen what the doosra did to the very man he was seeking to emulate.

We saw in the Introduction that Saqlain wasn't the first to bowl the doosra, Jack Potter having delivered it in the 1960s, assuming it *was* the doosra and not the carrom ball. It was on the 1964 Ashes tour that Benaud told Potter: 'If I had a ball like that, I'd be practising at Lord's before breakfast.' Wally Grout, Potter's wicketkeeper, to whom he occasionally bowled it in the nets for a joke, wrote:

You had no chance of detecting it from the hand and could only hope to pick the direction of the spin through the air, a dicey business, particularly on the many English grounds with sightscreens … [Gloucestershire's David] Allen muttered to me one day after Jack's wrong'un had him swiping fresh air: 'What's this fellow doing?' and though equally fooled I did my best to convince David that the ball had hit something on the wicket. In later matches the appearance of Potter at the bowling crease prompted a conference among the batsmen, one I should have been allowed to join. I was as much in the dark about Jack's pet ball as they were.

Just as Grimmett wasn't the first to bowl the flipper (was it Walter Mead? If not, Grace himself?), Saqlain didn't invent the doosra. But he did briefly master it, before it mastered him. He became addicted to it, reliant on it for the whole of his method, unable to operate without it, and so wholly did it consume him that, when combined with two major knee injuries, it pushed the career of one of the great spinners into a regrettably early retirement.

The romance of Saqlain's ascent, and his brief flirtation with a ball that threatened to consume the whole off-spinning tradition, and render the methods of the old masters incomplete, enhances the tragedy of his demise. It's hard not to be moved by Saqlain's recollections of playing with his brothers on the rooftops of Lahore. Younger and less academically inclined than them, he would wait until they came home from tuition, having drawn a line on a wall with a piece of chalk, and then use both table-tennis and tennis balls. He chanced on the doosra by accident, finding one day that by cocking his wrist inward he could get the ball to go the other way, undetected. Practising hardest with the smaller table-tennis ball, he soon acquired vast popularity on the rooftops of that magnificent city, and then in his local area. It took him between two and three years to graduate to a level where he could bowl it with a cricket ball, plagued all the while by lacerated fingers – 'most of the time, my fingers used to cut', he says – and by the time he was seventeen, though his hands were far from fully developed, he was beginning to control it.

In fact, Saqlain had learned different skills from each of his brothers. Sibtain, who played for Lahore, taught him off-spin; Zulqarnain taught him how to bat. Clearly the former was more influential than the latter. The three of them would get up at 4.30 in the morning, go to the local mosque and then scurry back to play what they liked to call a Test match. Sometimes, they would put electrical tape on one half of the ball, knowing that made it hack through the air in an unusual manner. Poor but precocious, they bet soft drinks or dinner on the outcome.

I suppose we should give thanks to Allah, as Saqlain does regularly in conversation, for the further lesson of the doosra, which is not to overbowl it. That 'thingy', as he calls it, can ruin a perfectly good career. Saqlain bowled it brilliantly on the tour of Australia in 1999, and there was a time in the following two years when he was one of the most accomplished spinners in the history of the game, turning his off-break sharply, and achieving quick turn, too, off the Pakistani wickets, and then bowling a ball that spun like a leg-break but was almost impossible to pick. To non-Asian batsmen, who he felt as a rule had poorer footwork, he got it in early. 'I used to bowl the doosra first [ball] to give them a *jhatka* ["shock"].' I remember watching super-super slo-mo video replays of Saqlain bowling during England's tour in 2000–2001, where he flummoxed endless Englishmen, and especially Hick. Even with the clearest videos moving at one frame every three seconds, it seemed impossible to work out how, with the subtlest of changes in his wrist position, he achieved break the other way. My own experiments left me baffled: to cock my wrist in sufficiently for the seam to be pointing towards slip, I simply had to bend my arm at the elbow. Even then, achieving the propulsion required with the wrist seemed very difficult.

Yet Saqlain could do it – legally. When he first bowled it on the county scene, many batsmen thought it was just a top-spinner that went away in the air. They were terrified when it transpired that he actually did make the ball turn, and at times quite sharply. Some joked that he would get into the England team even if he was banned from bowling the off-break – alas, Ian Salisbury, an underrated leg-spinner with a stiff, military precision to his action, was unable to hold a place down, though that was partly because he was treated insensitively by the captain and selectors.

Saqlain was the fastest bowler to one hundred one-day wickets, and so precise was his command of line and length, even while spinning it hard, that Wasim Akram regularly employed him to bowl both in the first fifteen overs and at the death. He had a shuffling, bustling run-up, like a schoolboy late for class. Sometimes, when opponents were well set on flat pitches, he would experiment wildly with his approach, first decelerating to a very slow amble, then running in super-fast, only to deliver the ball from next to the umpire, making it in effect slower than it seemed likely to be. Few spinners have ever used the crease more imaginatively.

Saqlain made his Test debut at nineteen, fast-tracked by Wasim, and took a wicket, that of Sri Lanka's Chandika Hathurusingha, with his seventh ball, at Peshawar in 1995. After the series in India in 1999, in which Kumble took his Delhi 10-fer, a spinner was adjudged 'Man of the Series'. It wasn't Kumble. Neither was it Harbhajan. With his five wickets in each of the innings in Chennai and Delhi, nobody was in any doubt that the real star of the series had been Saqlain. In the Chennai Test, he bowled thirty-four overs in sweltering heat, taking Tendulkar for a duck, and turning it sharply both ways. He nearly collapsed with heat stroke, but in the second innings, when Tendulkar's extraordinary century had brought India to within seventeen runs of victory, Wasim threw the ball to his star turn and said, 'You can do it. You're No. 1.' Saqlain did do it, getting Tendulkar caught in the deep – by Wasim – to secure an extraordinary win. Later that year he was almost the bowler of the tournament at the World Cup in England, taking seventeen wickets, including a hat-trick against Zimbabwe. But even his magic couldn't win the final, in which Warne excelled. Pakistan were thrashed, and Saqlain, then only twenty-three, was left scarred. 'I left the team hotel and went back to my London flat and cried,' he said. 'For two days I didn't speak to anyone apart from my wife. She helped me pull through.'

But even when in reasonable form for the Test side, in 2003, he was dropped ignominiously, and as usual it was over to the conspiracy theorists to explain what was going on with the selection of the Pakistan team. This time, it was thought he was being punished for blasting coach Javed Miandad on the phone after being dropped for a series against South Africa. He later apologised, but the damage was done. Grudges are rarely soon forgotten when it comes to cricket in Pakistan. Soon he would lose command of his stock ball, and it was left to the imagination as to what this devout Muslim, whose enormous beard nowadays distinguishes him from the callow youth of a decade ago, might otherwise have achieved.

Just as Indian fans were left to wonder what might have been if Kumble and Harbhajan had bowled together when both were at the height of their powers, so Pakistan's fans lamented the brevity of Saqlain's association, at Test level, with Mushtaq Ahmed. Doosra, as we have established, means 'the other one', and Saqlain really is best understood as 'Doosra Mushtaq', being the owner of a name that, when he broke into international cricket, had for several years already been synonymous with baffling and brilliantly executed spin.

If imitation is the highest form of flattery, Mushtaq Ahmed paid Abdul Qadir the biggest compliment he ever received by copying his bowling style to the smallest detail. There was that same bounding run-up, the same chest-on action, the same looped trajectory, loyally retraced with every ball; the same overreliance on over-spin, and the same brutal involvement of the googly. Except that Mushtaq's googly was even more deadly: indeed, no single bowler in the history of the game, going back to Bosanquet and the South African quartet, and even before, has used the googly with greater efficacy. The momentum Mushtaq's run-up gives him at the crease, together with the openness of his action and a wonderfully flexible wrist, make his googly at times impossible to decipher. He could generally turn it more than his leg-break, a rare quality among spinners, and his googly to dismiss Hick in the 1992 World Cup final deserves to be recognised as only one rung down from Warne's ball to Gatting in terms of sheer cricketing skill.

Time and again, the well-set batsman would fend off a series of leg-breaks pitching on his off-stump, then rock back at the ball much wider, fully expecting to cut it through point, only for it to spin sharply back into him and be his undoing.

However, exuberance getting the better of him, Mushtaq probably overbowled his googly, so that there came a time when batsmen, even if they didn't fancy themselves to pick it, could nullify him by playing each ball as if it would break from the off. This presented Mushtaq with problems, because so laden were his deliveries with over-spin that he didn't always turn his leg-break enough to trouble right-handers. 'Because his googly was so effective,' said Warne, 'we generally reckoned to play him as an off-break bowler if we were unsure of a delivery, knowing that a leggie would turn past the edge.' It was this approach that caused Mushtaq a rare dip in form in the mid-nineties. In 1995 specifically, under the advice of the great Martin Crowe, the New Zealander who played for Mushtaq's adopted home club of Somerset, batsmen just played him as an off-break bowler, negating a major line of attack. So discussed and debated was the success of this method that Mushtaq, much to his chagrin, was for some time nicknamed not 'Mushy', as he is generally known to the world, but Tauseef – after Tauseef Ahmed, the Pakistani off-spinner of the 1980s. It was more insult than compliment.

There were two immediate causes of the development of this batting technique against him. The first, ironically, was the fault of Warne himself:

The trouble when Pakistan came over in 1995 was that Mushtaq learned things too quickly for our own good. It came about after a long chat when I showed him how to bowl my flipper and he gave me his wrong'un. I thought that would be a good swap from my point of view, because even now he probably bowls the wrong'un (better known in England as the googly) better than anybody else in the world.

Unfortunately, by the time he came into the side, Mushtaq had got his head – or more to the point his fingers – around the flipper and kept using it to dismiss our batsmen! They couldn't believe it when they found out it was a ball he'd picked up from me.

The second reason was simply his phenomenal success at county level. If his first great claim to fame should be that he was the finest exponent of the googly ever to live, his second must be that not only did he prompt Angus Fraser to write of him, when he announced his retirement, that he was 'the most influential cricketer in the modern day county game', but nobody with an iota of knowledge about either the player or the sport could reasonably doubt it. At first for Somerset, and then from the 2003 season for Sussex, he made a greater impact on each club in each season he played than most overseas players would expect to make in five seasons. When Sussex signed him, it was initially on a modest salary, with bonuses for each wicket he took. The pay structure worked, incentivising him to take five ten-wicket hauls and become the first bowler for five years to take a hundred wickets in a domestic season, as Sussex won the Championship. They repeated the feat in 2006 and 2007, during which glorious years he took a magnificent 192 wickets at only 22.6. Between 2003 and 2007 he bowled just under 21,000 deliveries, testament to both his extraordinary stamina and the fact that so many of the finest spinners become better able to withstand the physical exertions with age.

He had by then come a long way from the child who, around the age of nine, began imitating the action of Pakistan's most glamorous cricketer, Qadir, in the streets of Sahiwal, not far from Lahore, where he grew up. He gave an early signal of his quality to English batsmen when, aged just seventeen, he took 6-81 for the Punjab Chief Minister's XI in his home town against Mike Gatting's infamous touring side of 1987–8. There was a kind of sporting romance, too, in the fact that when he was first called up to the Pakistan side, flying out in January 1990, it was as a replacement for Qadir that he had been selected. He took the torch of wrist-spin bowling from Qadir, and kept the flame alive until Warne's breakthrough against England – and for long after.

It's often said of Pakistan players that it's 'a mystery' why they didn't do better at Test level. Given Ahmed's exceptional talent, the same could reasonably be asked of a man who, in his fifty-two Tests, took 185 wickets at 32.97. But if what seems an isolated injustice keeps recurring to various players, and a pattern emerges, it's probably time to stop describing it as a mystery, and to start ascribing a cause. 'Given how long he played the game,' said Warne, 'it amazes me that he didn't play more Test matches, even taking into account the occasional madness of Pakistan selectors' – and you ought to feel no guilt about reading that final clause as diplomatic speak for: 'They're nutters.' The same backroom envies and dressing-room tribalism that did for Saqlain did, also, for Mushtaq. That he should have been 'hurt and angry' at being sacked as Pakistan coach just hours before the team left for a Champions Trophy tour of India in 2006 gives some indication of the lingering tensions that seem to account, eventually and inevitably, for the careers of so many of Pakistan's great talents. The public line was that his involvement in a match-fixing scandal in the 1990s had damaged his integrity irreparably. Mushtaq denied taking money from Salim Pervez, an illegal bookmaker well acquainted with the Pakistani authorities, but a report in 2000 suggested 'strong doubt' lingered over his version of events, and claimed he had brought his country's cricket into disrepute. He was fined £3,700 and censured. Like Saqlain, he acquired a deeper attachment to his faith in his playing days – both grew large beards as an outward manifestation of this – and it has been credibly claimed that his intensified piety was motivated by a desire for redemption from that episode.

It's especially sad given the vital energy that Mushtaq brought to the game. He really was a bowler who seemed to be constantly making the unexpected and untoward happen, irresistible to spectators and players alike. He once bowled a ball to South Africa's Pat Symcox in a Test match that passed through off and middle stump, rattling both, but failing to dislodge a bail. He was united, in this unfortunate occurrence, with 'Lumpy' Stevens, in the eighteenth century, whose deliveries kept passing between stumps and led eventually to the creation of a third, and middle, stump.

This bustling energy, together with the proficiency of his googly, made him very hard to play even on good wickets. Batsmen facing him had to respond to the full force of his personality before, during and after each delivery. Fraser, in that same career obituary for the *Independent*, conveyed the complete bemusement felt by any batsman tormented, and finally defeated, by the highest class of spin bowling:

I faced him once at Taunton when he was playing for Somerset and I have never felt more humiliated on a cricket field. For five balls I groped forward like a drunken teenager and failed to make contact with the ball. Nobody was happier than I when the final delivery of the over bowled me.

He shared with Arthur Mailey the notion that his job was to take wickets rather than bowl maidens, which is what the straight up and down men were in it for, after all. This meant that, unlike with Warne, Grimmett, Benaud or Kumble at their best, you could expect a four-ball every other over, and sometimes more regularly than that. But his occasional profligacy stemmed from his deeply held view that the first task of the spinner is to defeat the batsman with spin, and for that reason alone he deserves our gratitude. The greater cause for joy from an English perspective, however, is that whether motivated by guilt, faith or whatever, he seems to have taken it upon himself to devote the next phase of his life to getting the best out of England's finest spinners. In this noble task he is having tremendous success, as we shall see.

Looking back on these six bowlers, it is possible to divide them satisfactorily in rank. Warne and Muralitharan were giants, bestriding the world stage with unseen skills. They were followed by the pair of pairs from the Indian subcontinent, which yielded very different off-spinners in Harbhajan and Saqlain, and very different leg-spinners in Kumble and Mushtaq.

There is a bowler, currently playing for England, who seems likely to end up as worthy of equal status to the above. That is a joyful thing, but he's not there yet. And so, in the rank, below those six greats of the game, we alight on two more Antipodean maestros.

It's not altogether easy to be certain how to place Daniel Vettori, because it's possible that he is the only current player – Sachin Tendulkar aside – who, by the time his playing days are up, we'll have reason to call the greatest player his nation has ever produced.

Quite apart from the fact that he is the first New Zealander to do the double of 300 wickets and 3,000 runs in Test cricket; quite apart from the fact that he not only filled the gargantuan boots of Stephen Fleming, his predecessor as national captain; quite apart from the fact that he is the youngest cricketer to play for the All Blacks; quite apart from all that, he would, for his all-round ability, sober and shrewd cricketing brain, and brilliant adaptability to different forms of the game, be one of the first names on most team sheets, when compiling a World XI. That has been the case for the last couple of years; it looks as if it could be the case for several more. And to cap it all, he is, with the (hopefully temporary) demise of Monty Panesar, the best left-arm tweaker in the world just now, and the best since Underwood.

All this becomes at least doubly remarkable when considering what he has overcome to acquire such exalted status – testament to that ever-present quality of the great spinners, stamina. It is a curiosity not just of cricket but geography that, though so proximate in the atlas, New Zealand has a very different climate from Australia. Being a pair of small islands, it is buffeted by winds in a way that Australia is not; and its exposure to the Pacific is such that the effect of its rains lingers in a way they do not in Australia, large swathes of which are ravaged by drought for part of the year.

The consequence of all this is that the conditions for cricket in New Zealand are eerily similar to those in England: seam- rather than spin-friendly. Green tops, overcast conditions and moist surfaces are nothing like the baked mud common to Australian pitches. That makes Vettori's success all the more impressive; he has not been able to rely on helpful conditions for his wickets, and has therefore been required to innovate constantly.

The other major impediment to success that he has overcome is injury. At the age of twenty-three, he was struck down by stress fractures of his back, of the sort more familiar to fast bowlers who have 'mixed' actions, neither fully side-on nor fully chest-on (like Andrew Flintoff). It was stress fractures of the back, indeed, that so very sadly did for the searing pace of Vettori's compatriot, Shane Bond, a man who not only had a terrific name for a fast bowler, but the requisite raw materials, too.

Desperately disappointed, but not defeated, by the severity of his back problems, Vettori completely remodelled his action to reduce the strain on his body. This cost him some spin, but what he lost in revolutions on the ball he made up for in improved accuracy and variation. His career is therefore best understood as composed of two distinct passages.

In the first, he was an exceptionally exciting young talent, plucked from obscurity, able to spin the ball vigorously and pose problems for the best batsmen in the world. He added to this with exquisitely controlled variations in flight, pace and line. This was only amplified by his unlikely status as a sex symbol. The young star, every New Zealand housewife's dream, had the sort of inverse sex appeal that made Jarvis Cocker the bane of my adolescence. And that was long before Vettori's bespectacled appearance led to his being nicknamed Harry Potter by the mother-in-laws federation of his home country, who were acting in cahoots with sportswriters the world over.

He was fortunate to be selected so young for his had been an unlikely journey. Vettori is from a sporting family. On his mother Robyn's side are rugby league star Ken Stirling and Olympic swimmer Glenda Stirling; on father Renzo's side Daniel is a cousin of former All Blacks fly-half David Hill, while Joseph Hill, a first-class batsman, is his cousin, and Tony Hill, his uncle, is a former first-class all-rounder. Daniel took up cricket at the age of seven, when the family lived in Sydney, but only turned to spin when, at fifteen, he was proving an unexceptional medium-pacer in his school side. By then he was already a hugely talented footballer, though it was at that age that his football team's coach crashed, leaving him with a fractured vertebra.

Renzo's father had been a concrete worker in the Italian village of Roncone in the Dolomites, but moved when Renzo was six. Daniel's sudden ascent required of them that they learn quickly about a sport of which they knew very little. 'It was nuts. They suddenly became cricket experts,' Renzo told Cricinfo. 'It was the last thing they knew, or thought they knew.'

Robyn worked as a nurse, and Renzo worked for a dairy company. He recalls that he himself nearly crashed when picking up his car phone to be told that his son had been selected for the Test side. They live less than ten minutes' drive from Seddon Park, where their son made his debut for Northern Districts, aged just seventeen. In New Zealand, everything is local.

One newspaper headline, part of the mammoth set of cuttings still to be found in the Vettori household, screamed 'But He's Only 18!'. As Daniel put it himself, ever one for understatement:

I suppose I was a little bit lucky with the selection at that time. At thirty-eight, [off-spinner] Dipak Patel was close to the end of his career. They were looking for someone new and I had done well in the Under-19 tournaments. Steve Rixon watched me in my first first-class match and thought I had done enough and gave me a chance. It was pretty nerve-wracking, but pretty exciting as well to get a chance to play for your country at eighteen.

Rixon was the fabulously competitive, handlebar-mustachioed Australian coach who, together with the national selectors, had seen Vettori play for Northern Districts against England at the start of the 1997 tour. Aware of the tourists' difficulty against spin, they threw Vettori into the Test arena, and watched him perform creditably. Aged eighteen years and ten days, he bowled more overs than anyone else in England's only innings. Not long after, in the final Test at Christchurch, England won by four wickets chasing 305. But of the 146.4 overs they batted through, Vettori's young shoulders got through a mighty fifty-seven.

Their owner was a spinner with a fairly long run-up, a huge swivel into side-on position and a full pivot through the delivery stride, involving the body as much as possible in imparting spin. Obsessive, as all these spinners are, about how to maximise the revolutions on the ball, he watched videos of Warne, Muralitharan and Kumble (more recently, he has said that Harbhajan is the bowler he most enjoys watching). He supplemented a fiercely spun stock ball with one of the most brilliant disguised, and consistently effective, arm balls in cricket history. When he was at his best in bowling it, it's hard to think of another spinner whose arm ball was more deadly – and that's including 'Deadly' Underwood himself. (He was aware of his heritage: when assorted journalists congratulated him on his 300th wicket, Vettori sniggered, 'I can't believe you didn't mention me going past Derek Underwood' – clearly delighted at the competitive advantage he would thereafter hold over the English left-armer.)

I'll never forget what he did to the English batsman Darren Maddy on his Test debut, when he set him up with a ball outside off-stump that Maddy drove, another that spun sharply away to the slips, and then swung an arm ball into Maddy's off-stump as he shouldered arms, a delivery so delicious in its deception that I was briefly inspired to try bowling left-handed myself.

Then the back problems struck. 'In the early part of my career I had to make adjustments to my technique because of the problems I had with stress fractures in the back. All injuries are a low point,' Vettori says. 'When you're out of the game there's a frustration that comes in and you wonder whether you can get back to where you were. And when they're serious injuries you're remodelling your action and changing your technique, and that becomes a concern.' It led to a three-year spell without a five-wicket haul.

Vettori, who claims, 'I've always seen subtle variation as being the key to my success, using flight and pace rather than turn', did lose a substantial amount of his turn following the back trouble. With limited runs on the board and unexceptional support bowlers, he was often forced on to the defensive early, anyway, unable to set attacking fields. But by shortening his run-up and opening his action so that it was much more chest-on, he was able to take the strain off his more vulnerable parts. That has not only massively boosted his longevity as a player; it has also allowed him to bowl very long spells, often on thankless and unrewarding wickets in New Zealand, and to thrive in all three major formats of the modern game. He is a good enough batsman to get into the national side for his batting alone, and by adding the (delete as appropriate) duty/burden of being selector, he has ensured that he is easily the most powerful man in New Zealand cricket.

He is only the second spinning son of New Zealand to acquire one hundred wickets at Test level, after John Bracewell, and though the Kiwis have produced a modicum of competent spinners over the years – Tom Burtt, Hedley Howarth, Stephen Boock, Patel – none has come even close to the degree of success Vettori achieved. To that extent, he is a pioneer, both distinct from and superior to that which has gone before in his part of the world.

This could be understood as a sort of inverse of the situation in which Stuart MacGill found himself, and always will, in the annals of the game. Just remember, when the amateurish banter is underway in your local pub, and your interlocutors are claiming to know who turned the ball more than any other bowler in cricket history, that Warne himself reckoned MacGill turned his stock ball more than him. That is a subtle judgement, of course: Warne wasn't saying that he couldn't turn the ball more than his rival (they are friends now) had he wanted to; he was only saying that his own stock ball contained more over-spin, and so dipped more. Contained within that assertion is both a kernel of truth and a little dig: Warne was implying that MacGill was all about sideways turn rather than subtlety of spin – and it's the latter which Warne mastered, to devastating effect.

But you might add, when conducting this pub argument, that only Grimmett, Lillee and Younis have acquired a double century of Test wickets more quickly. MacGill was a volatile character to whom the nickname 'Cho' (cricket hours only), originally attached to Gleeson, might also apply, so voraciously did he read on tour. MacGill has been remarkably magnanimous about his career-long relationship with Warne, in which the latter prevented him from taking the three hundred Test wickets he deserved. But he presumably retains a constant sense of what might have been, and is particularly admirable for the way in which he refused to adapt his bowling style to make it more like Warne's.

Warne walked in; MacGill ran. Warne bowled at the right-hander's leg-stump, leaving mid-wicket open to get the batsman playing across the line; MacGill bowled at off-stump, and frequently left cover vacant, to get the right-hander driving. Warne reduced the amount of pure side-spinners he bowled late in his career, relying more on over-spin; MacGill kept trying to turn his stock ball square until the last. Warne abandoned the googly and the flipper in favour of the less physiologically corrosive slider; MacGill bowled googlies throughout.

On tour to the West Indies in 2008, he slept through an alarm – either that or it failed to ring, as he claims – and missed a team bus as a result, just like an Englishman we will shortly be reacquainted with. 'People ask me why I don't smile – it's because it's really hard,' MacGill said in 2003–4. 'Test cricket's hard ... I'll take a wicket and there'll be an explosion of emotion.' There was for Warne, too, but with MacGill it seemed – though it usually wasn't – as if each wicket was a means of vanquishing some long-held grudge or enmity.

Fiercely intelligent, as the wine connoisseur we know him to be he has hosted a pay television show called *Uncorked*, and learned later in life to enjoy the taste of beer. The son and grandson of Western Australian state players, he socialised with friends who weren't cricketers in his playing days, and was often portrayed as a thinker, a misfit, the odd man out, repeating yet again that tendency for spin pairings to include an extrovert (Warne) and an introvert (MacGill). Much like Ramadhin years before, he was a svengali, a mysterious outsider equipped with exceptional powers, uncomfortable with the demands of team membership.

In this, he was essentially the exact opposite of the man who, at the time of writing, is the best spinner in the world and who, wonderfully, is an Englishman. He, too, slept through alarms and put noses out of joint, though he is now, it seems, devoted to staying on what police officers still call the straight and narrow.

There are a few stories about Graeme Swann that you need to know. The first batch come from his disastrous tour of South Africa in 1999–2000. He suffered the fate of endless bowlers, and especially English spinners (think Richard Dawson), of being picked ludicrously early chiefly on the grounds that he could make the ball hit the strip and appeared to be a spinner. Swann had the added dimension of being able to make the ball turn square – and could bat usefully, too. But picked at the age of twenty, with only fifty-seven first-class wickets to his name, he wasn't yet a proper adult, never mind a proper bowler. This needn't have been fatal to his chances. The problem was that his youthful exuberance, and the sort of *joie de vivre* that illuminated Tiger O'Reilly's approach to the crease, rubbed up Duncan Fletcher, an austere disciplinarian who was then England coach, the wrong way. Then again, when you hear what Swann got up to, you can see that Fletcher might have had a point.

At Bloemfontein one morning during that tour, the selectors, coach and a few medical staff were in discussion, and happened to all be facing one way during practice. Swann was walking behind them when he decided to do a very funny thing. He stuck his right hand into his trousers, took his penis out, waved it at the selectors in mock invitation, twirled it round a few times, slipped it back in, and walked off, a giant smile moving across his face.

On that same tour, as Darren Gough was discussing the finer points of Kierkegaard with an attractive lady in a nightclub, Swann invited himself into the conversation – he's always been a keen amateur philosopher – and discovered he hadn't been formally summoned to do so. For this he received a faceful of Gough's right hand, fist clenched. Perhaps this was an unwarranted response by Gough. After all, he is the man alleged to have said to the physiotherapist Nigel Stockill, 'You know why they call me "Rhino" [referring to his nickname at Yorkshire]? Because I'm as strong as an ox.' But most accounts of the tour suggest Swann had it coming to him.

He also slept through two alarm calls, missing the team coach. Fletcher had his unflattering doubts about the young spinner's temperament confirmed. 'There was a lot of Jack Daniel's drunk on that trip,' Swann has opined more recently. He wasn't talking about Fletcher.

I would turn up at the next hotel and the first thing I'd find out was where the bar was located. I was young and stupid and I didn't realise that sometimes you need more than one alarm clock to wake you up. When you are nineteen you think you know everything there is to know. You are convinced you are right and that everyone else in the world is old and senile, out of touch and wrong.

Fast forward six years, and Swann has gone through a slump. He returned from that tour, where his cricket was no more than five overs in a game at Bloemfontein, thoroughly chastened, and playing on the turning tracks at Northamptonshire limited the development of his bowling. He was feeling low, his cricket in the doldrums and his potential seemingly being wasted. It was then he hit rock-bottom, as he told Stephen Brenkley in the *Independent*, the first time he confessed the extent of his anxieties. The following passage covers the dark days of 2005, when (before joining Nottinghamshire) he had constant and cutting arguments with Kepler Wessels, his militant coach at Northamptonshire.

The worst thing I ever did was going back [after the South Africa tour] and not learning immediately from that tour because we played on bunsens [turning pitches: bunsen burner, big turner] at Northampton all the following year. My cricket went into decline. I hated it. There then began not that long after what was a detestable state of affairs at Northampton. It was horrendous. I was probably clinically depressed.

I remember turning up in the car park one day, putting my head on the steering wheel and thinking, 'How can I go through this again?' I would have been more than happy to give the game up. If somebody had said come and work on a cruise ship for six months

I'd have probably bitten their hand off.

These tales, separated by several years, capture the essence of Swann's career, which is really just a Christian fable of redemption. Swann, who had three years earlier turned Nottinghamshire down, had been earmarked for greatness at a young age, along with his brother Alec, who specialised as a batsman. But by his own admission, his attitude as a young man, when he was known not so much as cock of the walk as a bit of a prick, conspired with the overhelpful wickets at Northamptonshire to limit his game. That, and his relationship with Wessels being harmoniously akin to that of the CIA and Che Guevara. As David Sales, Swann's former colleague at Northants (and a batsman who some thought could be as good as Gooch), put it: 'It was a shame for us he left, but he wasn't enjoying his game. He never really let on there was a problem, because that's the kind of guy he is, but there were regular bust-ups with Kepler.'

But, on arrival at Nottinghamshire, everything changed. He started to rediscover that inner confidence and love of attention that marked him out as a young player. It's a pleasant irony that he owed this largely to another player who never fulfilled his potential in an England shirt. Chris Read never recovered, in my mind at least, from Benaud's words into the microphone as he faced his first ball in Test cricket, against New Zealand. 'He doesn't look old enough to play Test cricket,' the master said, and it was true. Not long after that he ducked a Chris Cairns full toss that turned out to be an ingenious slower ball, which devastated his stumps. The rest of his England career was a case of high expectations never being fulfilled.

Yet later, at Nottinghamshire, he proved a wise head on young shoulders and gave the players around him the benefit of his experience. Few players profited more than Swann. Together with Mick Newell,

Nottinghamshire's director of cricket, he instructed Swann to be more patient, to think harder, to stop trying to turn every ball square, and to add a few different deliveries to his armoury. As Swann himself says, 'They said, "Maybe try to bowl straighter. Don't try to bowl so many magic turning balls. Try to frustrate the batsmen and use your variations." Now my line of attack is much straighter and I try to mix things up with the quicker ball, arm ball, slider, under-spinner.'

The result was a cricketer completely rejuvenated intellectually and physically – and to the benefit not just of himself, but his country, too. On 30 September 2007, seven years and 249 days, and 175 England one-day matches, since his solitary, desultory appearance in South Africa, he was back in the England side. This was helped by the fact that Peter Moores, the new England coach, had always rated Swann since his success against Sussex, where Moores had been coach – and by a brilliant spell in the nets against Strauss and Pietersen, which included his bowling the latter through the gate twice, at the Recreation Ground in Antigua. Swann was partnered with Panesar. But the Sikh of Tweak's struggle for form left Swann in possession of the sole spinner's slot soon enough, and the rest, as they say, is (unfinished) history.

Where will Swann end up in the list of greatest spinners? It is hard to know, partly because his career is so gloriously far from being finished; but, even more so, because Swann is in essence a bowler of his time. He, like Panesar, is a great beneficiary of the new willingness of umpires to give batsmen not playing a shot, but hit outside the line of the stumps, out leg-before wicket – a consequence of the penetration into the sport (almost all of it positive) of Hawk-Eye technology. The statistics bear this out. Compare him with other English off-spinners. Geoff Miller took 11.7% of his wickets lbw; John Emburey, 10.9%; Peter Such, 10.8%; Robert Croft, 16.3%. In contrast Swann has taken 42%

of his test wickets lbw. He has also been remarkably lucky in having so many left-handers to bowl to, and is open about the fact that, if he could choose, every batsman he bowled to would be a left-hander. His instinct is to go around the wicket to them immediately, deliver the ball from a wide angle and target the stumps before spinning it away.

It's from this angle that the under-cutter that he developed at Nottinghamshire, and which Warne taught Udal, is so effective. Instead of turning away to the slips, it hurries on to the left-hander and traps him leg-before wicket minutes before he can get the bat down. And the efficacy of the under-cutter is amplified, too, against the right-hander now that Swann is bowling a generally straighter line. Before, when he was tossing the ball up a long way outside off-stump to invite the drive, batsmen could guess that the straight one would hurry on; now, the straight(ish) deliveries might be looped, with plenty of over-spin; or they might be skidding, flipper-like deliveries, with pace off the wicket. Like Muralitharan, Swann conceals the ball in his left hand until close to the point of delivery. Unlike Muralitharan, he changes the position of the seam as he leaps into his delivery stride, according to the delivery he is going to bowl. So for anything other than the stock ball he'll push the ball round so that his finger is running along the seam (for the arm ball), or push it the other way so that it comes out as a 'flying saucer' for the under-cutter.

He bowls the ball faster than most – often up at 56mph for his stock ball – and yet still manages to make it dip and swerve. Perhaps most remarkable of all, Swann has become a world-class off-spinner by using a completely unconventional grip. This point seems to have escaped the attention of many commentators, who even now refer to his grip as if it were orthodox. In fact, rather than splaying the seam between his first and second fingers, Swann's hands are so huge that his fingers are much, much further apart than for most off-spinners. The effect of this – try it with a cricket ball – is that his index finger is nearly straight but his middle finger is bent right down to the side of the ball.

This has the rather extraordinary implication – which Swann brushes aside in conversation as if it were almost a distraction – that he spins the ball not between the inside top knuckle of his first and second finger, but, rather, between the inside top knuckle of his index finger and the middle knuckle of his middle finger. How on earth he manages to generate so much spin with this grip, let alone exert the degree of control his bowling now has, is difficult to know.

Swann has experimented at great length with the doosra, trying it on and off in the nets for nearly ten years. Journalists who watched him bowling for England at Chittagong in Bangladesh were convinced that he bowled one, but Swann claims that his extensive practice, and the experience of other bowlers, has convinced him not to bowl it. 'I don't bowl many of them,' he says (read: none at all), 'because it hurts my arm.' That is a wise decision.

Much like with Warne – who, in May 2010, went so far as to say the Englishman was the best spinner in the world – Swann takes many of his wickets by sheer force of personality. This is not just a cliché to account for any apparent discrepancy between his great success and the lesser achievements some might think his orthodox methods warrant; rather, the aggression, the pumping fists, the ingenuity and the willingness to take risks add hugely to the pressure on his opponents, and cause them to tremble with fear each time Swann's captain throws him the ball. No sportsman, after all, wants his opponent to sizzle with confidence, yet Swann has done so consistently since his return to the international fold.

One thrilling example of the power of personality is his preparedness, far greater than that of most off-spinning contemporaries, to go around the wicket to the right-hander. In doing this, he is invoking the spirit of his greatest forebear, Gentleman Jim, who took all those Australian wickets in 1956 from this unusually wide angle. Batsmen in today's game are less likely to prod forward as pathetically as the Australians did then, or even to take a half-step back; instead, modern players will tend to make a decisive push on to the front foot, and use the bat rather than the pad as the first line of defence.

Still, that Swann should be minded to experiment more readily with this different angle speaks of his aggressive, innovative nature. (His own solution to the perennial problem of lacerated fingers has been a traditional one: soaking them in a bucket of his own urine.) The fastest England spinner to a Test half-century of wickets is a very different man now from that tourist to South Africa – married, with two cats (Max and Paddy), but still devoted to his band Dr Comfort and The Lurid Revelations. Born in Towcester and a loyal Newcastle United fan, his nickname, 'Chin', would in his younger days have been a reference to his rather substantial jawline; these days it is a reference to his resilience, and his capacity to take one on the chin.

Aside from all that, he recommends himself to the public and to colleagues through being easily the best interviewee in recent English sporting history, making even an outraged Kevin Keegan seem like a tedious lecturer in statistical theory. This is related, no doubt, to his admission that '95 per cent of my discussions are me doing the talking'. His musings, by the way, can be read daily on one of the most brilliant of all Twitter accounts – @Swannyg66 – where he has roughly half the followers of Warne but boasts, in his biography, 'i play cricket, i'm in a band, and i recently stopped wetting the bed! oh and i'm funnier than Jimmy Anderson'.

When he was a little boy he imagined bowling the ball which clinched the Ashes for England. His final vanquished adversary was always Allan Border, then in his pomp for Australia, and after ensnaring him the young Swann would jump for joy in a fit of mock ecstasy.

This story becomes even more pleasing when one considers the present fate of England's second-best spinner, a man who, were he not equipped with a turban, would nevertheless bear comparison with Bedi, so beautifully have his left-arm twirlers accounted for the best batsmen in the world.

We have not yet had the full Monty. I once asked a former England Test match bowler why Panesar's form had dipped so sharply, after such an auspicious start to his career. 'I think there is a feeling in the England camp,' he said, 'that once Monty's confidence is knocked, it takes a lot to bring it back.' Panesar has been damaged by Warne's observation, a triumph of clarity and wisdom, that after his thirtieth Test match appearance he hadn't so much played thirty Tests as played one Test thirty times. This cutting remark – it was absolutely true – was proffered as an explanation of why, after an outstanding start to his international career, itself the culmination of a long schooling in youth teams including a successful England Under-19 side, he seemed to be in premature decline.

By the end of 2009, Panesar was looking back at a season where he had taken only eighteen wickets in first-class cricket, at sixty runs apiece. He had lost his place in the England side to Swann, lost his sense of purpose as a bowler and lost the confidence with a ball in hand that was so much the foundation of his fleeting fame. It was a sudden rise and fall for the first Sikh man to play for England, who had joined Northamptonshire as a seventeen-year-old in 1999. But the curious thing – the consolation, almost – is that his career seems closely to imitate that of Swann, albeit it lingers one stage further back.

Panesar, like Swann, was thrust into the England side at a young age, helped by the success he gleaned on the turning wickets at Northants, where Swann also experienced the illusion of success. Just as with Swann, he was the victim of Fletcher's straight talking. Fletcher was accused of 'damning Panesar with faint praise' during the 2006 series against Pakistan, an accusation that caused the Zimbabwean anguish. Indeed, Panesar was the third Northants spinner not to get on with Fletcher; not just Swann but the hugely talented Jason Brown, an off-spinner who went on the 2001 tour of Sri Lanka, had found themselves on the wrong side of his temper in the past.

Panesar, again like Swann, left Northants in search of better success elsewhere. In his case, he has moved to the seafront in Brighton, from where he is readying himself for a return to Test cricket by playing for Sussex. He was attracted there by the success of Mushtaq Ahmed on the pitches at Hove, the coach Mark Robinson, and, ironically, the captain, Michael Yardy, a left-arm spinner now ahead of Panesar in the running for the England one-day side at least, though sadly troubled by depression.

Whereas we know how dramatically Swann improved once he left Northants, there simply isn't enough evidence either way yet to say how well Panesar will take to the south coast. He was married in February 2010 to Gursharan Rattan, who was Graduate Pharmacist of the Year while working at the clinic inside Leyton Orient's Matchroom Stadium in east London. She now works as a locum, and those close to Monty say that marriage has had a settling effect on him.

There is enough evidence to allow us to speculate with reasonable certainty that moving was the right thing. Not only because he was struggling to make an impact at Northants, having spent a decade there, but because, if you ask those in the know, including Panesar himself, why his form dipped, two themes consistently recur: first, his bowling lacked variation; second, he is mentally fragile.

There is a revealing passage in his autobiography – a generally unsatisfactory book which lacked enough material really to merit that label – which concerns his unbearable excitement at having been selected for his debut against the Indians at Nagpur. He lay in bed, eyes closed, whispering to himself that he was about to play for England. Finding a couple of scraps of paper, he was compelled by adrenaline to scribble down some fielding positions and strategies for various batsmen. He wanted to show them to his captain:

When I knocked on Flintoff's door and handed over the results he seemed a bit bemused.

'This is what I'm thinking of doing,' I said.

'Ah, okay,' he replied, sounding as puzzled as he looked. 'No worries at all, mate. I'll take it all on board and you have a good night's sleep.'

I decided I ought to leave quickly because I wasn't sure whether he wanted me in his room.

This passage is sad long before it is either sweet or endearing. Far more than most bowlers, Panesar looks anxious and scared when batsmen start going after him; he looks ever ready for a consoling arm, or a sensitive captain. He becomes visibly uneasy when struggling in the face of some batting onslaught, a product perhaps of his innately shy nature. The mechanical reliability of his action seems to give way, so that, rather than bounding into the wicket, he hobbles reluctantly.

Prevailing opinion among batsmen is that he's worth attacking early on in his spell.

This vulnerability is compounded by the fact – now essential to the conventional wisdom about his career trajectory – that he was being bombarded with advice from all sides. As Udal put it to me: 'There's just a feeling that Monty is a fantastic natural talent, so able, but as soon as he has a bad spell he's got a physio talking to him, a captain, a coach, a spin bowling coach, a brain coach … it's just too much. He should be allowed to do what he does well, which is spin the ball hard and make the batsman play with quickish slow left arm.'

Panesar has recognised this himself. In November 2009 he said, 'I think I was trying to look for answers, and looking to better myself and move my game forward, and I think what I ended up doing was listening to a lot of people to try and improve my game.' Shortly before the 2010 season, he went further, in adding that an old English pro was instrumental in helping him to refocus. 'I was listening to too many people,' he said. 'I had played a lot of international cricket. I had a lot of experience under my belt, but I wasn't backing my own judgement and was listening too much to others. Then, on the fourth day at [the] Cardiff [Test], Geoffrey Boycott told me to ignore the advice I was receiving. He told me not to listen to anyone. "Trust yourself. People who do that survive", he said. From that moment, I started to change.'

It's a good thing, too. Because the criticism – especially, perhaps, Fletcher's reported frustration with his ongoing lack of utility as both a batsman and a fielder, despite one of the most laudable work ethics in the game – was starting to get to him. Warne's remark about his being the same bowler after thirty Tests stuck, and coming from the great man, for Panesar the greatest spinner he'd seen, it hurt. A conversation with Derek Underwood left me in no doubt that 'Deadly' felt that jibe was significantly below the proverbial belt, and a transgression of the unwritten code of conduct that binds Twirlymen.

It soon became the prevailing orthodoxy that Panesar lacked an arm ball and an under-cutter, and that the only variation in his bowling was really the product of natural variation on the pitch. He'd sometimes change his grip, so that his index finger ran along the seam rather than sitting perpendicular to it, meaning the ball came down to the batsman with a scrambled seam. But this was merely the stock ball with a different grip: hardly a different delivery altogether.

Then technical problems crept in. It cannot be said enough that Panesar has a wonderfully smooth, beautifully balanced action which, when it is working successfully, involves his very substantial physique in the imposition of spin. He starts with a walk, momentarily dropping his arms down to either side of his body – in clear imitation of Warne – before throwing himself into a side-on position. His giant fingers and wrist work in glorious union, imparting revolutions effectively.

But sometimes, when he's struggling for form or confidence, or both, Panesar's usually very high arm drops to a more round-arm position. When this happens, he tends to undercut the ball rather than spin it in the orthodox fashion. The result is a loss of the dip which made him hard to get comfortably forward to. Tufnell told me a few years ago, when Panesar seemed in his pomp, that it was this aspect of his bowling – late dip – which, though neglected, was possibly his greatest asset.

He depended heavily on it, such was his lack of variation. Panesar has claimed, rather absurdly, that he has 'no interest' in the technical side of the game and, even more absurdly, 'I get spin on the ball from the positive energy I generate', which sounds like a confession from life classes with Uri Geller. A few years ago, the spinner confessed, 'All I do is bowl stock ball, stock ball, stock ball, with little variations of pace.

Outwitting a batsman is a different skill and I'm still only twenty-five, which is pretty young for a spinner.' So Geoff Miller, the England selector, was merely ventilating a popular sentiment when he said, 'Monty had a cracking first year [in Tests], bowling with increasing confidence after claiming Sachin Tendulkar as his first Test wicket. But batsmen began to work him out. They could see what he could and, more importantly, couldn't do, and played him accordingly.'

None of which is to say we should despair. England have been blessed with many great left-arm spinners through the ages, from Rhodes and Verity, Wardle and Lock, through Underwood and Edmonds and, though a little less exalted, Tufnell and Ashley Giles. But, possibly setting the first two aside, Panesar is as naturally talented as any of them. He has set himself the task of rediscovering the form of his early Test career, not by reinventing himself altogether but by working out what he did best and seeing if he could add to it. In this task he will be aided by the consolations of family life, by his growing maturity, the less rewarding wickets at Hove, and by his deep faith, which, quite apart from causing him to be a teetotaller, makes him extremely disciplined. 'Sikhs are warriors and I am a fighter. I never give up,' he exclaims, giving his nod to the need for spinners to have stamina. He is naturally humble – when playing in the same series as Muralitharan, he asked, 'How can a student be a rival to the teacher?' – and there are strong grounds for thinking he'll be able to bring fresh delight to England's fans in the Test arena.

What is even more exciting, in fact almost unbearably exciting, is the prospect of what he and Swann could do together. It is eminently possible, given their ages and complementary styles, that Swann and Panesar will have a decent shelf-life as a spin partnership. The essentials are in place. They turn their stock balls in different directions, and tend to deliver them from different parts of the crease. And that potential partnership is wonderfully aligned with those of such spin twins as Grimmett and O'Reilly, and Ramadhin and Valentine, in being composed of an introvert (Panesar) and an extrovert (Swann). One of the great challenges of Andrew Strauss's tenure as England Test captain will be seeing if he can make the partnership work.

If he can he will have at his disposal two bowlers with the necessary basics in skill and control to be one of the most successful of all spin partnerships which, given England's lack of spinners in recent times, is a pleasing thought. What Panesar and Swann represent is the height of orthodoxy in their respective departments of spin: Swann doesn't bother with the doosra, and Panesar is so orthodox he waited until a decade into his career to add to his stock ball.

In this fashion the pair form an irresistible counterpoint to the other potentially exhilarating spin partnership in Test cricket – one which, at the time of writing, has also yet to be fully propagated in the international arena.

Not since the lanky Jack Iverson briefly flitted into view over half a century ago has a spin bowler been more deserving of the label mystery spinner than Ajantha Mendis. Paul Adams of South Africa was a remarkable proposition; but somehow his lack of success at the highest level seemed inevitable, given the absurdity of his action. Mendis, on the other hand, exploded on to the scene with a virtuoso display of spinning brilliance. In July 2008, he took 6-13 against the Indians (who know more than most about spin) in the Asian Cup final. Weeks later, his 8-132 in a Test against the same opposition was the best return of any Sri Lankan on debut. He took twenty-six wickets over the three-Test series, the best ever return over a three-match debut series (beating Alec Bedser by two). There wasn't much argument when he was named Man of the Series.

In his approach and delivery he is the most arresting sight in the modern game. His long run-up, around seventeen paces, would seem more at home with a military medium-pace bowler (the military link is pertinent – see below). This impression is confirmed by his bustling, hurried advance; though it is countered by the exceptionally bizarre hold he has on the ball, which sits between the tip of his fingers and thumb, as if it contained some toxicity which not even the most industrially powerful disinfectant could expunge. The batsman is likely to share this sense of the impending danger, given the range of deliveries in Mendis's armoury. As he moves into his delivery stride, the index finger of his left hand extends skywards, as if in confident expectation of the umpire's chosen finger doing the same shortly after.

Television producers have to refer to him in a way their viewers will understand, but are too patronising to go in for 'right-arm mystery' so have tended to stick with 'right-arm off-break'. How tedious. Mendis does bowl the orthodox off-break as his stock ball, but he mixes it up with a genuine googly, delivered out of the back of the hand, orthodox leg-breaks out of the side of the hand, a flipper and – oh gracious speciality! – a carrom ball. It was this, more than any other delivery, which flummoxed the Indians. Look on YouTube at what happens to Rahul Dravid: the man known as the wall has all the impenetrability of an open door when, in the fifth over of Mendis's Test career, he plays for a ball coming into his pads only to see it turn away from him and do violence to his stumps. The baffled expression on the Indian's face is wonderfully redolent of that on Mike Gatting's after his dismissal at Old Trafford by Warne.

The carrom ball is utterly brilliant if executed properly. It requires phenomenally strong digits and a willingness, probably, to risk arthritis, such is the devastation wrought on the knuckles of the middle finger in particular. It takes its name from the Indian board game in which players flick one disc against other discs; and to do the same with a cricket ball, and over twenty-two yards, is remarkable. Iverson and Gleeson had similarly strong fingers, as did Armstrong; but each of those involved their wrists heavily in the action of imparting spin. Iverson's stock ball, remember, was a googly which came into the right-hander from outside off-stump; to get that ball going he had to have a wonderfully supple wrist. Armstrong's stock ball was a leg-break, which also heavily involved the wrist.

Mendis, by contrast, bowls this skidding leg-break – which is what it is, in effect – out of the front of his hand, using his middle finger to flick it, and his index finger and thumb, dragging down and to the left, to aid the action. Since it comes out of the front of the hand, it is not altogether that easy to distinguish from the off-spinner. And because he bowls very, very straight – much as Ramadhin would on helpful wickets, or Tayfield, albeit with a much more parabolic flight – he gets many of his wickets with batsman playing down the wrong line (just as Dravid did in the above example).

Mendis always bowls straight. In this respect, he is just like Swann in being an ultra-modern bowler, somebody who has fundamentally conditioned his style to take advantage of umpires' increasing willingness to give batsmen out leg-before. And because batsmen now have to use their bats to play the ball, rather than their pads, the modern spinner doesn't really have to turn the ball square (though doing so helps to sow fear and doubt in a batsman's mind), especially if he can turn it both ways, as Mendis can.

He was just like Iverson in learning his trade while in the army. Mendis grew up in Moratuwa, a small fishing village, where his mother Ranjani worked in a clothing factory and his father Wenses was a carpenter.

Wenses wanted Mendis to accept the invitation of the Sri Lankan Army Cricket Committee, on the grounds that it would keep his son out of trouble while exposing him to top-class cricket. He died two weeks before the nineteen-year-old Mendis enrolled. Mendis, who like so many other spinners had practised with a tennis ball as a youngster, and used to bamboozle his brothers (shades of Saqlain here), was convinced to develop a stock ball, and chose the off-break.

There is a fanciful theory that his fingers developed the strength needed for the carrom ball through pulling triggers on army guns, but that is unlikely. Aruna, his brother, has claimed, 'he always had strong fingers'. In any case, his mother extracted a promise from the army authorities that he wouldn't be sent to the front line, on the grounds that 'His father wanted him to play cricket'. The army's panjandrums, conscious they had a star on their books, complied.

It was at an academy run by Australian Ashley Mallett that he started to work on other deliveries, but he was lucky (and rare) in being left largely alone by coaches, who seem to have realised his talent was too natural and unique to warrant much intervention. This has helped him retain an air of authenticity, as has the fact that he is a devout Christian in a Buddhist country (to match Muralitharan's being a Tamil in a Sinhalese country). Indeed, after his first, propitious series against India, he returned to Moratuwa by motorcade, the whole village coming out to welcome home their returning hero.

Mendis was severely wounded in the 2009 terror attacks in Lahore, requiring two rounds of surgery to have shrapnel removed from his scalp, and suffering from debilitating headaches for weeks after. His recovery was speedy: three months to the day after he was discharged from a hospital in Colombo, he took 3-9 against New Zealand in a Twenty20 match.

And yet the fastest bowler ever to fifty wickets in one-day internationals has threatened to disappear from the scene altogether. It is often said of mystery spinners – or, indeed, of any suddenly successful person anywhere – that they have had a 'meteoric rise'. This is one of the most abused phrases in English. The thing about meteors is not that they rise but that they fall. And the usage is doubly silly because meteors blaze in brief glory before falling into darkness – an outcome that is not usually factored in by those who bandy it about. And yet, in the case of Mendis, the metaphor sounds as if it might be appropriate.

There are two main reasons for this. First, as I've already said, mystery tends to run in inverse proportion to success: bowlers don't always remain unknown quantities, batsmen work them out, strategies are devised to nullify their threat, and then are swiftly promulgated. Atherton put it to me bluntly. 'The real mystery is why he should take so many wickets. He bowls it straight and moves it both ways; but if you play him straight – with a vertical rather than horizontal bat – you should be able to deal with him.' This is just what batsmen did with Kumble, making him much less dangerous on flat pitches. Pakistan's batsmen, who had some success by playing Mendis straight, also practised against spin on much shorter wickets, to simulate what it would be like playing his quicker carrom ball.

The second reason is video technology. A very quick search on YouTube reveals a bunch of what some people would call nutters, and we would call friends, dissecting Mendis's method in the smallest detail, and revealing such gems as his tendency to bowl the carrom ball after being hit for a boundary – showing his confidence in its execution. And these are the amateurs: modern teams devote vast sums to even more rigorous analysis, which they study at length before taking to the middle.

Some would posit a third reason too, which is recurring ankle trouble that has made transferring weight on to his front foot problematic. But that is a distraction: Mendis has struggled, inevitably, to rediscover the surprise factor that made his entry into the Test arena so spectacular. His time will almost certainly come again, as he learns to deploy more subtle variations of pace and line and degrees of spin, rather than simply flitting from one variant ball to another.

And yet, for those of us interested in the intellectual heritage of those different variations, the surprising thing about Mendis is that his biggest apparent surprise – the carrom ball – is a surprise at all. Pundits and players should have known better. There is another bowler, albeit one who is left-handed, who shot to prominence in 1999 with a mystery ball – briefly labelled the 'two-fingered' ball – which was nothing other than the left-armer's carrom ball. The oversight is particularly egregious because, like Mendis, this spinner is a Sri Lankan. Indeed, his rediscovery of form hastened Mendis's (hopefully temporary) demise.

Much as with so many of the spinners in these pages, including, most recently, MacGill, Rangana Herath must rue the fact that his career coincided with that of a true great – in his case Muralitharan. Herath made his debut seven years after Muralitharan, but played precious little cricket for the following decade. He also had to compete against other spinners who occasionally partnered Muralitharan, such as Kumar Dharmasena, and Upul Chandana, while opening batsman and sometime captain Sanath Jayasuriya bowled thoroughly useful, if defensive, left-arm spin. In 2009, unable even to retain his place in the Sri Lanka 'A' side, he was playing club cricket in Staffordshire. He had written a heartfelt letter to the Sri Lankan selectors before coming to England, reminding them of his existence, and so stirred were they by its message, and so concerned about Mendis's sudden ineffectiveness, that he got called up to play in the Test series against Pakistan. He bowled superbly on helpful tracks to claim 15 wickets at 26.93, including two 5-fers.

It was a welcome antidote to his previous experience of bowling against Pakistan, when, in 2000, they notched up over six hundred and the last column of his figures contained a nought. In the intervening years, he had carried on working in the credit card centre of Sampath Bank, a career beyond cricket which united him with both Chandrasekhar and Laker. The other thing he did over these years was develop his carrom ball.

There shouldn't be much doubt that Herath was bowling it first. He started practising it when he was fifteen, and by the time he made his debut six years later was clearly using it quite separately from his arm ball. We should dismiss as ridiculous the commentators who pronounced on his capacity to bowl the doosra: he was using the method of Interlude Nine, not Interlude Eight. Herath's stock ball has a seductive loop to it; by putting plenty of over-spin on the ball, he's able to drag batsmen forward to a ball landing well short of a half-volley. On helpful wickets, he can turn the ball sharply, too, and because he uses the crease far more than most left-arm spinners, sometimes getting very close to the stumps (whereas most left-arm spinners tend to end up bowling from a wide position), his arm ball is highly effective. Batsmen simply don't know what to play and what to leave. This makes the carrom ball a particular quandary.

He delivers it in a very different way from Mendis. That's not simply because he is left-handed whereas Mendis is not. Rather, Mendis bowls wicket to wicket, fast(ish) for a spinner, and hurries the batsman into playing down the wrong line. Herath, after setting up the right-hander with a few flighted, big-turning stock balls, throws up the carrom ball from wide on the crease, invites the batsman forward for a languid forward defensive, and then spins it through the gate. Both he and Mendis aim to beat the batsman in the air and then off the pitch, but with Herath the emphasis is on the former, whereas with Mendis it is on the latter.

He is also different from Mendis in regularly taking the new ball. Other spinners have done this, but not out of habit. Kumble was known to bowl with the new ball in his time with Northants. Swann took it against the West Indies, knowing their left-handed captain, Chris Gayle, much preferred fast bowling. A number of teams in the 2011 World Cup opened with spinners. Herath accounts for it himself by saying 'a left-arm spinner has the advantage over a leg-spinner in that he can bowl with the new ball and get batsmen out either bowled or lbw with his arm ball'. There is no reason why a leg-spinner shouldn't take the new ball, though the involvement of his first three fingers might dissuade him from risking further lacerations by a fresh seam.

Herath, however, has made a habit of taking the new ball, in part because he reckons he can swing his arm ball more with it. Indeed, for all the glamour of his carrom ball, he puts it lower down the pecking order than that older, more reliable variation: 'My wicket-taking ball is the arm ball,' he says, 'which gets a lot of batsmen out lbw. I also have a mystery ball, like Ajantha Mendis, which I have taken wickets with in Test matches.'

Herath is continuing the tradition of great spinners at Hampshire, where Warne so recently made such a profound mark. He was replaced halfway through the 2010 season by none other than Mendis, but the real hope must be that they too can be partnered together at the highest level, where, if they flourish, they will be one of the most unique spin bowling partnerships in history. Of all the left-hand, right-hand partnerships, Ramadhin and Valentine were probably the most successful, just ahead of Laker and Lock, while Bedi and Chandrasekhar complemented each other magnificently, and Swann and Panesar could yet earn their place among the pantheon of spin twins. But what a treasure it would be if the heirs to Muralitharan could be bowling at either end, each of them sending down carrom balls – one brisk and right-handed, the other looped and left-handed – in among their stock deliveries.

And what a glorious prospect too, for those of us whose championing of the merits of spin bowling was dismissed as so much misplaced faith just a few short years ago. The Wilderness Years of spin have been followed by an era of rare and special glories. That is a fact of both aesthetic and moral significance, and it does rather beg the question of where this venerable tradition is heading next.

Interlude Ten

RAJAN'S* MYSTERY BALL

Grip   *Batsman's Point of View*

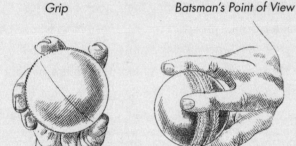

The grip is the same as for the flipper, with the spin imparted by a snapping of the middle finger and thumb. The inside of the top knuckle on the index finger will also naturally be involved in applying spin to the ball. On entering the delivery stride, the palm is over the ball, with the back of the hand facing the sky and the seam forming an equator around the ball. As the arm comes round, the thumb and middle finger snap. Unlike with the conventional flipper, in which the palm is over the top of the ball and it comes out like a flying saucer, now the back of the hand points towards the face. In other words – and crucially for deceiving the batsman – the release position is identical to that for the conventional leg-break, with the seam pointing towards third man. The right hand image shows the moment just before thumb and middle finger snap, to impart back spin.

---

* With a nod to Clarrie Grimmett.

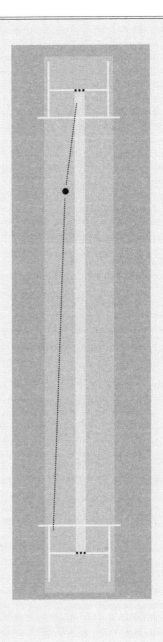

Perhaps harder to detect than the conventional flipper, this ball will float on to a fuller trajectory than the batsman is expecting, before cutting into the right-hander (from off to leg, by 'check-spin'). Though the ordinary flipper is usually bowled with extra pace, the more this delivery looks like a leg-break, the more likely it is to deceive the batsman. It is therefore worth bowling it at the same pace as the stock ball, and giving it plenty of air too.

Conclusion

INTO THE UNKNOWN

Surveying the vast canvas of the modern game, it is impossible not to conclude that today's spectators are extremely lucky. More cricket is being played than ever, with not just fifty-over but twenty-over matches providing a volume of entertainment that, even forty years ago, fans could not have dreamt of. The internet and satellite and cable sports channels beam live coverage into more homes than ever before, and the burgeoning market in India particularly is fuelling demand for ever more corporate investment in the sport. That is not an undiluted good, but it has thus far been a benefit to cricket.

Moreover, the standard of cricket being played is high. A slew of greats retired in the first decade of the twenty-first century, with the biggest impact being felt on an Australian side suddenly bereft of the giants who made them, under Steve Waugh's captaincy, the greatest of all sides. But across the world there are outstanding players who, through Twenty20 in particular, are innovating relentlessly and taking the game into new territory. In many countries, tickets are getting cheaper, and young fans are being encouraged to watch Test cricket.

And the penetration of technology into the game, from third umpires to Hawk-Eye, is giving armchair analysts and paying spectators deeper insights into this most cerebral and skilful of all sports.

But none of the above would resonate as powerfully were it not for a further, salient fact. Spin bowling, whose death was predicted so recently, has done more than defy the Grim Reaper. The Twirlymen of the game have vanquished him, and are now in the ascendant again. Led by Warne and Muralitharan, they have reinstated their role to its rightful position. Far from being peripheral characters, they seem central to the action once again.

We have seen how close they came to extinction. The advent of limited-overs cricket, with flat pitches to encourage batsmen, convinced many leading spinners to abandon spin for the sake of accuracy. Runs conceded, rather than wickets taken, became the dominant concern. They became slow bowlers, not spinners. But thanks in large part to Abdul Qadir, there remained a constituency in the game for genuine, attacking spin bowling, and a belief that despite the majesty of the West Indian pacemen, giving the ball a vigorous tweak was a worthwhile endeavour. The supreme careers of Warne and Muralitharan – with Kumble, Mushtaq, Saqlain, Harbhajan, Vettori, and now Swann in tow – make it very hard to see how that lesson can be unlearned.

This is not to say that some of us didn't try. Terry Jenner was far from alone in thinking that spin bowling and Twenty20 were irreconcilable. To my everlasting shame, I wrote a column for the *Salisbury Review* in September 2008 with the headline 'The Suicide of Cricket' condemning this new, adrenaline-fuelled game as a glorified form of rounders. Influenced by Jenner's gloomy prognosis for the future of spin, I lamented the inevitable decline of the Test arena, and with it those sacred practices the Twirlymen have undertaken for centuries.

It is long since time that the likes of Jenner and I admit error. Though there were early, worrying signs, Twenty20 has not caused lasting damage to Test cricket – at least not yet. More pertinently for our interest, it has not destroyed spin bowling. Jenner may feel that Twenty20 is a forum for slow bowling rather than spin, as the fifty-over game undoubtedly was in the 1980s. But it is hard to reconcile that view with the spectacle of the Indian Premier League and international Twenty20, let alone the domination of spin in the 2011 World Cup.

True, England's Michael Yardy is not the sort of bowler likely to pitch the ball outside leg-stump, beat the edge and dislodge the off-bail. But Swann, while varying his pace and angles cleverly, hasn't stopped giving the ball a violent rip in this shorter form of the game. Neither has Harbhajan, though he is not as prodigious a spinner of the ball as he was before his shoulder trouble and regrettable flirtation with the doosra. And what of Pragyan Ojha, the Indian left-arm orthodox bowler? He bowled so well for the Deccan Chargers of the IPL, under the captaincy of Adam Gilchrist, that he received the Purple Cap for the most number of wickets in a tournament – and then promptly took a call from the national selectors, asking him to play in the Test arena. His bowling in the IPL raised joyful memories of Bishen Bedi, with his superb command of flight, allied to a brisk snap of the fingers. The same positive message emanates from other alleged Twenty20 specialists, some of whom have made it into the Test arena (Saeed Ajmal) and others who haven't (South African Roelof van der Merwe).

Either way, it would be foolhardy to suggest that spin bowling is in terminal decline, when the opposite seems true. This raises the question of how the sudden proliferation of cricket will change the tradition of spin, and what further updates to the fashions and variations with which we are familiar can be expected.

All forecasters are frauds, of course. The future is unknowable. Predictions are a dangerous business, loaded with a serious risk of opening oneself to ridicule and even contempt. So let us have a go.

It will become much more commonplace, particularly in Test cricket, for off-spinners to go around the wicket to right-handers, especially early in their innings.

The carrom ball will replace the doosra as the alternative of choice for young off-spinners and slow left-arm orthodox bowlers. So clearly has the doosra hurt the prospects of those who became obsessed with it (Muralitharan aside), that most young bowlers will forget the fashions of the late 1990s and early 2000s and abandon this project. They will see that, provided they have sufficiently strong digits – as strong as Mendis and Herath – the carrom ball offers a more promising alternative. It too spins from leg to off; but it is less liable to disrupt the stock ball, or cause a bowler to lose it altogether, and with a little chicanery it can be easily concealed. The doosra will never leave us, having been practised to good effect by various exponents of recent years. And other bowlers, such as Ajmal, will go on using it liberally (and illegally, in many cases). But while the carrom ball flowers, the doosra shall wilt.

The dichotomies that have ruled spin bowling history, between left- and right-handed bowlers, and between those who impart off-spin and those who impart leg-spin, will continue to crumble. That is not to say that some bowlers will begin an over with three balls from their right arm, and then three from their left. I confidently predict that the vast majority of bowlers – spinners and otherwise – will continue to specialise with one arm. Ambidextrous bowling will not become fashionable. Rather, though bowlers will continue generally to spin the ball in one direction – generally into the right-hander and away from the left-hander as an off-spinner, for example – there will be an increasing number of spinners who bowl both off-spin and leg-spin in the orthodox fashion.

Sachin Tendulkar, that peerless ambassador for the game, has made himself even more useful to his captains of India in being capable of medium pace, off-spin and leg-spin. As if his record-smashing batting wasn't enough, he thinks it worthwhile to offer his captain three different types of bowler, who can be called upon according to conditions. It may be overcast, or sunny; it might be a grassy top, or a dustbowl; there might be two left-handers at the crease. Whatever the circumstance, Tendulkar has a form of bowling for the situation – and a cursory glance at his record in each form of the game proves just how much his captains have relied on this.

If Tendulkar can do it, why can't the Twirlymen? After all, Johnny Wardle could bowl Chinamen and orthodox slow left arm interchangeably, and Sir Garfield Sobers did the same, while throwing in medium pace, too. Muralitharan has bowled mini spells of leg-spin, especially when having two left-handers at the crease and plenty of rough to work with. The effect of these players' polymath abilities is to make conventional bowlers like Swann, Panesar and Vettori seem needlessly restricted by comparison. If the best spinners in the game have flexible, strong, callused fingers, and spend every other waking thought contemplating beating batsmen with spin, why should one half of the spin-bowling tradition be deemed off-bounds to them? So, though we cannot expect it to become the norm, look out for young bowlers who fill their overs with three off-breaks followed by three leg-breaks. That is a prospect to relish.

Closely related to this will be the resuscitation of a long dormant tradition. The Swift Pioneers will breathe again. Expect to see the ghost of Sydney Barnes stalk the Twenty20 arena. That most complete of bowlers – pace, spin, spin-swerve (which we now call drift), and movement off the pitch in both directions – is a shimmering example to modern bowlers. His mastery of all the rudiments of bowling also suggests that too many modern bowlers lack the imagination to deploy all the possibilities on offer to the cricketer with a ball in his hand. Fascinatingly, there is a suggestion that Barnes's lesson is already being learned – or, rather, relearned.

Harmeet Singh, a medium-pace bowler for the Deccan Chargers, is not yet a regular match-winner. But he has attracted considerable attention because of his fondness for throwing fast leg-breaks and off-breaks into the mix. He'll often bowl seam-up deliveries for his first few overs, and is capable of swinging the ball into the right-hander in doing so. But later in his spell, he'll still bring his arm round at full tilt, but roll his wrist and snap his fingers as if for a leg-break. These deliveries do in fact turn, and (even better) drift into the right-hander before doing so. Then he produces a fast off-break, which goes away from the right-hander in the air, before spinning back in, sometimes sharply. And then he has another, utterly brilliant, delivery bowled out of the front of the hand: flipper-like, squeezed between the thumb and first finger at pace. What is all this but the very panoply of variations with which Barnes rose to such giddy heights?

Harmeet will be of great interest to fans everywhere over the next few years. He is very much a product of his times, practising hard on a number of variations because of the demands of Twenty20, wherein raw pace and raw spin won't suffice. In that last variation of his, the flipper-like delivery squeezed out of the front of the hand, he also points to what I feel could prompt a new, great chapter in the history of spin. Energised by Twenty20, and heeding the nearly lost lessons of the twentieth century, the next great push by Twirlymen may come from the return of the thumb.

This is a part of the body whose general abandonment by spinners over the past three decades is almost inexplicable, whose redeployment is urgent and whose reignited utility could herald endless wicket-taking variations. A road map for its revival is best drawn by returning to the experiments of that brilliant little man Clarrie Grimmett. You may recall that in his book *Grimmett on Cricket* he documented a conversation with that defiant English lobster, George Simpson-Hayward, during which he learned the lesson that 'much more spin could be applied by holding the ball between the thumb and second finger'. Grimmett used this lesson not only to master his flipper, but to create different flippers that could turn in different directions off the pitch. In this same way he could bowl a variety of deliveries from the front of his hand.

Darwinists know that the advent of opposable thumbs was crucial to the evolution of *Homo sapiens*. And so it is for Twirlymen, too. There can hardly be a greater gift to the spinner than this fleshy lever – a fact which makes its general absence from modern coaching manuals shameful. The hand, we know, is not designed for spin bowling. As Brian Wilkins notes, 'the pressure points are in the wrong places. Not being on the pads of the muscular areas, but mainly on the sides of the fingertips or joints, the pressure is concentrated unnaturally'.

But not so with the thumb. The frontal pad of this special finger is not only made of thankfully plump tissue; it also provides the biggest lever on the hand, because of the distance between it and the other fingers when it is outstretched. It's highly possible that bowlers will emerge who bowl a variety of deliveries by snapping the ball between their thumb and middle finger – two fleshy pads working together to impart spin, but with minimal risk of lacerations to the skin. They might bowl an array of flippers, released either as 'flying saucers', with the hand over the top of the ball, or, as in Benaud's in-swerving flipper, with the seam pointing to fine leg. Another possibility is that these flippers will be released with the wrist in exactly the same position as for the leg-break – back of the hand pointing to the face, and seam pointing to third man – and these deliveries could be a major 'new' addition to the wrist-spinner's repertoire (indeed, Harmeet is bowling something similar already, albeit at medium pace).

This ball, Rajan's Mystery Ball, is best thought of as a slow flipper. In my own playing days it was easily my most effective variation: indistinguishable from the leg-break until the moment it pitches and zips in off the wicket. Whereas conventional flippers – Warne's flippers – are pushed through with extra pace, the deception of this delivery could be maximised by keeping it to the pace of the stock leg-break. Realistically speaking, this slow flipper might come to be known as 'the teaser'. You read it here first.

Nor should use of the thumb stop there. Spinners might use it to release the ball with the back of the wrist facing square leg, to create standard off-spin. Why restrict the thumb to membership of the flipper family, when it could be used for so much else? There are several possibilities: as Grimmett pointed out, in the development of bowling from under-arm and round-arm to over-arm, this exquisitely positioned and immensely capable tool has been needlessly lost. It is long due a return. If more thumbs in bowling means more spinners in cricket, it can't come soon enough.

Or not, as the case may be. These predictions might turn out to be so much bunkum. One of the excitements of cricket, and of spin in particular, is that we do not know how this or that practice will march forward, especially at a time when the game is changing so fast. Yet the evidence of these pages suggests certain customs, and recurring foibles, will remain with us. Off-spin will go on being the victim of silly snobbery. Allegedly 'new' deliveries will be unearthed – except that they'll be reheated versions of those that were bowled decades before. Mystery bowlers will emerge suddenly into the limelight, only to disappear just as fast; while masterful bowlers, who spin the ball hard and exert control over its line and length, will be world-beaters. And commentators will go on calling the flipper the googly, to the detriment of all but the spinner who profits from the confusion.

We can also be more confident that spin bowling will march forward than we had reason to be two decades ago. And we should be immensely grateful that this precious art has not been lost, despite the best efforts of generations of administrators and captains. In general, the former should have more sense, and the latter should have more faith.

In one of the interviews I did for this book, a legend of Fleet Street told me that he couldn't wait to read it, but wasn't there a danger that, in revealing the secrets of Twirlymen, their charm would be lost? This was akin to John Keats's claim that Isaac Newton and his fellow scientists were 'unweaving the rainbow' – destroying its beauty by explaining it.

Our present concern is not to unweave this rainbow. Rather, by documenting the patterns and habits of spin bowlers, we can reveal their many virtues. Understanding aids appreciation, and true knowledge enhances the spectacle. We may now see more clearly the eccentrics and heroes who have kept alive this tradition, and debunk some of the myths that have attended it. More crucially, we can create conditions under which those noble endeavours continue to flourish. Only by learning the glories of yesteryear, and the horrors by which spin bowling was nearly consigned to history's dustbin, will we sustain cricket's most beautiful pastime, and nurture the Twirlymen of tomorrow.

Acknowledgements

Dozens of books were useful to me in writing *Twirlymen*, but some I could not have done without. Two stand out. The first is David Frith's *The Slow Men*, a more erudite history than my own. The second is Brian Wilkins's *Cricket: The Bowler's Art* which, as I mention in the Introduction, had a very profound influence on me from the day I acquired it as a teenager. I'm hugely grateful to the authors of both those works, and fans of the game the world over should consider themselves fortunate to have access to two scholars of such distinction.

A fundamental cause of this book's existence is the inquisitiveness of my agent, Andrew Gordon. I shall never forget our first meeting in his Piccadilly Circus office, in which he shepherded me away from some of my more eccentric thoughts with far more diplomacy than they deserved. He has been a constant source of support, encouragement and decency. The same goes for my editor at Yellow Jersey, Matt Phillips. It is inconceivable that I could have had an editor more clever and patient than he has been. The sharpness of his editing massively improved the first draft of this book. Discussions with him never failed to yield brilliant ideas. And it has been a constant pleasure talking to him about subjects far beyond spin bowling. I am also hugely grateful to Andrew Davidson for his illustrations, Matt Broughton for his design, Richard Carr for his work on the layout, Richard Collins for his copy-editing skill and Myra Jones for her proof-reading. Their work has been vital to the publication of this book.

Conversations with Christopher Martin-Jenkins, Lawrence Booth, Simon Wilde, Jim Lawton, Brian Viner, Chris Maume, Simon O'Hagan,

Mark Steel, Matthew Norman, Roger Alton, Jim White, Peter Oborne, James Oborne, Mike Atherton, Mihir Bose, Shaun Udal, Bruce Anderson, Alex Deane, Alex Massie, William Keegan, Michael McCarthy and the White City XI in particular furnished me with utterly indispensable advice, information, quotes and leads. Of the others who I spoke to off the record, I hope they feel I have conveyed their many invaluable thoughts in a way that combines anonymity with accuracy.

Nor would I have written this book had not the legendary Graham 'Jacko' Jackson of my old club, Sinjuns CC, paid £20 of the £40 to put me on an after-school cricket course at Chestnut Grove School – or Kevin Molloy spent years in the nets with me at Sinjuns, guiding me affectionately even when my infant leg-breaks flew on to Burntwood Lane. At the *Independent*, I have been extremely lucky to have such generous support. In particular, Simon O'Hagan, Adrian Hamilton, Roger Alton and Katherine Butler showed me kindness far beyond what I deserved.

My comrades at Prospex – prospex.org.uk – have been a constant inspiration, as have so many friends – chief among them the crew formerly known as the Boozehounds. I have also been exceptionally fortunate to have in Mungo a flatmate with a keen feel for this book's intended audience. Explaining the merits of Richie Benaud's alternative flipper to him sharpened my own grasp of the subject considerably. He is a man of unbeatable charm and brains, who was born to be a diplomat and is now, thank goodness, paid to be one.

Of course, the debt I owe my father (Varada) and mother (Sunanda) is beyond measure. Perhaps the best I can say of them is that they are my biggest influence, along with my sister-in-law, Farrah, and brother, Keertichandra. Farrah has been a wonderful influence on us all, and I'm proud to call her family. As for Keertichandra, I think only he knows what I really mean when I say what a thrill it has been spending so much time together in recent years. Talking to someone so clever and kind would be a privilege even if it weren't for our common blood.

My biggest dose of gratitude is saved for my girlfriend, Charlotte. I doubt very much that, when she signed up to date this curious little Indian five years ago, she thought his idea of pillow talk was discussing the merits of Saqlain Mushtaq's doosra, or Clarrie Grimmett's disdain for the wrong'un. But she has endured such madness with the most extraordinary fortitude and kindness. In a realm as public as this, I think the most I can get away with saying is that I would have invented her were my imagination rich enough.

I reserve last mention for my late and dear friend Paul Nicolopulo, who was my boss at the Foreign Office a decade ago. Paul said he chose me ahead of another candidate because I declared cricket a hobby in my covering letter. He smoked over fifty cigarettes a day, and two years ago gave something like a full measure of devotion to his craft and calling when he died of lung cancer, while posted to Kingston, Jamaica, as Deputy Head of our Mission. It is of lasting sadness to me that we never watched cricket together in Sabina Park, as we had long planned. In my leaving card from the office, which was full of long, worthy best wishes, Paul wrote the shortest note of all. Crossing out the word 'crap', it said: 'Keep up the crap, I mean cricket'. Long after this book has been published, I fully intend to.

Amol Rajan

May, 2011

Bibliography

My biggest debt is to the indispensable espncricinfo.com, an extraordinary resource for fans of the game. I also relied heavily, of course, on *Wisden's Almanacks*, 1863–2010. My thanks to all those who contribute to both.

Austin, Ian – *Bully for You, Oscar* (Mainstream, 2000)

Altham, H S – *A History of Cricket* (Allen & Unwin, 1962)

Bailey, Trevor and Trueman, Fred – *The Spinner's Web* (Willow Books, 1988)

Barry, Paul – *Shane Warne: Spun Out* (Bantam Press, 2006)

Barry, Rowland – *Bradman's Invincibles* (Aurum, 2009)

Barker, Ralph – *Ten Great Bowlers* (Chatto &Windus, 1967)

Beckles, Hilary – *The Development of West Indies Cricket* (Pluto, 1999)

Bedser, Alex – *Twin Ambitions* (Stanley Paul, 1986)

Beldam, G W and Fry, C B – *Great Bowlers and Fielders* (Macmillan, 1906)

Benaud, Richie – *My Spin on Cricket* (Hodder & Stoughton, 2005)

Benaud, Richie – *Anything But... An Autobiography* (Hodder & Stoughton, 1998)

Benaud, Richie – *The Appeal of Cricket: The Modern Game* (Hodder & Stoughton, 1995)

Benaud, Richie – *Spin me a Spinner* (Hodder & Stoughton, 1963)

Benaud, Richie – *Willow Patterns* (Hodder & Stoughton, 1969)

Benaud, Richie – *Benaud on Reflection* (Collins Willow, 1952)

Berry, Scyld – *Cricket Wallah* (Hodder & Stoughton, 1982)

Birley, Derek – *A Social History of English Cricket* (Aurum, 1999)

Booth, Lawrence – *Cricket, Lovely Cricket?* (Yellow Jersey, 2009)

Booth, Lawrence – *Armball to Zooter* (Penguin, 2006)

Booth, Keith – *George Lohmann* (Sports, 2007)

Border, Alan – *Ashes Glory* (Swann, 1989)

Bose, Mihir – *A History of Indian Cricket* (Andre Deutsch, 2002)

Bose, Mihir – *Keith Miller* (Allen & Unwin, 1979)

Botham, Ian – *Botham's Century* (Collins Willow, 2001)

Botham, Ian – *Head On: The Autobiography* (Ebury, 2007)

Bowen, R – *Cricket: A History of its Growth and Development Throughout the World* (Eyre & Spottiswoode)

Boxhall, Thomas – *Rules and Instructions for Playing the Game of Cricket, as Practised by the Most Eminent Players* (Harold & Billing, 1801)

Boycott, Geoffrey – *On Cricket* (Ebury, 1999)

Bradman, Donald – *The Art of Cricket* (Hodder & Stoughton, 1958)

Brearley, Mike – *The Art of Captaincy* (Hodder & Stoughton, 1985)

Christakis, Nicholas and Fowler, James – *Connected* (Harper Press, 2010)

Close, D B – *Close on Cricket* (Stanley Paul, 1986)

Colquhon, Keith and Wroe, Ann – *The Economist Book of Obituaries* (Profile, 2008)

Duckworth, Leslie – *S F Barnes: Master Bowler* (Hutchinson, 1967)

Emburey, John – *Spinning in a Fast World* (Robson, 1989)

Fingleton, Jack – *Fingleton on Cricket* (Collins, 1972)

Fingleton, Jack – *Cricket Crisis* (Pavilion Books, 1984)

Fletcher, Duncan – *Behind the Shades* (Simon and Schuster, 2007)

Fowler, Graeme – *Fox on the Run* (Viking, 1988)

Frith, David – *The Slow Men* (Corgi Books, 1985)

Frith, David – *The Fast Men* (Van Nostrand Rheinhold, 1975)

Gilchrist, Adam – *True Colours* (Pan Macmillan, 2008)

Graveney, Tom – *Cricket over Forty* (Pelham, 1970)

Green, Benny – *Wisden Book of Obituaries 1892–1985* (Queen Anne Press, 1986)

Grimmett, Clarrie – *Grimmett on Getting Wickets* (Hodder & Stoughton, 1930)

Grimmett, Clarrie – *Grimmett on Cricket* (Thomas Nelson & Son, 1948)

Grimmett, Clarrie – *Tricking the Batsman* (Orbis, 1932)

Grout, Wally – *My Country's Keeper* (Pelham, 1965)

Haigh, Gideon – *Mystery Spinner* (Aurum, 2000)

Haigh, Gideon – *The Big Ship* (Aurum, 2003)

Haigh, Gideon – *The Ultimate Test* (Aurum, 2009)

Harvey, Neil – *My World of Cricket* (Hodder & Stoughton, 1963)

Haygarth, A – *Cricket Scores and Biographies, 1862–1925* (Southern,1999)

Hill, Alan – *Tony Lock: Aggressive Master of Spin* (The History Press, 2008)

Hilton, Christopher – *Bradman and the Summer that Changed Cricket* (J R Books, 2009)

Horden, Herbert – *Googlies* (Angus & Robertson,1932)

Hoult, Nick (ed) – *The Daily Telegraph Book of Cricket* (Aurum, 2007)

Hughes, Simon – *And God Created Cricket* (Doubleday, 2009)

Hughes, Simon – *A Lot of Hard Yakka* (Headline, 1997)

Hughes, Simon – *Jargonbusting* (Channel 4 Books, 2002)

Hussain, Nasser, Baxter, Peter and Brearley, Mike – *Cricket's Greatest Battles* (Generation, 2000)

Illingworth, Ray – *Spinner's Wicket* (Stanley Paul, 1969)

James, C L R – *Beyond a Boundary* (Stanley Paul, 1963)

Kilburn, J M – *Overthrows: A Book of Cricket* (Stanley Paul, 1975)

Koch, Richard and Lockwood, Greg – *Superconnect* (Little, Brown, 2010)

Mailey, Arthur – *10 for 66 and All That* (Allen & Unwin, 2008)

Major, John – *More Than a Game* (HarperSport, 2007)

Mallett, Ashley – *Clarrie Grimmett: The Bradman of Spin* (University of Queensland,1993)

Martin-Jenkins, Christopher – *The Top 100 Cricketers of All Times* (Corinthian, 2009)

Martin-Jenkins, Christopher – *The Complete Who's Who of Test Cricketers* (Guild, 1987)

McCool, Colin – *Cricket is a Game* (Stanley Paul, 1961)

Moyes, A G – *Australian Bowlers* (Angus & Robertson, 1953)

Marriott, C S – *The Complete Leg-Break Bowler* (Eyre & Spottiswoode, 1968)

Murphy, Patrick – *The Spinner's Turn* (Dent, 1982)

Nyren, John – *The Young Cricketer's Tutor* (David-Poynter, 1974)

O'Reilly, W J – *Tiger: 60 Years of Cricket* (Collins, 1985)

O'Reilly, W J – *Cricket Task Force* (Werner Laurie, 1981)

Peebles, Ian – *Bowler's Turn* (Souvenir, 1960)

Philpott, Peter – *The Art of Wrist-Spin Bowling* (The Crowood Press, 1995)

Philpott, Peter – *Cricket Fundamentals* (Batsford, 1982)

Pollard J (ed) – *Cricket – The Australian Way* (Landsdowne, 1961)

Pollard, Jack – *From Bradman to Border: Australian Cricket 1948 to 1989* (Angus & Robertson, 1989)

Pollard, Jack – *Bumpers, Boseys, and Brickbats* (Murray, 1971)

Pycroft, James – *The Cricket Field* (Virtue & Co, 1873)

Rae, Simon – *W G Grace: A life* (Faber & Faber, 1998)

Rayvern Allen, David (ed) – *Arlott on Cricket* (Willow Books, 1984)

Ross, A (ed) – *The Cricketer's Companion* (Hutchinson, 1979)

Rundell, M – *A Dictionary of Cricket* (Allen & Unwin, 1985)

Swanton, E W – *Cricketers of My Time* (Andre Deutsch, 1999)

Syed, Matthew – *Bounce: How Champions are Made* (Fourth Estate, 2000)

Thomson, A A – *Hirst and Rhodes* (Epworth Press, 1959)

Trescothick, Marcus – *Coming Back to Me* (Harper Collins, 2008)

Underwood, Derek – *Beating the Bat* (Stanley Paul, 1975)

Warne, Shane – *Shane Warne's Century* (Mainstream, 2008)

Warne, Shane – *My Autobiography* (Hodder & Stoughton, 2001)

Waugh, Steve – *Autobiography* (Michael Joseph, 2006)

Walker, P – *Cricket Conversations* (Pelham, 1978)

Wilde, Simon – *Shane Warne: Portrait of a Flawed Genius*
(John Murray, 2007)

Wilde, Simon – *Number One: The World's Best Batsmen and Bowlers*
(Victor Gollancz, 1998)

Wilde, Simon – *Ranji* (Kingswood, 1999)

Wilkins, Brian – *Cricket: The Bowler's Art* (Kangaroo, 1997)

Whitington, R S – *Bradman, Benaud, and Goddard's Cinderellas*
(Bailey Bros & Swinfen, 1964)

Woodcock, John – *100 Greatest Cricketers* (Macmillan, 1998)

Index